Portraits of Lady Jane Grey Dudley, England's 'Nine Days Queen'

Revised Edition

John Stephan Edwards

Old John Publishing
Palm Springs, California

Publisher's Cataloguing-in-Publication data

Names: Edwards, J. Stephan [John Stephan]
Title: Portraits of Lady Jane Gery Dudley, England's Nine Days Queen, Revised Edition
Description: Palm Springs, California : Old John Publishing, 2024
Identifiers: Library of Congress Control Number: 2024903396
ISBN 979-8-9900377-0-0 (hardcover)/ 979-8-9900377-1-7 (softcover)
Subjects: LCSH : Grey, Jane, Lady, 1537-1554 – Portraits | Portrait Painting, English – 16th Century | Great Britain – Kings and Rulers – 16th Century – Portraits
Classification : DA345.1.D9 E39 2024
Library of Congress record available at https://lccn.loc.gov/2024903396

CONTENTS

PORTRAITS OF THE BERRY HILL TYPE

APPENDICES

BIBLIOGRAPHY

PREFACE TO THE REVISED EDITION

Throughout the nine years since publishing the first edition of this book under the lengthier title *A Queen of a New Invention: Portraits of Lady Jane Grey Dudley, England's Nine Day's Queen'*, I have continued to pursue research on the iconography of Jane Grey Dudley as new evidence has emerged and new material has become available. The most significant of that new evidence and material is the re-discovery in November 2021 of the Berry Hill Portrait after exactly 60 years in obscurity. I have entirely rewritten the entry on that portrait and revised the entries on the others of the Berry Hill Type in an effort to present the reader with the most up-to-date findings on the subject of portraiture of Jane Grey Dudley.

Additionally, the Introduction presented in this revised edition differs from that of the first edition in that it here reflects my latest thinking on the Succession Crisis of 1553. I plan to offer a more complete presentation of the evidence, my analysis of that evidence, and my conclusions related to the succession crisis in a separate volume that I hope to publish in the near future.

I have also sought to correct the many unfortunate mechanical errors that inadvertently found their way into the first edition. I hope that this revised edition will constitute a more refined and polished printed product.

An Important Note Regarding Subjectivity and Bias

Portraits, whether drawn, engraved, painted, or otherwise rendered, are liminal objects that often occupy two or more cultural spaces simultaneously. Among political and socio-cultural historians, for example, portraits are historical artifacts that may provide primary source evidence to document the past visually, especially the physical appearance of historical actors, satisfying the basic human sense-need to see things with one's own eyes. Art historians may analyze portraits to illuminate the development and evolution over time of compositional motifs and technical and creative processes, for example, while costume historians may utilize portraits to track the history and develvpoment of fashions and trends in clothing and clothing construction. Scholars and academics assign relative and predominantly abstract values to most types of artifacts, including historical portraits, based largely on how and to what extent the given object contributes evidence useful to a particular area or field of study.

But historical artifacts may also carry concrete monetary or financial values. Numerous factors govern the relative monetary value of any given artifact and include—but are not limited to—age, rarity, raw materials used, identity of the creator(s), and/or various subjective aesthetic considerations. And as any fan of the international television series *Antiques Roadshow* will undoubtedly know, the monetary value of even common, mundane objects often increases significantly whenever those objects have demonstrable associations with persons of high status. A mass-produced sweater or jumper retailing for less than USD/GBP 50 recently commanded an astonishing USD 1,143,000, for example, because it had belonged to and been publicly worn by the late Diana, Princess of Wales.[1] A 1995 commemorative edition of the 1960 novel *To Kill a Mockingbird* sold in February 2023 for USD 35,000 largely because the author had signed and presented the volume to Gregory Peck, the actor who won an Academy Award for his portrayal of the story's main character in the 1962 film adaptation of the book.[2] Researchers in consumer science refer to the phenomenon of objects carrying extreme relative value owing primarily to their past owner associations as "celebrity contagion."[3]

A similar phenomenon occurs in relation to painted portraits. All other factors being equal, the market for paintings (both buyers and sellers) commonly assigns greater financial value to portraits of known sitters than to those of unknown sitters. And the market assigns still greater value to portraits of famous or historically significant sitters. I believe we are too often culturally driven as a result to **wish** portraits to depict famous individuals and are therefore too often biased, both consciously and unconsciously, when identifying unknown sitters. Many of the sitters in the portraits discussed in this volume were at one time or another identified quite subjectively, to be discussed in association with each relevant portrait. Examiners have sometimes proposed identifications based on little more than personal 'feelings' or 'gut instinct.' But identifications are also too often influenced, I believe, by undue consideration of purely financial advantages that may accrue through naming a particular person as the sitter. The art market will usually support a higher, sometimes even significantly higher, financial price for a portrait if the sitter is a 'historical celebrity.' This, too, will be discussed in regard to several portraits presented herein, particularly the Berry Hill Portrait that stimulated this revised edition.

I therefore ask you, the reader, please to consider carefully as we proceed any biases you may have (e.g.: favoritism toward an individual Tudor historical figure), to set aside those biases, and to evaluate the evidence as objectively as possible, as I have striven to do myself.

---

[1] "Princess Diana's Sheep Jumper," Sotheby's (New York), 14 September 2023, Lot 1.

[2] "*To Kill a Mockingbird* inscribed by Harper Lee to Gregory and Veronique Peck," Heritage Auctions (Dallas, Texas), 23 February 2023, Lot 89088.

[3] George E. Newman, Gil Diesendruck, and Paul Bloom, "Celebrity Contagion and the Value of Objects," *Journal of Consumer Research* 38:2 (August 2011), 215-228.

ACKNOWLEDGMENTS

Throughout the lengthy process of researching and writing this book I have been repeatedly overwhelmed by the generosity of so many people who have given of their time and knowledge and who have offered such unrelentingly enthusiastic assistance. One of course runs the risk when naming names of leaving out someone and thereby offending, so please know that those named here are but the tip of a large iceberg of wonderful people connected in various ways to this study. I am grateful to each and every one.

Many individual private collection owners were extraordinarily welcoming in allowing me access to their paintings, as were the staff members and volunteers at numerous estates and institutions. Even in those instances when a site visit was not feasible, others generously provided me with available archival information and high-resolution photographs of the paintings. I would therefore like to thank His Grace the Duke of Northumberland; Leslie Feore, Clare Baxter, and Chris King at Syon House; the Right Honorable the 6th Earl of Normanton and the Right Honorable the Viscount Somerton; the Right Honorable the Baroness Willoughby de Eresby; Ray Biggs at Grimsthorpe Castle; the Right Honorable the Baron Hastings; Hugh Dixon, Julie Hawthorne, and the staff at Seaton Delaval Hall; David Scrase and Janet Munro at the Fitzwilliam Museum; Mike Webb at the Bodleian Library; Anna Spender at Hever Castle; the Right Honorable the Earl Spencer; Caroline Dwyer at Althorp House; the Right Honorable the Earl of Jersey; Bendor Grosvenor; Nicole Wankel at the Minneapolis Institute of Art; Gareth Sandham at Anglesey Abbey; Chris Penney at Hartlebury Castle; Peter Hughes at Madresfield Court; Rupert Colville; and Diogo Maia at the Fundação Eva Klabin.

One of the more challenging aspects of this study has been the effort to locate portraits not in public collections and on which little or no substantive information has ever been published. I am especially grateful to the many people who responded so generously to my letters and emails of enquiry, as well as to those who contacted me of their own accord after learning of the project. Very often, they offered critical information that allowed me to track down numerous otherwise "lost" portraits. Those people include His Grace the Duke of Somerset; the Right Honorable the Earl of Scarbrough; Stuart Band and James Towe, Devonshire Archivists; Lee Porritt; Amy Baker; Marianne Stienbauer; Sandra Stock; Mandy Henchcliffe at the Derby Local Studies Library; Lewis Chapman; Dr. Terry E. Rogers; Lance Biesele and Alison Kolb; Andrew Loukes at Petworth House; James Berry Hill of Berry Hill Galleries; Frances Mouton of AuctionAugur.blogspot.com; and the staff at Butterscotch Auctioneers and Appraisers of Bedford Village, New York.

Others offered invaluable assistance in the actual research process as I gathered documentation and evidence related to the various portraits, including Dr Ian Tyers and Cathy Tyers at Dendrochronology Consultancy Ltd; Christopher Foley at Lane Fine Art; the staff of the Heinz Archive and Library at the National Portrait Gallery; Matthew Bailey in the Reproductions and Images Department at the NPG; the staff of the Getty Research Institute Library; Harvey Proctor at Belvoir Castle; Susan Higginbotham; Mary Lovell; Richard Philp of Philp Gallery; Sonja Marie Isaacs of the Lady Jane Grey Internet Museum; Lara Eakins of TudorHistory.org; Tamise Chaplin of the Lady Jane Grey Reference Guide; Peter and Leanda de Lisle; and Stuart Tabbron.

I owe a separate and very special debt of gratitude to Hope Walker, who was so very helpful in introducing me to the specialized world of art history.

My heartfelt thanks to Professor Robert Tittler for his thoughtful comments on an early draft of the manuscript for this book.

Professor Marjorie Keniston McIntosh. No graduate student could ever ask for or even dream of a more personable, skillful, attentive, enthusiastic, protective, and committed supervisor. Her guidance was invaluable, her advice never flawed, and her counsel much appreciated. I am truly grateful for having been able to work under her tutelage.

My heartfelt thanks to David L. Newell for encouragement throughout the entire process and for 40 years of friendship.

And lastly, I am truly most grateful to the late Lavada A. Bryant, who so generously funded much of the research that went into this book, including the expenses associated with numerous transatlantic journeys, lengthy hotel stays, and train tickets and car hires throughout the UK. This project could never have been completed without her ongoing assistance and unstinting encouragement. This book is therefore dedicated to her memory.

J. Stephan Edwards
December 2015 and February 2024

ILLUSTRATION CREDITS

Plates:

1. Called Jane Grey by Willem and Magdalena van de Passe
   © The National Portrait Gallery, London, UK

2. Queen Katherine Parr attributed to Master John
   © The National Portrait Gallery, London, UK

3. Queen Katherine Parr by Unknown Artist
   © Use by kind permission of the Rt. Honorable the Baron Hastings
   Seaton Delaval Hall, Northumberland, UK

4. Queen Katherine Parr by Unknown Artist
   © Use by kind permission of the Rt. Honorable the Earl of Jersey
   Photograph by Peter Trenchard, 2014

5. Probably Queen Katherine Parr by Unknown Artist
   © Photograph by the author

6. Called Lady Jane Grey by Unknown Artist
   © The National Portrait Gallery, London, UK

7. Called Lady Jane Grey by Unknown Artist
   © The National Portrait Gallery, London, UK

8. Called Princess Elizabeth Tudor by Unknown Artist
   © Photograph by the owner

9. Called Portrait of Lady Jane Grey by English School
   Private Collection / Photo © Philip Mould Ltd, London / Bridgeman Images

10. Anna of Bohemia and Hungary after Hans Maler
    © Private Collection

11. Unknown Lady by Hans Eworth
    © The Fitzwilliam Museum, Cambridge, UK

12. Unknown Lady by Unknown Artist
    © Photograph by the author

13. Portrait of a Noblewoman by Unknown Artist
    © The Minneapolis Institute of Art, Minnesota, USA

14. Unknown Lady by Unknown Artist
    © The Bodleian Library, University of Oxford, UK

15. Unknown Lady by Unknown Artist
    ©The National Portrait Gallery, London, UK

16. Portrait of a lady, previously identified as Lady Jane Grey by circle of François Clouet
    Private Collection / Photograph © Christie's Images / Bridgeman Images

17. Unknown Lady attributed to Levina Teerlinc
    © The Yale Center for British Art, New Haven, Connecticut, USA

Figures:

INTRODUCTION

Among the twenty six monarchs that have ruled England or the United Kingdom over the past 500 years, authentic portraits created from the life survive for all but one. The lone unrepresented individual is Lady Jane Grey Dudley, the so-called Nine Days Queen of 1553. No life portrait of Queen Jane is currently known to exist, and neither is any posthumous copy taken from such a life portrait known. Adding to our lack of knowledge regarding her appearance is the recent discovery that the single purported written physical description of Jane is almost certainly nothing more than the colorful imaginings of the late-Victorian novelist-historian Richard Davey (see Appendix One, p.177). The reliable historical record describes Jane using only the very vague and subjective adjectives "pretty" and "well-made," terms applied with frequency to a wide range of women of the Tudor period but useless in objectively identifying a sitter in any portrait.

Documents from the sixteenth century contain only two mentions of portraits that may be accounted authentic likenesses of Jane Grey Dudley. The first is an inventory taken early in the 1560s of the possessions of the widow Elizabeth Hardwick St Loe (known to history as Bess of Hardwick) housed at Chatsworth House, Derbyshire. Listed among the items in Bess's personal bedchamber was a portrait of "my Lady Jane."[1] This was certainly Lady Jane Grey Dudley. Bess had no relatives in the 1560s who were named Jane and who might also be styled Lady. Bess herself had resided in the Grey household during the 1540s, however, serving as a lady in waiting to Jane's mother Frances Brandon Grey, Marchioness of Dorset and later Duchess of Suffolk. Indeed, Bess's second marriage, to Sir William Cavendish, had been solemnized in the Grey family's private chapel at Bradgate in 1547. Jane, her parents, and her younger sister Katherine each variously stood godparent to all but one of Bess's many subsequent children by Cavendish.[2] Bess remained close to the entire Grey family, even after the family's disgrace in 1553/4. She seems to have been particularly fond of Jane, and Bess's choice to display the portrait in her most private chamber marked it as a prized and very personal possession. In light of the continuing intimate association between Bess of Hardwick and the Greys of Bradgate, it is entirely reasonable to conclude that any portrait of "my Lady Jane" owned by Bess was a reliably authentic image of Jane Grey, probably even a life portrait. The Chatsworth Portrait, as I have chosen to call it, did not appear in a second inventory of Bess's possessions taken in 1601, however.[3] The disposition of the portrait was not recorded, and its current whereabouts remain unknown despite exhaustive efforts to locate it (See Appendix Two, p. 183).

The second mention of what may well have been an authentic likeness of Jane Grey Dudley occurred in the Lumley Inventories.[4] Well known to art historians, the inventories were compiled in about 1590 to enumerate the collection of John Lumley, 1st Baron Lumley, an important collector of portraits during the Elizabethan period. A "scantlinge" or small painting identified as "Lady Jane Graye, executed" was included in the Lumley collection. And as with Bess of Hardwick, the Lumleys had a connection to Jane Grey that made it altogether likely that the Lumley Portrait was an authentic likeness, if not a life portrait. Baron Lumley's wife, Jane Fitzalan, was the daughter of Catherine Grey Fitzalan, herself a sister to Jane Grey's father, Henry Grey. Thus Jane Lumley and Jane Grey were first cousins. Further, the two Janes were the same age, both having been born in about 1536/7, and it is probable that the two cousins knew each other well. Therefore, any portrait of Jane Grey owned by Jane Fitzalan Lumley and her husband John Lumley was very possibly a likeness that the Lumleys recognized as accurate and genuine. But like the Chatsworth Portrait before it, the Lumley Portrait of Jane Grey disappeared from the historical record after the inventory was taken. Its survival and current whereabouts remain similarly unknown (see Appendix Two).

Until now, no systematic scholarly analysis of the numerous putative portraits of Jane Grey has ever been undertaken. Though her nineteenth-century biographers did sometimes provide lists of portraits said to depict Jane, they made no real attempt to authenticate any of the likenesses. Writing in the 1860s, Agnes Strickland cited an engraving from 1620, the van de Passe Engraved Portrait, supposedly based on an original by Hans Holbein. She noted only that the portrait contrasted strongly with anecdotal descriptions of Jane's character, though those same anecdotes made no mention of her physical appearance. Strickland also cited a painted portrait then owned by the Earl of Stamford, copied from the Wrest Park Portrait, praising that depiction as "quietly elegant."[5] Richard Davey provided a much more extensive list in his biographical novel on Jane published in 1909, a list totaling twenty images, but he characterized them as "probably not a single one ... authentic."[6] By the second half of the twentieth century, biographers began to include in their volumes a number of photographic illustrations rather than mere lists of unseen pictures. For example, the flyleaf of Hester Chapman's *Lady Jane Grey*, published in 1962, displayed a small portrait from the National Portrait Gallery, NPG764. Chapman referred to the image as only a "supposed" portrait, implying a conscious awareness that it was likely not authentic.[7] Some years later, the book jacket for the second of Alison Plowden's two biographies of Jane was illustrated with a photograph of a painting from a private collection, the Hastings Portrait, though the analysis of that portrait included here will demonstrate that it is instead a portrait of Queen Katherine Parr.[8] Neither Chapman nor Plowden provided any commentary on the reliability of the images they reproduced.

More recently, two historians writing on Jane Grey have offered in their individual works some brief discussion of the issue of portraiture, but neither writer pursued the point as a separate topic of focused research. In a lengthy footnote to her collective biography of Jane and her two sisters, Leanda de Lisle extended tentative support for identifying as a posthumous portrait of Jane a miniature now in the collection of the Yale Center for British Art, the Yale Miniature Portrait.[9] That miniature served as the only illustration of Jane Grey in de Lisle's volume. Almost simultaneously, Eric Ives lent just over two pages of discussion in his own biogrpahy of Jane to eight portraits, ranging from the van de Passe engraving of 1620 to the Yale Miniature and others. Ives reproduced each of those portraits as illustrations to his volume, concluding that an acquisition by the National Portrait Gallery in 2006, the Streatham Portrait, together with two variants of it, the Houghton and Norris Portraits, must together be accounted "persuasive likeness[es]."[10]

This volume details the results of over fifteen years of research focused very narrowly on a goal of distinguishing a reliably authentic image of Jane Grey Dudley from among the many surviving portraits associated with her name. From the outset, I made a very deliberate methodological choice to limit the study to that narrow goal alone and simply to cast a critical eye on the portraits themselves. The result is a volume devoted primarily to fundamental connoisseurship rather than to the production of a historiographical research monograph. I consciously elected to defer to others for the application of complex methodologies that might utilize popular analytical theories to situate the portraits in some broader art historical context. But in any such larger historiographical endeavor, whether involving the history of art, politics, religion, or some other field of human activity, scholars ordinarily begin by "interrogating" (to use the academic jargon) the primary source materials. For example, interrogation of manuscripts or printed documents may entail investigation of such issues as the source's origin and nature, credibility, authorial bias, etc. For art historians, the individual art objects are themselves a class of primary source material, and they must be similarly analyzed. One avenue of investigation should include correctly identifying and authenticating the objects, if only to avoid using them inappropriately as evidence in some wider argument and study. The process of interrogating the primary source material is essentially the "grunt-work" of the historiographical process, and this volume seeks to accomplish that fundamental task for the portraiture of Lady Jane Grey Dudley.

A Brief History of Lady Jane Grey Dudley

Lady Jane Grey, more correctly referred to by her married name Lady Jane Dudley, was born of semi-royal blood. She was the great-granddaughter of Henry VII, founder of the Tudor dynasty. Through her mother Frances Brandon, herself the daughter of Henry VII's fifth child and third daughter Mary, Jane was the grandniece of Henry VIII. And Jane's father Henry Grey was a cousin to Henry VIII, Grey's grandfather Thomas Grey having been half-brother to Henry VIII's mother, Elizabeth of York. In other words, Jane, her mother, her father, and King Henry VIII were all close kinsmen and all descended from a single common ancestor, Elizabeth Woodville, Queen Consort to King Edward IV.

Jane was born in the winter of 1536/7, entering the world at an exceptionally dynamic point in English history.[11] Only two years previously the English Church had ended its allegiance to the Roman Catholic system of church governance. English monasteries were beginning to be closed *en masse*, and new doctrines challenged the long-established system of religious belief and practice. Henry Grey was a supporter of the new system and patronized numerous reformers both within England and on the continent. One of those was the young John Aylmer, whom Grey hired in the early 1540s to tutor his daughters.[12] Jane soon became famously very fond of her tutor. For his part, Aylmer persuaded Jane to correspond with various leading men of the reform movement, including Martin Bucer and Heinrich Bullinger. Jane even translated a large number of Bullinger's sermons from Latin into ancient Greek. By 1553, Jane had herself become an uncompromising follower of a reformist confession of faith known today as Zwinglianism.[13]

Jane's ability to translate Bullinger's sermons reflects a second area of significant change then occurring in England, in the field of education. A larger percentage of the male population began to receive an education beyond basic literacy, and a growing proportion of the educated were non-clerics. But most importantly for Jane, families began making advanced academic study available to an appreciable—though still very limited—number of women for the first time in English history. By the time she was fourteen years of age, early in 1551, Jane had earned a reputation across Europe as a significant scholar. Even the pedagogue Roger Ascham, tutor to Elizabeth Tudor, acknowledged Jane as second only to Elizabeth among feminine intellects. Shortly after Jane's death, the English ambassador and poet Thomas Chaloner would extol her ability to function in at least eight languages, including English, Latin, ancient Greek, Hebrew (in which she was apparently self-taught), Spanish, French, Italian, and even Chaldean, or Aramaic.[14] She also studied rhetoric, theology, moral and natural philosophy, logic, and history while reading many of the ancient Roman and Greek classical authors, from Cicero and Livy to Plato and Aristotle.[15]

Numerous political changes accompanied the social and cultural shifts. Queen Anne Boleyn was executed in May 1536, just months before Jane's birth, and a new queen, Jane Seymour, took Anne's place. Henry VIII's only children to survive from his previous marriages, daughters Mary and Elizabeth, were both declared illegitimate and removed from the royal succession by separate Acts of Parliament. Despite a near-obsessive pursuit, Henry VIII had, as of Jane's birth, failed to sire a legitimate male heir that could survive infancy. The Second Act of Succession passed in June of 1536 empowered Henry to set aside traditional inheritance patterns and to name a successor of his own choosing, and many believed his only acknowledged illegitimate son, Henry Fitzroy, was the likely candidate.[16] But Fitzroy died unexpectedly in July 1536, leaving only the descendants of Henry's two sisters, Margaret and Mary, within the legitimate Tudor blood line. The birth in October 1537 of a son, Edward, to Henry's third wife Jane Seymour seemed literally heaven-sent. Prince Edward duly became King Edward VI upon the death of his father in January 1547.

Edward's brief reign coincided with Jane's transition from childhood to young adulthood and brought further religious reform aimed at completing the break with Roman Catholicism initiated under Henry VIII. The changes were led first by Edward Seymour, Lord Protector and the new King's uncle, aided by clerics such as Thomas Cranmer, Archbishop of Canterbury and Nicholas Ridley, Bishop of London. The two successive Books of Common Prayer of 1549 and 1552 replaced the traditional Roman liturgy. The reformed religion, the various sects of which would later collectively be called Protestantism, became the official state religion. Altars and religious images were removed from churches, sermons replaced the Mass, and the Lord's Supper replaced the Eucharist. Edward's half-sister, the Lady Mary, remained a firm practitioner of the old religion, however, bringing her into sharp conflict with her brother and his advisors. Seymour fell from power in 1551, however, and was eventually executed. John Dudley, Duke of Northumberland after November 1551, replaced Seymour at the head of the king's Privy Council. Though Dudley continued the religious reforms, he was a newcomer of relatively humble origins and many disliked him. Nonetheless, he was a skilled politician and thus able to form an effective ruling coalition of supporters from amongst the members of the Council.

Edward VI unexpectedly fell ill in March of 1553, and, in the absence of any heirs of his own body, the succession issue sprang to the fore. The line of succession to the English throne early in 1553 consisted of eight female cousins descended from Henry VIII's elder sister Margaret and younger sister Mary, plus one male cousin, just seven years old, descended from Margaret.[17] English political culture found rule by women abhorrent, however, while the accession of a minor child opened the door to a contested regency. Further, all but one (Francis Brandon Grey) of the eight surviving female heirs remained unmarried: Mary and Elizabeth Tudor; Jane, Katherine, and Mary Grey; Margaret Clifford; and Mary Stuart. Were any to succeed Edward while still unmarried, international relations might require them to take a foreign husband. English political culture assumed a queen's husband would bear rule in right of his wife, presenting the spectre of the realm falling under the domination of a foreign power. These circumstances, coupled with a desire to preserve the reformed English church, motivated Edward to produce his 'Devise for the Succession.'

Edward's 'Devise' explicitly removed his half-sisters Mary and Elizabeth from the succession on the combined grounds that both were illegitimate under the Second and Third Acts for the Succession and either might marry a foreign prince and thereby bring the English kingdom under foreign domination. The 'Devise' also implicitly removed the three descendants of Henry VIII's sister Margaret Tudor through failure of mention, mirroring the Third Act for the Succession of

1543 and Henry's Last Will and Testament of 1547. And in its final form, the 'Devise' also set aside Frances Brandon Grey through failure of mention. Edward's crown thus descended to Frances's eldest daughter Jane, with Jane's younger sisters to follow should she fail to produce issue.

John Dudley acted in his capacity as Edward's principal advisor and President of the Privy Council to support the king's 'Devise.' First, he created an intricate system of marriage alliances woven between several of the leading noble families. Each of four marital pairs included a potential female heir to the crown wedded to a non-heir male drawn from among families of leading members of the Privy Council. The marriages were intended to give each of Edward's four English female heirs under the 'Devise' (i.e., Jane, Katherine, and Mary Grey, plus Margaret Clifford) a domestically English husband who was also a committed follower of the Edwardian religious settlement.[18] Jane was herself wedded to Dudley's younger son Guildford, the only candidate available who was both unmarried and of sufficient rank.

The king and Dudley then planned a parliament for September to codify the 'Devise' as a formal Act for the Succession. In the interim, the dying king compelled the members of the Privy Council, the senior law judges, leaders of the City of London, and others to subscribe to letters patent drawn up under the Great Seal in an effort to enforce the terms of the 'Devise.' Edward died just two weeks later, on 6 July 1553. News of the king's death was initially withheld until Dudley and the Privy Council could put the 'Devise' into practical effect, but they failed in those preparations to take Mary into custody. Instead, they allowed her to flee to her own extensive estates in the north in the days just before Edward's death. That oversight would prove fatal to the Janeian regime.

Four days later, on 10 July 1553, Jane ceremonially processed into the Tower, as was customary upon the accession of a new monarch, and she was proclaimed throughout London as the new Queen of England. The proclamation was not well received by the populace, but most political observers assumed for the moment that Mary had been successfully displaced and that Jane would indeed remain as Queen, with Guildford as her king-consort. Nonetheless, as soon as Mary arrived at her Suffolk estate of Framlingham, she had herself locally proclaimed Queen and wrote to the Privy Council to assert her right to the throne. Mary's self-proclamation was far better received by the general population, and many began to travel to her in a tangible show of support. Members of the gentry likewise began showing their support for Mary, some of whom described Jane as nothing more than "a quene of a new and pretie [i.e., crafty, devious] Invencon."[19] Even the crew of a naval vessel sent by Dudley to prevent Mary from fleeing into exile instead defected to Mary and offered her the cannons and ammunition from their ship.

The Privy Council reacted on 14 July to this unanticipated turn of events by appointing Dudley to lead an army north to seize Mary. But no sooner had he left London than his alliance began to crumble. The Council fractured, and a significant portion shifted their allegiance to Mary. Even Dudley's own army quickly fell into disarray almost as soon as it passed beyond sight of London. Many of the soldiers abandoned Jane's cause and either returned to their homes or continued north to aid Mary. Upon hearing of the dissolution of Dudley's army, those Council members thus far remaining loyal to Jane quickly declared instead for Mary. By 19 July, the reign of Queen Jane had ended and that of Mary had begun, with Mary proclaimed Queen in London to great public rejoicing.

Jane and Guildford remained in the Tower, but as prisoners rather than as possessors. Jane was held in the private domestic quarters of two successive resident-employees of the Tower, while Guildford, his brothers, and his father were held primarily in the Beauchamp Tower. John Dudley was tried and executed for treason late in August 1553. Queen Mary pardoned and released Jane's father Henry Grey, however, as well as most of Jane's other supporters. But Mary did not include Jane and Guildford among those pardoned. Instead, they stood trial in November, and the court found them guilty of treason. Mary initially resisted allowing their execution, believing them to be guiltless puppets of John Dudley. Only when a rebellion broke out late in January of 1554, known today as Wyatt's Rebellion, did Mary consent to Jane's execution. Jane's father participated in Wyatt's Rebellion and called for the restoration of Queen Jane, effectively sealing his daughter's fate. Jane and Guildford were duly executed on 12 February 1554, she within the precincts of the Tower. Her remains are traditionally said to have been interred inside the Chapel of St Peter-ad-Vincula within the Tower.

The Afterlife of Lady Jane Grey Dudley

Almost immediately following Jane's death, a popular mythology began to develop around her name. She quickly became—and remains—one of the most popular female historical figures of the Tudor era, surpassed only by Elizabeth Tudor, Anne Boleyn, and Mary Stuart. And like Elizabeth, Anne, and Mary, Jane has "lived ... many lives ... since, in drama, poetry, historiography, propaganda, fiction, and the cinema, from the aspiringly epic to the frankly kitsch."[20] Only recently have scholars begun to look critically at the large body of literature devoted to her and to recover a life narrative that is supported solely by the surviving contemporary sources and freed from later legend and myth, replacing fawning hagiography with scholarly biography.[21] But the enduring hagiography of Jane Grey has, at key points in British history, driven her iconography as well. As Jane's popularity in literature waxed and waned, so too did interest in portraits of her. At times of peak interest, collectors re- or mis-identified existing portraits of other persons or created entirely new ones in an effort to fill a visual void, giving Jane "many lives" through portraiture.

In order to understand this impulse to rechristen portraits "like children at a foundling hospital," as the art historian Horace Walpole once observed, we must first understand the related impulses that drove the hagiography of Jane.[22] Over the course of the four centuries following her death, Jane evolved into an increasingly fictionalized literary character deployed by successive generations of writers attempting to further diverse national religious, political, and social agendas. Jane developed into an easily recognized trope-like figure around whom issues of succession politics, religion, and the relationship between religion and the state could be debated and challenged. Portraiture said to depict her was likewise used to support a given political or religious agenda and even to associate the owners of specific portraits with particular sides of the various debates.

By the time of Jane's execution in February 1554, the First Act of Repeal had reversed virtually all of the Edwardian religious reforms. Leaders of the reform movement, both those who remained in England and those who had fled into religious exile on the continent, sought ways to subvert the complete restoration of Roman Catholicism within England. One popular method was through the production of printed pamphlets that could be widely distributed and read by large numbers of people. Within weeks of Jane's death, a sample of her writings, carefully selected specifically for their exposition of reformist religious doctrines, was printed and circulated.[23] Notably, those pamphlets said almost nothing about Jane as a person, relying on her words rather than her actions, character, or physical appearance to convey the desired message.

Even the sixteenth-century martyrologist John Foxe, whose widely read and highly influential *Acts and Monuments* (commonly referred to as *The Book of Martyrs*) did much to establish Jane as a specifically religious heroine, actually said very little about Jane as a person. Foxe gave no details whatsoever of Jane's physical appearance. Instead, he offered only a single descriptive sentence that focused exclusively on her intellect. Jane's knowledge of languages was superior to that of Edward VI, according to Foxe, and she possessed "trimness of wit." She might have been compared, he said, "not only to the house of the Aspasians, Sempronians, or mother of the Gracchis, yea to any other women beside that deserved high praise for their singular learning: but also to the University men, which have taken many degrees of the schools."[24] Foxe's fulsome praise for Jane's intellectual achievements served a very particular and necessary purpose in that it sought to establish Jane as a credible female voice in the otherwise exclusively male sphere of theological discourse. In the paternalistic culture of mid-Tudor England, Jane's feminine writings were useful to reformers only if they could reliably show her to be on a par intellectually with the men of the universities. Thus in the decades immediately following her death, Jane's words and intellectual abilities were of greater importance to the collective cultural memory than was her distinctly female physical appearance, so that no painted portrait was yet required.

Demand for portraits of Jane did not emerge until the last decade of the sixteenth century, in association with the debate on who should succeed the childless Elizabeth I. With the death of that last surviving issue of the loins of Henry VIII, two rival lines of descent from Henry VII asserted their respective claims to the Crown of England. If judged solely in terms of blood lineage, the senior claimant was King James VI of Scotland, son of Mary Queen of Scots and great-grandson of Henry VIII's elder sister Margaret Tudor. But some argued that English Parliamentary law dating back to the fourteenth century barred those of foreign birth from inheriting within England.[25] Others maintained that the Succession Act of 1543 and the last will and testament of Henry VIII, in failing to mention the descendants of Margaret Tudor, had effectively barred them collectively from the legal succession, regardless of bloodline or realm of birth.[26] This second argument eliminated not only James VI of Scotland from inheriting the English crown, but also his English-born cousin, Arbella Stuart, a great-granddaughter of Margaret Tudor. The Succession Act and Henry VIII's last will instead vested the crown in the successors of Henry's younger sister, Mary Tudor Brandon, from whom Jane and her two sisters Katherine and Mary Grey descended. The senior surviving claimant in the Tudor-Brandon-Grey line during the 1590s was the eldest son of Katherine Grey, Edward Seymour (*b*.1561), Viscount Beauchamp of Hache. The relative legitimacy of Jane's brief tenure as queen thus became a focal point of the debate on the Elizabethan succession issue, especially during the last decade of the sixteenth century and the first decade of the seventeenth.

The poet Michael Drayton was among the first writers to utilize Jane for asserting a particular political opinion on the succession issue, doing so in an otherwise literary context. In 1597, he published *England's Heroical Epistles*, a collection of pairs of fictional letter-poems supposedly passed between famous male-female couples of English history, one of those pairs being Jane and her husband Guildford Dudley. Jane's letter to Guildford voiced support for a succession in 1553 in strict accordance to the will of Henry VIII, i.e., first Mary, then Elizabeth, then the descendants of Mary Tudor Brandon, implying support in 1597 for the Seymour faction. Drayton skillfully pre-empted any religious objections to an accession in 1553 by Catholic Mary by having Jane utter a prophetic prayer for Mary's continued barrenness and an eventual return to "right religion" if God would allow the Protestant Elizabeth to succeed Mary. Drayton noted Jane's "wisdom and learning" but made no attempt to describe her appearance, leaving that effort to others.[27]

The London stage soon provided a more public forum for the conduct of the Elizabethan debate on the succession. Several playwrights wrote and produced plays in which they presented Jane

Grey as a leading character and the succession issue a central topic, albeit couched in the politically safer and historically distant context of 1553. The playwright Thomas Dekker co-authored at least two of those plays. The first, *Lady Jane, or The Overthrow of Rebels,* he wrote in 1602, but it is now lost. The second, *The Famous History of Sir Thomas Wyatt*, also written in 1602, proved sufficiently popular to merit printed publication in 1607 and again in 1612.[28] In the second play, as in Drayton's earlier *Epistles*, the stage character Jane explicitly advocated against her own interests and in favor of a succession following the dictates of the will of Henry VIII. Dekker and his co-authors thus echoed Drayton in implicitly promoting a pro-Seymour, anti-Scottish succession to Elizabeth I.[29] But unlike Drayton's *Epistles*, through which a reader simply read Jane's disembodied words on a printed page, Dekker's plays presented those words as audible speech delivered by a living person adopting the stage persona of Jane Grey. It was a highly visual experience, one that perhaps led viewers to question the extent to which the physical appearance of the person taking the role of Jane Grey matched that of the historical Jane.

It is no coincidence that portraits said to depict Jane Grey first began to emerge in exactly this period of debate on the Elizabethan succession, as both sides looked back to the last contested succession for guidance. Sets of portraits of English monarchs began to include images of Jane Grey, several of which are discussed in this volume and at least one of which, the Streatham Portrait, has been reliably dated to no earlier than 1594. Another, the Syon Portrait, was even produced very specifically for the Seymours who were laying claim to the crown as the senior descendants in the Tudor-Brandon-Grey line. Yet another was included among the political heroes in the *Heroωlogia Anglica*, a collection of engraved portraits of both political and religious heroes of English history published as a printed volume in 1620 (see The van de Passe Engraved Portrait, p.18).[30] The historical Jane Grey had by then been transformed from a faceless writer of words of religious inspiration into a political hero whom the educated public wanted to see as well as to read or to hear.

Demand for portraits of Jane Grey seems to have waned following the death of King James VI & I in 1625 and the uncontested accession of his son, Charles I. Even during the tumultuous 1630s and 1640s, as the three kingdoms of England, Ireland, and Scotland were riven by both political and religious civil war, the historical figure of Jane Grey remained a seemingly distant memory.[31] Abolition of the monarchy in 1649 rendered the issue of the royal succession moot. And following the establishment in the 1650s of the austere republican Commonwealth and the domination of the English Church by ardent reformists, religious debate was largely quieted for a time, removing any need to deploy Jane as an advocate for religious reform. Indeed, she merits only the very briefest of notices in Thomas Fuller's *The Church History of Britain* of 1656, where she is characterized by only the single adjective "dutiful."[32] And no surviving portraits of Jane are known to have been re-identified or newly produced in this period.

Following the demise of the Commonwealth and the Restoration of Charles II in 1660, the English Church set about renegotiating its doctrinal identity after the severities of the previous period. The adapted history of Jane Grey was once again brought forward into the public consciousness, though this time solely in the context of the debate on religion, Charles II being the undisputed heir of his father. Writers began to utilize Jane to provide an "ancient" model of the "true" English Church. Peter Heylyn published *Ecclesia Restaurata, or, the Reformation of the Church of England* in 1661, for example, in which he enunciated in the form of a history his agenda for the re-establishment of the post-Puritan English church. Heylyn presented a lengthier and more detailed account of Jane and her role in the succession dispute of 1553 than perhaps any writer since the early Elizabethan period.[33] Heylyn intended the Edwardian reforms of the 1550s, to which Jane was an adherent, to serve as a prescriptive model for the Restoration Church.[34] This was in opposition to those who sought a more "high church" settlement of the type that had existed early in the reign of Charles I. Heylyn did not attempt to describe Jane's appearance, however, other than to note that she "seemed to have been born with those attractions which seat a sovereignty in the face of most beautiful persons."[35] Neither did Heylyn provide any portrait illustrations in his volume.

In contrast, Gilbert Burnet offered a handful of engraved portraits to accompany his exceedingly popular *History of the Reformation of the Church of England*, one of which depicted Jane Grey as Queen.[36] Burnet published two of the three volumes of his *History* at the height of the Exclusion Crisis of 1679-1681, an unsuccessful Parliamentary effort intended to prevent the Roman Catholic James, Duke of York from succeeding his childless elder brother King Charles II. Burnet's *History* was so well received that Parliament passed a motion of thanks and the University of Oxford awarded him a Doctorate in Divinity in specific recognition of his effort. Burnet was no hardline Puritan, however, which may help to explain the obvious embellishments added to the costume of the sitter in his engraved depiction of Jane Grey. The engraving was based on the Wrest Park Portrait (p.60), owned until the 1690s by Dorothy, Lady Dacre of Herstmonceux Castle, whose second husband Chaloner Chute had briefly been a politically moderate Speaker of the House of Commons.[37] But whereas the original painted portrait depicted the sitter in austere attire consistent with the modern stereotype associated with English Puritans, the engraving contained added embroidery work on the chemise and partlet, fur trim and numerous *ouches* or decorative jeweled buttons on the gown, and large pearls on the headgear. This was actually more in keeping with the earliest depictions of Jane, most of which had shown her clothed in the same finery commonly seen in other portraits of the English aristocracy of the sixteenth century. Jane had not yet been transformed into the plain-dressing proto-Puritan maiden that she is so often today perceived to have been, though that transformation was underway.

The public debate on the Act of Settlement of 1701 provided the next occasion for evoking a mythologized memory of Jane Grey in service to religious and political agendas. It also witnessed her full transformation into a purely religious heroine of a decidedly Puritan stripe. The Catholic James II had succeeded his nominally Protestant brother Charles II in 1685. James's two female heirs, daughters Mary (*b.*1662) and Anne (*b.*1665), had both been safely raised as Anglicans. But the belated birth to James of a son in June 1688 and the announcement that the child would be raised Catholic so compounded existing concerns over James's own Catholicism that he was forced to abdicate later that same year in favor of his daughter Mary and her husband, William of Orange. That childless couple would eventually be succeeded by her sister Anne in 1702, but the last of Anne's five live-born children, Prince William, died at age eleven in July 1700, initiating a new succession crisis even before Anne herself came to the throne. One faction favored the return of the Catholic son born to James II in 1688, while another favored the Protestant German descendants of Elizabeth of Bohemia (*b.*1596), the Hanoverian Electress Palatine and eldest daughter of James VI & I.

As during the Elizabethan succession debate a century earlier, literature and the stage both provided venues for conducting the debate over whom should succeed Queen Anne. Transcripts of Jane's pre-execution theological debate with John de Feckenham were reprinted as chapsheets and broadsides beginning in 1688.[38] Those publications "querie[d] the legitimacy of replacing the hereditary, if Catholic [heir], with a Protestant who ha[d] a more distant claim to the throne."[39] The playwright John Banks issued a legitimist response in 1693 with his play *The Innocent Usurper*, but the stage production was immediately banned for its support of a hereditary succession without regard to the heir's religion. It was, however, successfully published in print in the following year.[40] The Act of Settlement of 1701 eventually attempted to settle the matter, at least in law, by vesting the succession in the Protestant Sophia of Hanover, daughter of Elizabeth of Bohemia and granddaughter of James VI & I.

The Act did not require enforcement until Anne's death in 1714, at which time Sophia's son George of Hanover became King George I of Great Britain. But both before and after his accession George faced significant challenges from Stuart loyalists, often called Jacobites.[41] The Crown's military response to the Jacobite Rebellion of 1715 was supplemented by an anti-Catholic propaganda campaign in which Jane was again trotted out in pamphlets, poems, and plays, leading to an "intense obsession" with Jane by the general public.[42] Initially, many of these works were not overtly political, but their content did much to influence public perceptions of Jane Grey as a historical figure and to stimulate demand for portraits of her. Edward Young's book-length poem, *The Force of Religion; or, Vanquish'd Love*, for example, was undoubtedly the source for the modern myths that Jane was offered full pardon should she convert to Catholicism and that she died solely on account of her religion.[43] Ironically, at least in the context of religious martyrdom, Young presented Jane as what one historian has characterized as "an object of frankly libidinous male gaze," encouraging all literally to "fix [their] eyes on a fair example of piety" and to contemplate an image conjured in the reader's imagination.[44] Those conjured images led directly to a demand for tangible and reliable ones in the form of portraits, and the demand was often met by simply rechristening portraits of other women, as will be demonstrated later in this study.

Subsequent propaganda evoking Jane Grey quickly became more overtly political, especially in the poet and playwright Nicholas Rowe's stage-play *Lady Jane Grey: A tragedy, in five acts*, a markedly pro-Hanoverian, pro-Protestant work. The play has been described as the most successful of the 1714-1715 season, and it enjoyed significant subsequent popularity in print.[45] A dedication in one of the printed editions included an acknowledgement by Rowe that he had used "Poetical Colouring ... aim'd at heightening and improving some of [Jane's] Features."[46] One such change was in the nature of the relationship between Jane and her husband Guildford, which Rowe explicitly characterized as entirely chaste, rendering Jane a specifically virgin martyr, another myth that has endured and influenced the Janeian iconography. It is in precisely this period, for example, that Sarah, Duchess of Marlborough re-identified as a depiction of Jane Grey the Althorp Portrait of a studious maiden isolated in her chamber, and in which engravings of the Wrest Park Portrait included in later editions of Burnet's *History of the Reformation* were restored to their original Puritan-like simplicity of costume.

Rowe's play spawned a number of pro-Jacobite responses, including the re-issue of Banks's play of 1693 and an anonymous pamphlet entitled *Remarks on the Tragedy of Lady Jane Gray* [sic]; *In a Letter to Mr Rowe* (1715). The latter attacked attempts by Rowe and others to glorify Jane Grey through false amplifications of her piety, chastity, and even beauty. Similarly, Charles Gildon's *Remarks on Mr Rowe's Tragedy of the Lady Jane Grey, and all his other plays* criticized Rowe for "seem[ing] to be afraid, that a connubial Love in a young Lady of 15, should lessen her Character."[47] Gildon further argued that Rowe's choice to transform Jane from a political to a religious martyr was nothing more than a calculated effort to heighten her feminine attractiveness.

Rowe's characterization was nonetheless well remembered, such that Jane is today perceived almost universally as a specifically *religious* martyr.

These debates sparked an entirely new development, with monograph biographies of Jane Grey emerging for the first time. The bookseller James Roberts issued the first of these in 1714, an anonymous account lengthily entitled *The Life, Character, and Death of the most Illustrious Pattern of Female Virtue, the Lady Jane Gray, Who was Beheaded in the Tower at 16 Years of Age, for her Steadfast Adherence to the Protestant Religion*.[48] Most of these early biographies made liberal use of fictional material drawn from the above mentioned poems and plays, presenting that material as historical fact and further complicating the mythology of Jane Grey. Overtly fictional accounts also began to be published, starting with *The History and Fall of the Lady Jane Grey* issued by Roberts in 1725.[49] Many included woodcuts or engravings depicting various scenes from the life of Jane Grey, though virtually all of those images were distinctly anachronistic in content. Nonetheless, they both fed and fueled a public demand for images of Jane Grey, especially portraits.

Even as these various broadsides, chapsheets, poem, plays, and early biographies fostered the early-eighteenth-century obsession with Jane Grey, the work of one additional writer did more to change public perceptions of Jane's character than perhaps any other. The antiquarian John Strype published a series of works, beginning in 1694 with a collection of the works of Thomas Cranmer, that focused on the doctrinal and liturgical form taken by the "primitive" English church in its first idealistic years after the break with Rome. The third in the series was published in 1701, the same year as the Act of Settlement, and narrated the life of John Aylmer, tutor to Jane Grey and later Bishop of London under Elizabeth I. Strype included a number of anecdotal tales supposedly found "somewhere" among Aylmer's papers, one of which involved an anonymous "great lady" who refused a gift of luxurious fabrics proffered by Queen Mary by stating a preference for following the habits of dress practiced by Elizabeth, "which followeth God's word."[50] Though the story is entirely apocryphal and not corroborated by any other source or evidence, it nonetheless led to a belief since 1701 that Jane must necessarily have favored extremely plain attire constructed of simple fabrics and entirely free of embellishments or jewels. This is in striking contrast to virtually every supposedly authentic portrait put forward between her death and 1700, all of which depict her in rich textiles, furs, and jewels. Portraits newly presented in the three centuries following the Hanoverian succession debate as depictions of Jane Grey instead showed her in relatively plain attire without significant jewels or other adornments.

Demand for images of Jane Grey continued throughout the eighteenth century as antiquarianism became the new pursuit of many members of the leisure classes. Men such as Richard Gough (godfather of John Gough Nichols, the nineteenth-century antiquarian editor of *The Chronicle of Queen Jane*), Maurice Johnson (co-founder in 1717 of the Society of Antiquaries of London), and Sir Hans Sloane (donor of the Sloane Manuscripts to the newly-founded British Museum in 1759) pursued an intense new interest in recovering the documents of Britain's historical past. In the process, they published innumerable volumes of source materials, many of which included content related to the life narrative of Jane Grey.[51] Antiquarian interest in Jane also helped to fuel an entirely new genre of literature: historical fiction. The mythological figure of Jane Grey now came into its own as books of acknowledged fiction and featuring her as the central character were published with regularity throughout the eighteenth century.[52] By the end of that century, artists were also meeting an apparent demand for historical scene paintings featuring Jane, supplementing the continuing demand for portraits of her.[53]

The perception of Jane Grey as a fundamentally religious martyr was solidified at the turn of the nineteenth century as the British nation debated the future role of Roman Catholics in British society. The earlier Test Acts of 1673 and 1678 required that holders of public office, including members of both Houses of Parliament and the military, must take an oath of conformity to the doctrines of the established Church of England. The effect was to bar Roman Catholics and other non-conformists from holding office of any kind. Further acts attempted to bar Catholics from owning or inheriting land, and since the voter franchise was determined by property ownership, the effect was to disenfranchise Catholics.[54] The first Relief Act of 1778 restored property rights to Catholics, but was so opposed by the general population that it resulted in the Gordon Riots of 1780. Nonetheless, continuing pro-Catholic advocacy, coming especially from Ireland, led eventually to the Roman Catholic Relief Act of 1829, which largely restored the political rights of Catholics. Throughout the reform process, however, those seeking to preserve the anti-Catholic measures often brought Jane's martyrdom forward as an example of the dangers posed by Catholics. Demand for images of her once again spiked, and existing portraits of other persons were again copied and rechristened as Jane to meet the demand, such as the Fulbeck Portrait (see p.66).

Both antiquarian historians and popular writers embraced Jane Grey in the nineteenth-century with considerable vigor. Some found a romantic identification with her as an innocent and heroic young female victim who had died with admirable dignity. Others, especially the large percentage of antiquarians who served simultaneously as Anglican priests, gravitated to her story because her faithful commitment to Protestant Christianity alleviated their own anxieties in the face of the rising secularization of English society. In the process those writers produced a large body of biographical studies of both her and her era. The mythologized Jane Grey, innocent, virtuous, and compliant, also played perfectly into Victorian constructions of idealized Christian femininity.[55] Women writers, especially, engaged with this discourse of idealized femininity, producing biographies of historical female figures, including Jane Grey, who were perceived to exemplify the Victorian ideal of Christian womanhood. Agnesw Strickland was the most influential of those writers, in many respects. She produced in the middle of the nineteenth century a twelve-volume collective biographical series on the queens of England, including Jane Grey, that remains readily available even today.[56] She later penned a single-volume collective biography of the Tudor princesses, again including Jane.[57]

Strickland presented Jane as a young woman favored with the principal attributes that many people during the Victorian era thought ideal in a woman and worthy of emulation. Strickland identified these Victorian-era values as piety, learning, courage, and virtue.[58] She described Jane, in the context of a discussion of her potential marriage to Guildford Dudley, as possessing "rare accomplishments and high attainments which were, in after days, to render her the wonder and boast of her native land."[59] Strickland implied that Jane was distinctly and uniquely gifted with the desirable Victorian-era feminine ideals. Strickland and others were so diligent in their praise of Jane's virtues that they imbued her with a metaphorical halo of Protestant sanctity, a construction that has since been exceedingly difficult to put aside. And that holy aura heavily influenced the iconography of Jane Grey during the late-nineteenth and early-twentieth centuries. Portraits of her that reflected in some manner the Victorian feminine ideals of piety, learning, courage, and virtue, such as the Althorp (p.130), Bodleian (p.88), and Wrest Park Portraits (p.60), were reproduced more often than others that might potentially convey the undesirable traits of vanity or haughtiness, such as the many portraits of Queen Katherine Parr long misidentified as Jane.

By the beginning of the twentieth century, writers began to acknowledge the accumulated mythology, but they often found themselves seemingly powerless to set it aside. Ida A.Taylor, a noted novelist and author of numerous biographies of high-status women, including Jane Grey, explicitly addressed the Janeian mythology, but her observation itself nonetheless reinforced that same mythology.

> The eulogies of her panegyrists have, as a natural effect of extravagant praise, done in some sort an injury to this little white saint of the English Reformation .... To a figure defaced by flattery and adulation, whose very virtues and gifts were made to minister to party ends, it is difficult to restore the original brightness and beauty which nevertheless belonged to it.[61]

So it is with Jane's iconography. In the general absence of any reliably authentic portrait of Jane Grey Dudley, visual images of her have been adapted from other sources, whether from existing portraits of her contemporaries and co-religionists or from the imaginations of artists. Others were obtained by simply rechristening existing portraits of persons with no connection whatsoever to Jane. The result today is a confusing plethora of images that make it exceedingly difficult to recover any notion of what Jane may actually have looked like. For some of the portrait images discussed herein, the supporting documentation is frustratingly thin. It is, however, much easier to prove a negative than to prove a positive, so that many of the portraits are quite easily shown *not* to be authentic likenesses of Jane Grey. Demonstrating beyond a reasonable doubt that a given portrait *is* an authentic likeness is somewhat less easily accomplished. Only one portrait in this study, the Syon Portrait, has sufficient circumstantial evidence associated with it to enable declaring it a potentially reliable likeness. But unless one or both of the Chatsworth and Lumley Portraits can be recovered and definitively authenticated, providing a fully-documented genuine depiction of Jane Grey, perhaps the best we can ever realistically hope for is qualified reliability.

The portraits discussed in this volume are presented in groups, with each group defined by a common attribute. The first group is comprised of portraits that can reliably be re-identified as some other historical figure of the sixteenth century. One important subgroup here consists of eight portraits that can each be identified as a depiction of Queen Katherine Parr, the last of Henry VIII's six wives. The second of the large groups consists of portraits that very probably depict real persons, but those persons cannot today be readily identified. A third group includes portraits of either fictional or Biblical persons. Lastly, a portrait with a singular provenance linking it to Jane's sister Katherine Grey Seymour is presented, together with its many known copies and variants.

[1] Chatsworth Devonshire MSS, Hardwick Hall Drawers H/143/6, f.3v. The inventory is available in transcription in Gillian White, *'That whyche ys nedefoulle and nesesary': The Nature and Purpose of the Original Furnishings and Decoration of Hardwick Hall, Derbyshire* (Ph.D. diss., University of Warwick, 2005), II: 389-415.

[2] Arthur Collins, *Historical Collections of the Noble Families of Cavendishe, Holles, Vere, Harley, and Ogle* (London: 1752), 11-12.

[3] National Archives (UK), PROB 11/111, ff. 196v–208r, inventories of Chatsworth House, Hardwick Old Hall, and Hardwick New Hall, property of Elizabeth Hardwick Talbot, Dowager Countess of Shrewsbury.

[4] Mark Evans. ed., *The Lumley Inventory and Pedigree: Facsimile and Commentary on the Manuscript in the Possession of the Earls of Scarborough* (Roxburghe Club, 2010).

[5] Agnes Strickland, *Lives of the Tudor Princesses, including Lady Jane Gray* [sic] *and her sisters* (London: Longmans, Green, and Co., 1868), 137-138.

[6] Richard Davey, T*he Nine Days Queen: Lady Jane Grey and her Times* (London: Methuen, 1909), 359-362.

[7] Hester Chapman, *Lady Jane Grey* (London: Jonathan Cape, 1962).

[8] Alison Plowden, *Lady Jane Grey: Nine Days Queen* (Stroud: Sutton Publishing, 2003). The portrait used previously by Chapman, NPG 764, was also included.

[9] Leanda De Lisle, *The Sisters Who Would Be Queen: The Tragedy of Mary, Katherine and Lady Jane Grey* (Hammersmith: Harper Press, 2008), 340-341, note 25.

[10] Eric Ives, *Lady Jane Grey: A Tudor Mystery* (Oxford: Wiley-Blackwell, 2009), 15-17, illustrations 1, 2, and 5-9, plus the book jacket.

[11] Jane Grey's date of birth is usually given as sometime in October 1537, but this is a modern invention not supported by the primary-source evidence. See J. Stephan Edwards, "On the Date of Birth of Lady Jane Grey," *Notes and Queries* 54:3 (September 2007), 240-242; "A Further Note on the Date of Birth of Lady Jane Grey," *Notes and Queries* 55:2 (June 2008), 146-148.

[12] John Aylmer was notoriously uncompromising in matters of religion, and would go on to serve a controversial term as Bishop of London from 1576 until his death in 1594.

[13] Zwinglian doctrines and practices included infant baptism, denial of transubstantiation, and civil or secular rule under divine authority.

[14] See Thomas Chaloner, *Elegy on the untimely death of the most Protestant divine Lady Jane Grey* (London: Thomas Vautrollerius, 1579).

[15] See J. Stephan Edwards, *'Jane the Quene': A New Consideration of Lady Jane Grey, England's Nine Days Queen* (Ph.D. diss., University of Colorado at Boulder, 2007), 36-84.

[16] See Beverley A. Murphy, *Bastard Prince: Henry VIII's Lost Son* (Stroud: Sutton, 2001).

[17] Edward's heirs through his aunt Margaret Tudor were Margaret Douglas Stewart, Countess of Lennox and her seven-year-old son Henry, plus 10-year-old Mary Stuart, Queen of Scotland and fiancée of the Dauphin Francis of France. Those descended from Edward's aunt Mary Tudor were Francis Brandon Grey, her daughters Jane, Katherine and Mary, and Margaret Clifford (only child of the late Eleanor Brandon Clifford).

[18] Katherine Grey wed Henry Herbert, the son and heir of Dudley's ally William Herbert, Earl of Pembroke. Mary Grey, though only about eight years old, was betrothed to Arthur Grey, son of Dudley's ally William Grey of Wilton. Dudley's own daughter Katherine was betrothed to Henry Hastings, son of Francis Hastings, Earl of Huntingdon and yet another Dudley ally. Young Hastings was a potential non-Tudor claimant to the crown through his descent from a younger brother of Edward IV. Lastly, Dudley's brother Andrew was reportedly betrothed to Margaret Clifford, the only additional heir of Mary Tudor Brandon.

[19] British Library Additional Manuscripts 33230, f. 21, letter from Henry and Charles Neville, Thomas Wyatt, Robert Southwell and others to Queen Mary, July 1553.

[20] Michael Dobson and Nicola J. Watson, *England's Elizabeth: An Afterlife in Fame and Fantasy* (Oxford: Oxford University Press, 2002), 2.

[21] The most reliable biographies of Jane currently available are de Lisle, *The Sisters Who Would Be Queen* and Ives, *Lady Jane Grey*. See also Edwards, *'Jane the Quene'* (n.15 above).

22 Horace Walpole to Richard Bentley, undated 1752, *The Letters of Horace Walpole, Earl of Orford*, ed. Peter Cunningham (London: Henry G. Bohn, 1861), II: 302-304. On a visit to Penshurst.

23 Lady Jane Grey, *An epistle of the Ladye Iane, a righte vertuous woman, to a learned man of late falne from the truth of Gods most holy word, for fear of the worlde read it, to thy consolacion: whereunto is added the communication that she had with Master Feckenham vpon her faith, and belefe of the sacraments: also another epistle whiche she wrote to her sister, with the words she spake vpon the scaffold befor she suffered, anno. M.D.Liiii* (London: John Day, 1554). Leanda de Lisle has argued that production of the pamphlets was facilitated by Jane's mother Frances and by William Cecil. Cecil would later become chief minister to Elizabeth I and a supporter of the claims of Jane's sister, Katherine Grey, to succeed Elizabeth I. See de Lisle, *Sisters Who Would Be Queen*, 159 and 234.

24 John Foxe, *The Unabridged Acts and Monuments Online* or *TAMO* (1563 edition) (HRI Online Publications, Sheffield, 2011), Book 5: 969. <http//www.johnfoxe.org> Accessed 27 April 2014. The mother of the Roman tribunes Tiberius and Gaius Gracchus (late 2nd century BCE) was Cornelia Africana, a woman noted even during her own lifetime for her knowledge of Latin and Greek literature and for patronizing scholars, as well as for the chastity she maintained during her widowhood. Foxe's somewhat vague reference to the "house of the Aspasians [and] Sempronians" is more problematic. There being no Roman gens or family of the nomen Aspasian, the term would seem to indicate Aspasia, the 5th-century-BCE Greek patroness of Socrates mentioned in the works of Plato and Xenophon. Yet that Aspasia was reputedly also a brothel-keeper and notorious mistress to Pericles. There were numerous Roman women named Sempronia, some of whom were also members of the gens or "house" Sempronia, but none are noted for their intellect. Sempronia Gracchus, for example, was famed primarily for her status as sister to the Gracchi brothers mentioned above. She was accused by some of contriving the death of her husband, Scipio Amelianus Africanus. Another Sempronia, mother of Julius Caesar's assassin Decimus Junius Brutus Albinus, was reputed of poor character by the Roman historian Sallust. None of these Aspasian or Sempronian figures is appropriate in Foxe's context of positive historical comparisons to Jane Grey.

25 25 Edward III c.2, *De natis ultra mare*. See also Keechang Kim, *Aliens in Medieval Law: The Origins of Modern Citizenship* (Cambridge: Cambridge University Press, 2000), 103-125.

26 Eric Ives, "Tudor Dynastic Problems Revisited," *Historical Research* 81:212 (2008), 255-279.

27 Michael Drayton, *The Works of Michael Drayton, Esq.* (London: Printed by J. Hughes for W. Reeve, 1753), I:372-383.

28 Thomas Dekker and John Webster, *The Famous History of Sir Thomas Wyatt* (London: Thomas Archer, 1607). The play continued to be restaged and reprinted periodically down to the present day.

29 See Musa Gurnis-Farrell, "Martyr Acts: Playing With Foxe's Martyrs on the Public Stage" in *Religion and Drama in Early Modern England: The Performance of Religion on the Renaissance Stage*, ed. Jane Hwang Degenhardt and Elizabeth Williamson (Farnham: Ashgate Publishing, 2011), 179-189. The play is also the first known instance in which Jane and her husband Guildford Dudley are portrayed as sentimentally romantic lovers, a theme that would be repeated often by successive writers, most recently in the ahistorical Paramount Pictures release, *Lady Jane* (1986).

30 Henry Holland, *Herωologia Anglica hoc est, clarissimorvm et doctissimorvm aliqovt* [sic] *Anglorvm qvi florvervnt ab anno Cristi M.D. vsq' ad presentem annvm M.D.C.XX viuae effigies vitae et elogia*, with engravings by Willem, Crispin, and Magdalene van de Passe (Arnhem: Jan Janson Arnemuiden, 1620).

31 One notable exception is the re-issue in 1629 and 1636 of a pamphlet originally published in 1615, *The life, death and actions of the most chast, learned, and religious lady, the Lady Iane Gray, daughter to the Duke of Suffolke. Containing foure principall discourses written with her owne hands. The first an admonition to such as are weake in faith: the second a catechisme: the third an exhortation to her sister: and the last her words at her death* (London: G. Eld, for John Wright, 1615; London: printed by I. H[aviland] for John Wright, 1629 and 1636).

32 Thomas Fuller, *The Church History of Britain: From the Birth of Jesus Christ Until the Year MDCXLVII*, ed. J.S. Brewer (Oxford University Press, 1845), IV:136.

33 Peter Heylyn, *Ecclesia Restaurata, or, the Reformation of the Church of England* (London: H. Twyford, T. Dring, J. Place, W. Palmer, 1661), II:3-44.

34 Joseph H. Preston, "English ecclesiastical historians and the problem of bias, 1559-1742," *Journal of the History of Ideas* 32:2 (April-June 1971), 203-220; John Drabble, "Thomas Fuller, Peter Heylyn and the English Reformation," *Renaissance and Reformation*, New Series, 3 (Spring 1979), 168-188.

35 Heylyn, *Ecclesia Restaurata*, 4.

36 Gilbert Burnet, *The History of the Reformation of the Church of England: The second part, of the progress made in it till the settlement of it in the beginning of Q. Elizabeth's reign* (London: printed by T[homas]. H[odgkin]. for Richard Chiswell, 1681), leaf numbered 172 between pages 272 and 273 of the text. This first edition included 16 engraved portraits. Burnet's History was re-issued, in both full length and abridgment, dozens of times between 1681 and the present.

37 Chute was elected to the Second Protectorate Parliament in 1656, but was barred from taking his seat (along with over 100 others) owing to suspicion that he held Royalist sympathies. He was re-elected to the Third Protectorate Parliament in 1658 and chosen Speaker of the Commons by unanimous acclaim. He died in office less than four months later, on 14 April 1659, aged 61.

38 See, for example, *A conference between the Lady Jane Grey and F. Fecknam a Romish priest, concerning the blessed sacrament; whilest she was prisoner in the Tower of London, and was beheaded on the Green there, Feb. 12. 1554. Together with her behaviour and last speech and prayers at her suffering* (London, 1688).

39 Edith Snook, "Jane Grey, 'Manful' Combat, and the Female Reader in Early Modern England," *Renaissance and Reformation* 32:1 (Winter 2009), 66.

40 John Banks, *The Innocent Usurper* (London: printed for R. Bentley, 1694).

41 James Stuart, son of James II, unsuccessfully attempted to invade Scotland in 1708. Shortly after the accession of George I in 1714, the so-called "Rebellion of the Fifteen" was put down. Several other rebellions arose between 1715 and 1745, effectively ending with the defeat of James Stuart's son, "Bonnie Prince Charlie," at the Battle of Culloden in 1746.

42 Jean I. Marsden, *Fatal Desire: Women, Sexuality, and the English Stage, 1660-1720* (Ithaca: Cornell University Press, 2006), 171.

43 Edward Young, T*he Force of Religion; or, Vanquish'd Love (*London: Printed by E. Curll and J. Pemberton, 1714).

44 Marsden, *Fatal Desire*, 177.

45 Marsden, *Fatal Desire*, 174.

46 Nicholas Rowe, *Lady Jane Grey: A Tragedy, in five acts* (Edinburgh: Apollo Press, 1782). Like Burnet's *History of the Reformation*, Rowe's play has seldom been out of print since its first publication.

47 Charles Gildon, *Remarks on Mr Rowe's Tragedy of the Lady Jane Grey, and all his other plays*, The English Stage Series, vol. 48 (New York: Garland Publishing, 1974).

48 *The Life, Character, and Death of the most Illustrious Pattern of Female Virtue, the Lady Jane Gray, Who was Beheaded in the Tower at 16 Years of Age, for her Steadfast Adherence to the Protestant Religion* (London: James Roberts, 1714).

49 *The History and Fall of the Lady Jane Grey* (London: Printed by J. Watts for J. Roberts, 1725).

50 John Strype, *Historical Collections of the Life and Acts of the Right Reverend Father in God John Aylmer* (London: printed by W Bowyer for Brabazon Aylmer, 1701), 297.

51 See, for example, *A collection of proceedings and trials against state prisoners; ... from the Norman conquest to this present time* (London: printed for J. Wilcox, 1741); Delahay Gordon, *General History of the Lives, Trials, and Executions of All the Royal and Noble Personages, that have Suffered in GReat-Britain and Ireland for High Treason, and other crimes* (London: J. Burd, 1760).

52 See, for example, *The history and fall of the Lady Jane Grey* (London: J. Watts, 1729); George Keate, *An Epistle from Lady Jane Grey to Lord Guildford Dudley* (London: printed for R. and J. Dodsley, 1757); *Lady Jane Grey: An Historical Tale in Two Volumes* (London: Minerva Press, 1791). The last is an example of the degree to which eighteenth-century historical fiction continues to be cited as factual history. It was extensively quoted by James D. Taylor in 2003 for his publication, on the 450th anniversary of Jane's reign, of *The Letters of Lady Jane Grey, the Nine Days Queen, 1553: Containing letters from, to, and about Lady Jane Grey* (Jefferson, N.C.: MacFarland Press, 2003),

a book sold under the guise of "historical reference" and unwittingly purchased as such by numerous universities and other academic institutions.

[53] See, for example, *The Dukes of Northumberland and Suffolk Praying Lady Jane Grey to Accept the Crown*, Giovanni Battista Cipriani, before 1785, oil on canvas, dimensions unknown, private collection; *Lady Jane Grey and Abbot Feckenham*, James Northcote, 1792, oil on canvas, dimensions unknown, private collection; *Lady Jane Grey the Night Before her Execution*, William Ward after Robert Fulton, 1793, mezzotint engraving, 20 in. x 13 $^7/_8$ in., British Museum, London, 1878.0713.152; *The Death of Lady Jane Gray, A.D. 1554*, Valentine Green after Johann Gerhard Huck, 1786, mezzotint engraving, 19 $^1/_8$ in. x 24 $^1/_4$ in., Victoria and Albert Museum, London, E389-1959.

[54] Wealthy Roman Catholic landholders sometimes circumvented these laws through the creation of estate trusts.

[55] On the Victorian discourse on idealized femininity, see M. Jeanne Peterson, *Family, Love, and Work in the Lives of Victorian Gentlewomen* (Bloomington: Indiana University Press, 1989); Anne Digby, "Victorian values and women in public and private," *Victorian Values*, ed. Thomas C. Smout (Oxford: Oxford University Press for the British Academy, 1992); Angela Schwarz, "They cannot choose but to be women: Stereotypes of femininity and ideals of womanliness in late Victorian and Edwardian Britain," *Political Reform in Britain, 1886-1996: Themes, Ideas, Policies*, eds. Ulrike Jordan and Wolfram Kaiser (Bochum: Brockmeyer, 1997), 131–50.

[56] Agnes Strickland, *Lives of the Queens of England: From the Norman Conquest*, 12 vols. (London: H. Colburn, 1841-48).

[57] Agnes Strickland, *Lives of the Tudor Princesses, including Lady Jane Gray* [sic] *and her sisters* (London: Longmans, Green, and Company, 1868).

[58] Strickland, *Tudor Princesses*, 94.

[59] Strickland, *Tudor Princesses*, 94.

[60] Ida A. Taylor, *Lady Jane Grey and Her Times* (New York: D. Appleton and Company, 1908), 190-191.

IANA GRAYA

Regia stirps tristi cinxi diademate crines
Regna sed omnipotens hinc meliora dedit

Leiden 296

1   The van de Passe Engraved Portrait

Queen Katherine Parr (inscribed Iana Graya)
Willem and Magdalena van de Passe

Line engraving printed on paper; 6 ½ in. x 4 ⅝ in.

Published 1620 in Henry Holland's *Heroωlogia Anglica*.

Our study of the portraiture of Jane Grey begins with this engraved portrait owing to its reputation over the past four centuries as a reliably authentic portrait of Jane. It first appeared in 1620 in Henry Holland's *Heroωlogia Anglica*, a collection of laudatory accounts of fifty-nine political heroes and "divines," or religious heroes, of the Tudor period. A preface to the work states that the engravings were created by members of the van de Passe family of noted Dutch engravers, drawing where possible upon pre-existing authentic painted life-portraits.[1] And of the fifty-nine engraved portraits in the *Heroωlogia*, twenty-eight can in fact still readily be matched to surviving authenticated portraits of those same individuals.[2] The engraving representing Jane Grey incorporated into the image itself the Latinized form of Jane's name, Iana Graya, leaving no question as to whom the engraver intended it to depict.

The statement in the preface to the *Heroωlogia* attesting to the authenticity of the images, especially the engraving labeled "Iana Graya," went largely unchallenged until the end of the twentieth century. Writing in 1965 as Director of the National Portrait Gallery (NPG), Sir Roy Strong declared the engraving to be "the only authentic portrait" of Jane then known.[3] He presented as corroborating evidence the claim that an ancient painted portrait (the Hastings Portrait, p.28) had "always been known as Lady Jane and came from her father's castle of Astley" and closely resembled the engraving, including its inclusion of a coronet-shaped bodice jewel exactly like that seen in the engraving. Strong thus deduced that the engraving must have been based upon the painting, and the engraving must therefore have been authentic.[4] Yet subsequent research published in 1996 directly correlated the seemingly unique coronet brooch with the written description of a brooch of identical design found among the jewels owned and worn by Katherine Parr, the last of Henry VIII's six wives.[5] That research focused, however, on the Glendon Hall Portrait (NPG4451) discussed below and addressed the van de Passe engraving only tangentially. Yet if the coronet brooch was as unique as was implied by the later study, the lady depicted in the van de Passe engraving must be Katherine Parr rather than Jane Grey. Nonetheless, the identification of the sitter in the engraving remains officially unresolved. The National Portrait Gallery's online database descriptions of its own copies of the engraving continue to identify the sitter as Jane Grey Dudley, qualified by an non-committal notation that "the source for this portrait of Lady

Jane Grey remains in doubt and it is possible that the original portrait was misidentified."[6]

The question arises as to how and why a portrait of Katherine Parr became incorrectly identified as Jane Grey less than 75 years after both their deaths. The answer may lie in the relative presence of the two women in the general cultural memory during the late Tudor and early Stuart periods. Katherine Parr was certainly still present as a historical figure, but she was not the object of popular admiration nor the subject of myth-building to the same degree as was Jane Grey. Parr's two devotional works, *Prayers or Meditations* and *The Lamentation of a Sinner*, were repeatedly reissued well into the seventeenth century, and portraits of her were reproduced, but she was neither the principal subject of numerous poems and plays nor a conduit for conducting the public debate on the royal succession. Yet throughout the reign of Elizabeth I, memories of Jane were repeatedly resurrected in poetry, prose, and drama, particularly in relation to the Elizabethan succession issue. Jane was inevitably remembered, for example, in the rhetoric and propaganda of the 1560s and 1570s supporting the claims of Jane's sisters Katherine Grey Seymour and Mary Grey Keyes as potential successors to Elizabeth.[7] And by the last decade of the sixteenth century, when it was apparent that Elizabeth's reign would soon end, Jane became a focal point around which the succession could be metaphorically argued in the public sphere with less fear of incurring official censure, as discussed in the introduction to this volume. Jane became an enduringly popular historical figure, stimulating a demand for portraits of her, while memories of Katherine became increasingly limited to her status as the last of Henry VIII's wives. It is therefore likely that the portrait of Katherine Parr from which the van de Passes engraved their depiction of Jane Grey had, for any number of reasons, simply lost its identity following Parr's death and become erroneously re-identified as her more-popular and better-remembered friend and ward, Jane Grey (see The Hastings Portrait, p.28).

The van de Passe Engraved Portrait became a popular image of Jane Grey and was reproduced repeatedly, especially as a fashion for the collecting of engravings arose late in the eighteenth century and early in the nineteenth. Some reproductions were faithful to the original by the van de Passes, including those by William Marhsall (1648) and Gaspar Bouttats (1658). Others embellished the image with added background drapery and scenery (Edme de Boulonois, late seventeenth century) or royal robes draped over the sitter's shoulder (Cornelis Martinus Vermeulen, 1697). In the most extreme example, Edward Hargrave (1840) extended the original bust length portrait into a full length one, complete with ermine-lined royal robe and flowing train. But as a result of the popularity of the engraving and the many later copies, the basic image became firmly cemented in the collective cultural and historical consciousness as an authentic likeness of Jane Grey rather than of its true subject, Queen Katherine Parr. And that early error by the van de Passes enabled further error in later years by owners and evaluators of at least three other portraits said to depict Jane, all discussed below.

The painted source from which the van de Passes derived their engraving of Jane Grey has never been properly identified. Manuscript marginalia in a single copy of the first edition of the *Heroωlogia* identified the owner of the painting as "Mr Jo: Harison" and the artist as Hans Holbein.[8] Art historian Arthur Hind speculated that Harison was perhaps John Harrison (*d*. after 1638), Groom of the Privy Chamber to James I's son and heir apparent, Prince Henry Frederick (*d*.1612).[9] Hind's speculation has been accepted and repeated over the years, most notably by Roy Strong.[10] Yet in light of the deployment of Jane near the turn of the sixteenth century as a vehicle for advocating for or against specific lines of royal succession, Hind's association of "Mr Jo. Harison" with the Groom Harrison seems highly improbable. Since Jane was most commonly put forward to argue for the Seymour line and against the Scottish line of Prince Henry's father, James Stuart, possession by a Groom of the Privy Chamber of a portrait of Jane would, in the gossip-prone world of Stuart court politics, have undoubtedly led to questions regarding the owner's true loyalties.

Hind seems to have assumed that the marginalia of the *Herωlogia* was written at about the same time as the publication of the volume in 1620. Yet the specific content of the marginalia allowed for it to have been written somewhat later. The first three engravings in the volume, for example, were all described as being taken from paintings by Holbein held at Richmond Palace. That palace was still an active royal residence until 1650, so that the marginalia could date to any time between 1620 and 1650. But it was in that later year that Parliament began liquidating the royal art collection of the recently-executed Charles I, a process that involved the creation of inventories and even public exhibitions of the works seized. These were quite probably the circumstances through which the marginalist acquired his information.

Jerry Brotton published in 2007 a careful study of the sale of Charles I's art collection during the period between 1650 and 1652.[11] Brotton noted that the collection was used as a form of payment-in-kind to settle the debts of the former king, with creditors receiving paintings and other art objects in lieu of cash. Many of those creditors were formerly suppliers of goods and services to the royal household, including one Edmund Harrison, until 1649 the King's Embroiderer. Harrison became a commissioner in the sale and was thus in charge of the distribution of a significant portion of the collection. Harrison was also the brother-in-law of another of the commissioners, Edmund Godfrey, a large-scale London woodmonger who supplied the royal households. Godfrey's business partner was, in turn, one James Harrison of Sellinge, Kent.[12] Further, James Harrison had a brother John Harrison who was a lawyer at Gray's Inn, London.[13] This cluster of inter-related Harrisons (and Godfreys) is important because they were mentioned by the Civil War-era diarist Richard Symonds, who in December 1652 inspected the Harrisons' groups of paintings removed from the Royal Collection.

Symonds left only very vague accounts of the Harrisons' paintings, written in the pages of a small manuscript volume of notes on painting that survives today in the British Library. Symonds recorded simply that one "Harison the wood-monger of the Kings" sold to the Spanish Ambassador, Alonso de Cardenas, a collection of paintings worth one hundred English pounds sterling.[14] And on 30 December 1652, Symonds visited a wharf-warehouse owned by "Harison the Kings Embroyderer" situated on the Thames near Somerset House. Symonds noted explicitly that this second group was the seized property of the former king, Charles I.[15] Though Symonds did not enumerate the precise contents of either Harrison's collection, they undoubtedly contained a wide sampling of the many works amassed by the Crown over the preceding century. And while we can today only speculate, it is entirely possible that the collections included one or more portraits of Katherine Parr attributed to Hans Holbein, and that any one of the three Harrisons – whether embroiderer, woodmonger, or lawyer – acquired the painting between 1650 and 1652 as payment for a debt owed to one or more of them by the Crown.[16] It is far more likely that the "Mr Jo: Harison" of the marginalia in Holland's *Herωlogia* was one of the Harrison tradesmen of 1650–1652 rather than the Harrison Groom of the Privy Chamber before 1612.

[1] Holland, *Heroωlogia Anglica*, f.5r. "In vobis delineatas Anglicanae gentis heroum effigies, quas curavi (quod maxime potui) ut ab ipsis illorum vives imaginibus olio depictis, effigerentur."

[2] Fifteen can be precisely correlated with surviving life portraits of the given individuals. An additional thirteen bear a strong facial resemblance to otherwise dissimilar surviving life portraits of the same individual (i.e., the costume or position is significantly altered in the engraving). Of the remaining thirty-one engravings, five are copies of other engravings created by other artists before 1620 and two are probably misidentified (those of John Harrington [I and II] of Exton). Others, such as those of Edward Seymour, Henry Prince of Wales, and Robert Montagu, are described as having been in buildings that were destroyed by fire or neglect later in the seventeenth century, likely also destroying the reference portraits. The remainder depict mostly persons who are today relatively obscure and for whom no painted portrait seems to have survived.

[3] National Portrait Gallery, Heinz Library and Archive, Object File NPG4451, Pre-Purchase Assessment signed by Roy Strong, 25 June 1965.

[4] National Portrait Gallery, Heinz Library and Archive, Object File NPG4451, letter from Roy Strong dated 24 August 1965.

[5] Susan E. James, "Lady Jane Grey or Queen Kateryn Parr?," *The Burlington Magazine* 138: 1114 (Jan., 1996), 20–24.

[6] National Portrait Gallery, Online Collection Database, NPG D19952, *Jane Dudley (née Grey)*, Magdalena de Passe, by Willem de Passe, after Hans Holbein the Younger.

[7] Katherine Grey Seymour died in custody in 1568. Mary Grey Keyes died in 1578.

[8] Marginalia photographically reproduced in Arthur M. Hind, *The Reign of James I*, Volumes 2 of *Engraving in England in the Sixteenth and Seventeenth Centuries* (Cambridge: Cambridge University Press, 1955), 32, 153, and plate 87.

[9] Hind, *Engraving*, 153.

[10] Roy Strong, *Tudor and Jacobean Portraits* (London: HMSO, 1969), I: 78.

[11] Jerry Brotton, *The Sale of the Late King's Goods: Charles I and his Art Collection* (London: Pan Books, 2007).

[12] Alan Marshall, "The Westminster Magistrate and the Irish Stroker: Sir Edmund Godfrey and Valentine Greatrakes, Some Unpublished Correspondence," *The Historical Journal* 40:2 (1997), 501.

[13] John Foster, *Alumni Oxonienses 1500-1714: Abannan-Kyte* (London: Parker and Co, 1891), s.v. "Harrison, John," 652–678.

[14] British Library Egerton Manuscripts 1636, f. 101r.

[15] British Library Egerton Manuscripts 1636, f. 90v.

[16] Any original portrait of Parr attributed to Holbein could easily have been lost or destroyed during the turbulent period between the break-up of the Royal Collection in 1651/2 and its re-assembly after 1660, with only copies surviving. No portrait of Parr (or of Jane Grey) resembling the van de Passe Engraving is currently known to be in the Royal Collection.

2   The Glendon Hall Portrait

Queen Katherine Parr
Attributed to Master John

Oil on wood panel; 71 in. x 37 in.

Ca. 1545

Provenance:

> By descent with the Lane family of Glendon Hall, Northamptonshire, to 1758;
>
> when acquired by John Booth with purchase of Glendon Hall;
>
> thence by descent to Mrs Vincent Gompertz, 1953;
>
> National Portrait Gallery, London, accession number NPG4451, 1965.

The National Portrait Gallery acquired this painting in 1965 and, upon comparing it to the van de Passe Engraved Portrait discussed above, immediately rechristened it as Lady Jane Grey.[1] Previously, it had been part of the collection at Glendon Hall, near Kettering in Northamptonshire, for well over three centuries, throughout which time it had always been identified as a portrait of Katherine Parr.[2] The owners of Glendon Hall in the sixteenth century were the Lanes of Horton, cousins by marriage to Katherine Parr.[3] The painting remained at Glendon Hall until the 1950s, at which point the collection was broken up and sold.

The new identification applied in 1965 stood essentially unchallenged for three decades, during which time the image was reproduced repeatedly as a portrait of Jane Grey. The NPG itself used the image for commercial purposes, producing pictorial souvenir posters, postcards, refrigerator magnets, and key chains all labeled "Lady Jane Grey."

Historical novelist Deborah Meroff adapted the image in 1979 for the book jacket of her popular fictional tale *Coronation of Glory: The Story of Lady Jane Grey*.[4] Mary Luke did the same in 1986 for her book, *The Nine Days Queen: A Portrait of Lady Jane Grey*.[5] But most importantly, the Glendon Hall Portrait was used in the same capacity by Alison Plowden for her best-selling *Lady Jane Grey and the House of Suffolk*, a work that continues to be cited by scholars of Tudor history.[6] A detail of the head was even used on commemorative postage stamps issued in the early 1970s by the British territorial dependency of Barbuda. Though the portrait was correctly restored to its original identification as Katherine Parr after three decades, the association with Jane Grey remained deep-rooted in international popular culture for many years thereafter. The Internet-based reference work Wikipedia even felt compelled until April 2009 to include the Glendon Hall Portrait as a portrait of Jane.

The seemingly authoritative identification of the portrait as Lady Jane Grey was very convincingly and ultimately successfully challenged by Susan James in 1996. While working on a biography of Katherine Parr, James had occasion to study numerous inventories of royal jewels, including an inventory of "the Quene's Jewells" dated 1550. James identified the "Quene" as Katherine Parr specifically, though Parr had died in 1548. Notable among the items listed was a brooch "with a crown containing two diamonds, one ruby, one emerald; the crown being garnished with diamonds [and] three pearls pendant."[7] The crown motif was seemingly unique, and the colors of the diamonds, ruby, and emerald noted in the inventory matched the stones depicted in the coronet (or crown) brooch seen in the Glendon Hall Portrait. James also noted that others of the jewels depicted in the portrait can be reliably associated with items listed in various royal inventories, especially the necklace pendant and the beaded girdle-chain.[8] The painting's prior longstanding identification as Katherine Parr and its provenance linking it to Parr's sixteenth-century relatives, when coupled with the evidence drawn from the jewel inventory, make it very difficult to refute James's conclusion that the sitter is indeed Parr rather than Jane Grey.

James carefully noted a strong correlation between the Glendon Hall Portrait and three others—the engraving from Holland's *Heroωlogia*, the Hastings Portrait, and the Jersey Portrait—leading her to suggest that they too might best be re-identified as Katherine Parr. James asserted that the jewelry, especially the coronet-shaped brooch, "is most unlikely to have passed through the hands of Jane Grey," but she offered no evidence or argument to support that critical assertion. She did note, however, that an inventory of jewels presented to Jane out of the Royal Treasury in July 1553 did not contain any items identifiable with the jewels in the Glendon Hall Portrait, though that presentation was made at least six years after the Glendon Hall Portrait is thought to have been created. James failed to rule out explicitly the possibility that Parr or others may have simply loaned the jewels to Jane very briefly for the purpose of having a portrait executed in which Jane could be depicted in attire appropriate to a potential royal bride.

The fact that Jane did borrow jewels from the Royal Treasury on at least one occasion, her wedding to Guildford Dudley late in May 1553, is well documented.[9] This is all the more crucial when it is remembered that Jane lived in Parr's household for perhaps as much as two years, late 1546 to 1548, having entered the Queen's household as a maid of honor prior to the death of Henry VIII in January 1547. A few months after the king's death, Parr married Thomas Seymour, who was already actively courting Jane's father Henry Grey with promises to bring about a marriage between Jane and Seymour's royal nephew, King Edward VI. To that end, Seymour acquired guardianship of Jane in 1547, and she remained in the Parr-Seymour household until after Parr's death in September 1548.[10] It would have been consistent with Seymour's own plans for either himself or Parr to have commissioned a portrait of Jane. Yet as James noted, many of Parr's jewels were locked away in the Royal Treasury during 1547 and 1548, forcing Seymour to pursue legal avenues in an attempt to have them restored to Parr.[11] Both Parr and Seymour died before the dispute was settled, she in childbirth and he for treason related to his plans to exploit his nephew the King. But James was correct that the jewels are most unlikely to have passed through Jane Grey's hands, even as a brief loan and despite Jane's presence in the Parr household during 1547 and 1548, since they were never in Parr's own hands after January 1547. It seems entirely correct that the Glendon Hall Portrait depicts Katherine Parr at about age 32 rather than Jane Grey at age 8 or 9.

[1] "An Authentic Portrait of Lady Jane Grey?," *The Times of London*, 5 July 1965, 14; Strong, *Tudor and Jacobean Portraits*, I:78 and II: pl. 142.

[2] See, for example, *Jones' Views of the Seats, Mansions, Castles, Etc. of Noblemen and Gentlemen in England, Wales, Scotland, and Ireland* (London: Jones and Company, 1829), s.v. "Glendon Hall, Northamptonshire," page marked "FF2."

[3] James, "Lady Jane Grey or Queen Kateryn Parr?," 20.

[4] Deborah Meroff, *Coronation of Glory: The Story of Lady Jane Grey* (Grand Rapids: Zondervan Publishing, 1979).

[5] Mary Luke, *The Nine Days Queen: A Portrait of Lady Jane Grey* (New York: William Morrow, 1986).

[6] Alison Plowden, *Lady Jane Grey and the House of Suffolk* (New York: Franklin Watts, 1986).

[7] James, "Lady Jane Grey or Queen Kateryn Parr?," 22.

[8] James, "Lady Jane Grey or Queen Kateryn Parr?," 23-24.

[9] British Library Royal MSS 18C XXIV, ff. 340v and 363v.

[10] de Lisle, *Sisters Who Would Be Queen*, 28-52.

[11] James, "Lady Jane Grey or Queen Kateryn Parr?," 21.

3   The Hastings Portrait

Queen Katherine Parr
Unknown artist, formerly attributed to Hans Holbein

Oil on canvas; 38 in. x 26 in.

Undated

Provenance:

   By descent with the Astley Barons Hastings since the 18th Century.

The sitter depicted in this painting has been identified as Lady Jane Grey since at least the eighteenth century. It bears an exceptionally strong resemblance to the van de Passe Engraved Portrait discussed previously and was almost certainly the source for the engraving. Comparison of the jewels depicted in the painting to those seen in the engraving reveals a positive and complete match. Further, the brocade patterns of the dress fabrics match those in the engraving so closely that any slight differences can reasonably be attributed to artistic license in the hand of the engraver. Equally tellingly, the jewels (other than the crown brooch) and fabric patterns seen in the engraving do not match in any way the same elements seen in the Glendon Hall Portrait, though the engraving is far more commonly associated with that better-known picture.[1]

Neither is the Hastings Portrait likely to have been adapted after 1620 from the van de Passe engraving. The painted portrait contains significant background detail not seen in the engraving and is three-quarter rather than bust length. Further, the sitter in the painting faces the opposite direction from the lady in the engraving. This would be expected if the engraving had been based on the painting, but not if the painting were based on the engraving. Paintings derived directly from the engraving are known, but they more nearly mimic the engraving.[2] Yet the close correlation between the Hastings Portrait and the van de Passe Engraved Portrait labeled "Iana Graya" cannot be taken as proof that the sitter in the painting is indeed Jane Grey. The Hastings Portrait must be considered on its own merits, without reference to the engraving.

Provenance is often key to identifying the sitter in a portrait, and in the case of this portrait, an Astley family tradition holds that it came originally from Astley Castle, built by the family's thirteenth-century ancestors. Ownership of the castle was transferred by marriage to the Greys early in the fifteenth century, however, eventually passing in the sixteenth century to Jane's father Henry Grey. Astley Castle was one of many Grey estates in the area and was a mere twenty miles from the Grey family seat at Bradgate Park. But while the association between Astley Castle and the Greys was a strong one prior to the executions of both Jane and her father in February 1554, the house and manor were soon thereafter acquired by Edward Chamberlaine, who had no discoverable direct connection with either the Astleys or the Greys. The house was let out to tenants over the next century, until it was sold to the Newdigates of Arbury Hall in 1674.[3] In other words, Astley Castle was never in Astley hands after the early 1400s, a full century before Jane's birth. The disposition of the sixteenth-century furnishings of Astley Castle is not documented. It is therefore impossible to confirm reliably the Astley family tradition regarding the origins of the portrait.

Circumstantial evidence actually dictates against the Astleys having owned a portrait of Jane Grey in the second half of the sixteenth century. During that period, Thomas Astley possessed both Hillmorton and Melton Constable Hall, two residences through which the portrait is documented to have passed in the eighteenth century. Thomas's first wife had been Catherine (called "Kat") Champernown Astley, famously a beloved companion to Princess Elizabeth Tudor. The Astleys remained in high favor throughout the reign of Queen Elizabeth, making it extremely unlikely that they would have possessed a portrait of Jane Grey, whose sisters Elizabeth regarded as a threat. But because Elizabeth had been fond of Parr, there would have been no risk associated with owning a portrait of her.

The portrait first entered the historical record in 1770 at the manor of Hillmorton near Rugby, Warwickshire, upon its removal to Melton Constable Hall, Norfolk.[4] Sir Jacob Astley (d.1729), 1st Baronet Astley of Hillmorton, had inherited the estate of Melton Constable in 1659 from his uncle, Sir Isaac Astley, 1st Baronet Astley of Melton Constable. Sir Jacob came to prefer Melton Constable over Hillmorton and therefore rebuilt the former in the 1660s using the latest architectural styles. Hillmorton was let out to a series of tenants.[5] Sir Edward Astley, the 4th Baronet, finally sold Hillmorton outright in about 1770, prompting the removal of its contents to Melton Constable Hall. The Astleys subsequently succeeded in 1841 in reclaiming the long-abeyant barony of Hastings and retained Melton Constable as their primary residence until it was sold in 1948 by the 21st Baron Hastings. The portrait is now held at Seaton Delaval Hall, inherited by the Astleys early in the nineteenth century but not routinely occupied by them until the 1980s. While the Hastings Portrait can be traced through the three Astley residences of Hillmorton, Melton Constable Hall, and Seaton Delaval Hall, its provenance prior to 1770 is unknown. Its history may well be connected to the sale of King Charles I's art collection in 1650-52, however.

The royal collection liquidated early in the Commonwealth period included large numbers of portraits of royal figures of the sixteenth century, those portraits having been held in the various royal palaces of Whitehall, Richmond, Greenwich, etc. It is exceedingly likely that one or more portraits of Parr were held in those palaces, it being well documented that she commissioned numerous portraits of herself.[6] And in his study of the dissolution of the royal collection, Jerry Brotton noted that many members of the aristocracy were keen to take financial advantage of the death of Charles I by acquiring from the former royal collection, at what amounted to bargain-basement prices, works of art that were both aesthetically appealing and monetarily valuable. The sale of the king's goods posed an ideal investment opportunity for anyone who could afford to participate.[7] It is not inconceivable that any one of several Royalist Astleys, two of whom earned titles specifically for service to the embattled Charles I, acquired this and perhaps other paintings both as investments and as mementoes of the executed King. Several of those Royalist Astleys died childless, so that their collected estates eventually descended to a single heir, Sir Edward Astley, 4th Baronet Astley of Hillmorton and owner of this portrait in 1770.

According to an article published in *Country Life* magazine in 1928, the Hastings Portrait had originally been painted on wood panel, consistent with sixteenth-century practices. It was reportedly transferred to canvas in 1893, a conservation technique not uncommon in that era. In the process, the original painted surface was damaged, requiring considerable restoration and "somewhat detract[ing] from the picture's appearance of authenticity."[8] The painting was examined in 1965 by

Joyce Plesters, a pioneer in the use of technology in studying art objects, who determined that the painting had apparently always been on canvas. She further identified the surface painting technique as consistent with the eighteenth century rather than the sixteenth.[9]

Examination of the painting in August 2010 did nonetheless reveal that it had at least been relined and placed on new stretchers in the not-too-distant past. A paper label attached to the stretcher indicates unknown work was performed at some point by W. Boswell & Sons of 48 London Street, Norwich. Boswell was situated on London Street between 1883 and 1929, but the trading name did not become "W. Boswell & Sons" until about 1916, suggesting that Boswell worked on the painting sometime between 1916 and 1929. Whether this work by Boswell is the source for the report in 1928 that the painting was transferred from wood to canvas is unclear pending technological examination using modern methods and the removal of any overpainting.

If it is determined that the painting was always on canvas and was created in the late seventeenth or early eighteenth century, the question arises as to why a family by then distinguished as Tories, and thus supporters of a succession based solely in blood and without regard to religion, would have commissioned a portrait of Jane Grey, an icon of the Whig and anti-Catholic cause. If, however, it can be definitively established that the painting was originally on wood panel, it would become all the more likely that the painting was a life portrait of Parr sold out of the royal collection early in the 1650s, acquired by an Astley, installed at Hillmorton until 1770, removed to Melton Constable until 1948, and held now at Seaton Delaval. Possession at the end of the seventeenth and beginning of the eighteenth century of a historical artifact associated with Charles I, even if that object depicted Jane Grey, was undoubtedly politically less questionable than newly commissioning a copy of an ancient portrait thought to depict an icon of one's contemporary political enemies.

Regardless of whether the Hastings Portrait is a sixteenth-century original or a late seventeenth- or early eighteenth-century copy, several similarities between it and the Glendon Hall Portrait indicate that the sitter is the same individual. There is, of course, the seemingly definitive presence of the coronet-shaped brooch. But the two ladies also appear to be essentially identical in physical appearance. The overall facial shape, together with the appearance of such individual facial elements as the chin, cheekbones, lips, and eyes are all but indistinguishable between the two. Both sitters have slender necks and gently sloping shoulders. Each has reddish-brown with waves or a tendency to curliness. Based on physiognomy alone, there can be little doubt that the two portraits depict the same woman.

Further, James's methodology of comparing the jewels depicted in the portrait to those described in inventories of the royal jewels actually produces a stronger correlation for the Hastings Portrait than for the Glendon Hall Portrait. For example, the pendant attached to the necklace in the Hastings Portrait could easily correspond to an "ouche or flower with a diamond, a ruby, an emerald, and a pearl pendant [i.e., hanging]" listed among "the Quene's Jewells."[10] The upper billiment seen in the portrait has, seen and unseen, approximately ten red stones and thirty-five pearls. In comparison, the inventory lists an "upper habiliment containing nine rubies and thirty pearls," a difference of just one span of settings.[11] Multiple gold rings set with table (flat topped), pointed, and rock (cabochon or uncut) rubies are listed in the inventories, and while none are described in sufficient detail to be definitively correlated with those in the portrait, the sheer quantity in the inventory indicates that ruby rings were one of Parr's favorites.[12] The double-looped necklace might easily correspond to one listed in the inventory: "Item a lace for the neck containing twenty-nine rubies and eighty-four pearls."[13] If the number of stones visible in the portrait is doubled to account for portions unseen behind the neck and beneath the bodice, the result is ninety pearls and twenty-six red stones, a very close approximation to the necklace itemized in the inventory.

The double-looped necklace and others of the jewels depicted in the Hastings Portrait also correspond closely or exactly to items seen in portraits of other of Henry VIII's wives and of his daughter Elizabeth. The necklace, though with a different pendant, can be seen in both the full-sized portrait of Jane Seymour, Henry's third consort, and in the miniature thought to depict Henry's fifth wife, Katherine Howard, both by Hans Holbein.[14] The girdle chain is identical to the one worn by Seymour in the Holbein portrait, while the attached strands of ewer beads are strikingly similar, though not identical. And the design of the girdle chain, consisting of clusters of five pearls interspersed with goldwork quatrefoils set with red stones, is a seemingly perfect match to the design of the necklace worn by Elizabeth Tudor in the Clopton Portrait.[15] The girdle chain would be of sufficient length that, if "re-purposed" as a necklace, it would indeed have to be worn double-looped. Through this close correlation between multiple jewels depicted in the portrait to corresponding items both from inventories of Parr's possessions and from portraits of other members of the immediate family of Henry VIII, the evidence for identifying the sitter as Katherine Parr becomes overwhelming. We must therefore conclude that the Hastings Portrait depicts Queen Katherine Parr rather than Lady Jane Grey.

[1] See, for example, James, "Lady Jane Grey or Queen Katherine Parr?," 22.

[2] See, for example, *Called Queen Jane Seymour or Lady Jane Grey*, unknown artist, eighteenth or nineteenth century, 26 in. x 21 in., oil on canvas, King's College, Cambridge.

[3] *A History of the County of Warwick*, ed. Louis F. Salzman (Oxford: Oxford University Press, 1951), VI:18.

[4] Christopher Hussey, "Melton Constable, Norfolk, the Seat of Lord Hastings" in *Country Life* 64:1653 (22 September 1928), 404.

[5] *History of the County of Warwick*, 258.

[6] James, "Lady Jane Grey or Queen Katherine Parr?," 20.

[7] Brotton, *The Sale of the Late King's Goods*, 309.

[8] Hussey, "Melton Constable," 404. For a concise but illuminating discussion of overpainting, see Philip Mould, "Overpaint Uncovered," *Lost Faces: Identity and Discovery in Tudor Royal Portraiture* (London: Philip Mould Ltd, 2007), 13-15.

[9] Roy Strong to Lord Hastings, 20 December 1965, Picture File for Lady Jane Grey, Heinz Archive and Library, National Portrait Gallery.

[10] Susan E. James, *Kateryn Parr: The Making of a Queen* (Stroud: Ashgate, 1999), Appendix V, 423. Though an "ouche or flower" was usually a brooch pinned to a garment, they were sometimes equipped with loops or bales so that they might double as pendants suspended from necklaces.

[11] James, *Kateryn Parr*, Appendix V, 429.

[12] James, *Kateryn Parr*, Appendix V, 430. Three ruby rings are therein listed. Also Appendix VII, "The Sudeley Chest," 436, itemizing jewels removed from the Parr residence of Sudeley Castle, including five more ruby-set rings.

[13] James, *Kateryn Parr*, Appendix V, 428. The arrangement of the pearls and the settings for the rubies are not explicitly described in the inventory. Inventorists were concerned only with intrinsic monetary value, not with aesthetics.

[14] *Jane Seymour*, Hans Holbein, 1536/7, oil on wood panel, 25 ¾ in. x 16 in., Kunsthistorisches Museum, Vienna, GG-881; *Probably Kathrine Howard*, Hans Holbein the Younger, ca. 1541, watercolour and bodycolour on vellum laid on playing card, 2 ⅓ in. diameter, Royal Collection, RCIN 422293.

[15] *Portrait of Queen Elizabeth I*, unknown artist, sixteenth century, oil on wood panel, 26 ½ in. x 19 ¼ in., Philip Mould Ltd.
<http://www.historicalportraits.com/InternalMain.asp?ItemID=451> Accessed 6 August 2010.

4   The Jersey Portrait

Queen Katherine Parr (labeled Queen Mary I)
Attributed to Master John

Oil on wood panel; 36 ⅜ in. x 28 ½ in.

Circa 1544−1545

Provenance:

John Dent (*d.*1826), MP, FSA, Barton Cottage, Christchurch, Hampshire and heirs;

Thomas Baylis, Esq., Prior's Bank, Fulham, *ca.*1831−1841;

Richard, 2nd Duke of Buckingham and Chandos, Stowe House, 1841−1848;

Lady Sarah Sophia Fane Child-Villiers, Countess of Jersey, Osterley Park, Middlesex;

Thence by descent with the Earls of Jersey at Radier Manor, Isle of Jersey;

Sotheby's, London, 5 July 2023, Lot 6.

Art historians understood for over 65 years that the Jersey Portrait had been destroyed in a fire. The 9th Earl of Jersey, George Child Villiers, donated his London home of Osterley House and Park to the British Nation in 1949 but removed many of the valuable art objects beforehand. He stored them temporarily in a warehouse on the Isle of Jersey, location of the current family seat, Radier Manor. A series of random arson fires plagued Jersey that same year, one of which involved the storage facility for the Earl's collection. On Friday, 1 October 1949, a fire broke out in the furniture depository of F. Gallais and Sons in St Helier, Jersey, resulting in the loss of an estimated £100,000 worth of the Earl's property (roughly £2,500,000 in current value, without consideration for appreciation as collectible objects of art).[1] Subsequent scholarship directly related to the painting assumed it to have been among the objects lost, and no notice to the contrary was published until the first edition of this study appeared in 2015.[2] Prior to that year, historians relied solely on a single photograph of the portrait that had been reproduced in various formats, from picture postcards to reference works on art history.[3] The portrait re-emerged intact in 2023, however, when it was sold through Sotheby's, London.[4]

For most of its existence, the owners understood the portrait to be a depiction of Queen Mary I, with attribution to Lucas de Heere (1534-1584). The current gilt frame, dating to at least as early as the eighteenth century, even bears an engraved label identifying the sitter as Mary. The painting was sold three times during the first half of the nineteenth century as a portrait of Mary, though when it was acquired by the Countess of Jersey in 1848 the execution had been re-attributed to Hans Holbein. It was not, however, included in either Paul Ganz's or Arthur Chamberlain's studies of Holbein, both published before World War I, though the latter was certainly familiar with the Jersey collection.[5] As late as 1956, seven years after its supposed destruction, it was still

Figure 1: *Jersey Portrait, detail*   **Fig. 2:** *Hastings Portrait, detail*   **Fig. 3:** *Glendon Hall Portrait, detail*

being reproduced as a portrait of Queen Mary, though the attribution had by then been reduced to "Holbein School."[6] The re-identification of the sitter as Jane Grey came about in the 1960s in connection with the publicity surrounding the Glendon Hall Portrait, but the change was only very tentative. In 1969, Roy Strong actually rejected the notion that the Jersey Portrait depicted either Queen Mary or Lady Jane Grey on the grounds that the face of the sitter was "that of a much younger woman [than Mary] and not apparently to be reconciled with" those of the ladies in the Glendon Hall or the Hastings Portraits.[7]

The Jersey Portrait is, however, clearly linked very closely to not only the Glendon Hall Portrait and the Hastings Portrait, but also to the van de Passe Engraved Portrait. Despite Strong's reservations to the contrary, the three faces in the painted portraits bear an undeniable similarity to each other (Figures 1-3). Indeed, but for the very regular nature of the waves in the hair of the lady in the Jersey Portrait, her face and headgear are otherwise virtually identical in every respect to the those of the lady in the Hastings Portrait. Likewise, only the tip of the nose is slightly smaller in the Glendon Hall Portrait. The headgear in the Glendon Hall Portrait is very similar but not quite a perfect match.

The other jewels are virtually identical among the Jersey, Hastings, and van de Passe Portraits, while the coronet-shaped brooch is identical in all four in the group. And though the gown worn by the lady in the Jersey Portrait is dark with no discernible brocading, the undersleeves are essentially identical to those seen in the Hastings Portrait, in both coloration and patterning. By all appearances, the Jersey and the Hastings Portraits are simply seasonal variations taken from a common pattern, the Jersey costume being suitable for cooler weather that that of the Hastings. Lastly, the hands are so similarly arranged in all three painted portraits, and the rings on the lady's fingers so similar in appearance and placement, that is seems altogether likely that the three images were derived from a single sitting. If the lady in the Glendon Hall Portrait is indeed Katherine Parr, as Susan James so persuasively argued, and so too is the lady in the Hastings Portrait, it necessarily follows that the sitter in the Jersey Portrait is also Katherine Parr.

[1] "Art Treasures in Fire," *The Times of London*, 1 October 1949, 4.

[2] See, for example, Strong, *Tudor and Jacobean Portraits*, I:79 and II: pl.148.

[3] Ibid; and Soho Gallery Card #231, "Called Queen Mary, Holbein School," issued December 1956.

[4] The portrait fetched a remarkable £3,436,000 ($4,368,000), including premiums, against a pre-sale estimate of £600,000—£800,000 ($768,000—$1,015,000), setting a record for a Tudor painting. See "A Rare Portrait of Henry VIII's Sixth Wife Breaks Auction Records," *Observer*, 6 July 2023. <https://observer.com/2023/07/portrait-henry-viii-sixth-wife-breaks-auction-records/>, Accessed 9 January 2024.

[5] Paul Ganz, *Hans Holbein D.J.: Der Meisters Gemälde in 252 Abbildungen* (Stuttgart: Deutsche Verlags-Anstalt, 1912); Arthur B. Chamberlain, *Hans Holbein the Younger* (New York: Dodd, Mead and Company, 1913).

[6] Soho Gallery Card #231, "Called Queen Mary, Holbein School," issued December 1956.

[7] Strong, *Tudor and Jacobean Portraits*, I:79 and II: pl.148. Strong was perhaps unable to detect in pre-1949 photographs the dark circles under the sitter's eyes. Those same dark circles are apparent in x-radiographs of the face of Katherine Parr in the Glendon Hall Portrait, though they have since been covered during various restorations. Mary was much closer in age to Parr than to Jane Grey, effectively negating Strong's objection.

5   The Northwick Portrait

Probably Queen Katherine Parr

Unknown artist

Oil on wood panel; 21 ¼ in. x 16 ½ in.

Undated

Provenance:

Mr George Fripp, Kent, by 1939, as *Queen Elizabeth when Princess*, by Holbein;

Christie's, London, 23 July 1948, Lot 144, as *Portrait of Queen Elizabeth*;

Sotheby's, London, 28 October 1953, Lot 28;

George Spencer-Churchill, Northwick Park, Gloucestershire;

Sotheby's, London, 5 June 1965, Lot 2;

Sir Hugh Wontner;

Private collection.

This portrait has been identified at different points over the past six decades as both Jane Grey and Katherine Parr.[1] After a rapid succession of sales and re-sales, it was purchased in 1953 by the Spencer-Churchills of Northwick Park. The sale catalogue indicated that the painting "may represent Katherine Parr" and attributed the work to "School of Hans Holbein."[2] The identification as Parr remained somewhat tentative when the Northwick Park collection was liquidated through Christie's in 1965, though the attribution to Holbein was seemingly confirmed.[3] The portrait was resold later in the same year to Sir Hugh Wontner of the Savoy Hotel Group, who promptly rechristened it as Lady Jane Grey, perhaps after comparing it to the Glendon Hall Portrait then being popularized in the British press. Roy Strong confirmed the rechristening in 1969 when he published the Northwick Portrait as a depiction of Jane Grey.[4] Eric Ives went a step further in 2009, observing that comparison of the Northwick Portrait to the Streatham and Houghton Portraits (discussed later in this volume) led him to a conclusion that "a single sitter does, superficially, not seem impossible."[5] Ives further noted that an inventory compiled in 1590 of the collection of Baron Lumley included a portrait said to be "of the Lady Jane Graye, executed."[6] Finally, in 2010, Tarnya Cooper, Curator of Sixteenth-Century Portraits at the National Portrait Gallery, was apparently herself sufficiently convinced that the portrait depicted Jane Grey to label a photograph of it as such in The Lumley Inventory and Pedigree. She did nonetheless note that "doubt remains over the identity of the sitter."[7]

Ives's reference to the Lumley Inventories was prompted by the presence in the upper right-hand corner of the Northwick Portrait of a *trompe-l'œil* painted label that is consistent in general

Fig. 4: *Face details from (left to right) the Northwick, Glendon Hall, Hastings, and Jersey Portraits.*

appearance with similar labels Baron Lumley added to many of the pictures in his collection. Often called *cartellini*, such labels are sometimes taken today as evidence that a given painting was once part of the Lumley collection.[8] Strong identified the *cartellino* on the Northwick Portrait as a genuine Lumley label and, apparently unaware of the Chatsworth Inventory of the 1560s, declared the Lumley Inventory to be the first instance in the surviving historical record in which a portrait of Jane Grey was mentioned.[9] The *cartellino* had become illegible prior to the Sotheby's sale of 1953, however, so that proper identification of the sitter has always been uncertain.[10] The picture is currently held in a private collection, and its owner believes the portrait to depict Katherine Parr.

In *The Northwick Rescues*, George Spencer-Churchill noted that the painting had been "completely overpainted, except for the lower parts of the sleeves."[11] That work was carried out by the highly-reputable New Bond Street firm of William Drown Ltd, though the degree to which the effort may have altered the original image is as yet unclear.[12] Assuming the repainting faithfully reproduced the original, it is useful to compare the face of the Northwick lady to the faces of the sitters in the Glendon Hall Portrait, the Hastings Portrait, and the Jersey Portrait (Fig.4). While the Northwick lady's nose is slightly straighter along its spine than is seen among the other three sitters, the four faces are otherwise exceedingly similar in appearance. Based on facial depiction alone, it seems altogether probable that all four portraits depict the same sitter.

We must also consider the Northwick Portrait within the specific context of the Lumley Inventories of 1590 and the history of the Lumley family in the sixteenth century. John Lumley married Jane (or Joan) Fitzalan in 1552. She was the daughter and co-heiress of Henry Fitzalan, 19th Earl of Arundel, one of the first to turn against John Dudley during the succession dispute of July 1553. Arundel became one of Mary's leading officials and was rewarded in 1556 with license to purchase Henry VIII's unfinished palace of Nonsuch. Lumley then inherited Nonsuch Palace from the Earl of Arundel in 1580, in right of his wife and together with its contents. The Lumley Inventories were created in about 1590, the year in which Lumley gave the palace to Queen Elizabeth as a demonstration of personal loyalty. Yet it is not entirely clear from the original manuscripts whether the objects described were held at Nonsuch Palace, at the Lumley family's ancient seat of Lumley Castle in County Durham, at Baron Lumley's London residence near Tower Hill, or all three. Nonetheless, it is usually said that the paintings at Nonsuch formed the nucleus of the Lumley collection through inheritance from the Earl of Arundel in 1580. As a former royal palace, Nonsuch probably did contain numerous royal portraits, but the Lumley Inventories of

1590 include in their entirety almost three hundred paintings. In contrast, Nonsuch held just thirty three paintings by 1649.[13] This massive quantitative difference over a span of just sixty years, especially for a royal palace still very much in use, indicates that the Nonsuch collection was itself always a small one and thus never represented more than a mere fraction of Lumley's holdings.

The Northwick Portrait was, in all statistical likelihood, acquired separately from the Nonsuch inheritance.[14] And it was included in the Lumley Inventory of 1590, whether as Katherine Parr or Lady Jane Grey, because it was intended by the inventorist to remain in Lumley possession even after Nonsuch was remitted to the Crown. The portrait would then have passed by descent to his heirs, the Lumley Earls of Scarbrough. The fifth Earl sold off much of the Lumley art collection in 1785 and 1807, though no portraits identified as either Katherine Parr or Jane Grey were included in those sales.[15] But a significant percentage of the Lumley portraits had already lost their *cartellini* inscriptions, as evidenced by the large number described generically in those sales as simply "A Lady" or "A Gentleman." In all probability, the Northwick Portrait did appear in the Scarbrough sales as one of the many unidentified portraits, from which it eventually passed to Sir Hugh Wontner. No other portrait from the Lumley collection has ever been identified as either Jane Grey or Katherine Parr. Yet despite any urge in the 1960s to name Jane Grey as the sitter depicted in the Northwick Portrait, the available evidence supports instead restoring it to its earlier identification as Katherine Parr.

1 The Lady Jane Grey Sitter File at the National Portrait Gallery's Heinz Archive and Library contains black and white photographs of two later copies of this portrait, both of which include the Lumley cartellino and both of which are identified as Katherine Parr. Which of the three is the original version has yet to be determined. One of the photographed versions was, according to notes penciled on the photograph, owned in the 1960s by P.J. Ely. The other is marked as whereabouts unknown.

2 E. George Spencer-Churchill, *Northwick Rescues*, 1912-1961 (Evesham: Sharp Bros, 1961), 46 and pl. 169.

3 *Catalogue of Important English Pictures circa 1550 – circa 1880 from the Northwick Collection*, Christie's (London), 25 June 1965, Lot 23, as "Portrait of a Lady, said to be Katherine Parr, by Holbein."

4 Strong, *Tudor and Jacobean Portraits*, I:78 and II:pl.145.

5 Ives, *Lady Jane Grey*, 17.

6 Ives, *Lady Jane Grey*, 16-17. Ives apparently understood the portrait listed in the Lumley Inventory to be lost and thus did not directly associate it with the Northwick Park Portrait, which he describes as a separate and distinct item originating in the Lumley collection but not included in the inventory of 1590.

7 Catharine MacLeod, Tarnya Cooper, and Margaret Zoller, "A list of Portraits in the Lumley Inventory," *The Lumley Inventory and Pedigree*, 164. Cooper explicitly cited the authority of Strong without challenging his identification.

8 See Evans, *The Lumley Inventory and Pedigree*.

9 Strong, *Tudor and Jacobean Portraits*, I:78.

10 Evans, *The Lumley Inventory and Pedigree*, 164.

11 Spencer-Churchill, *Northwick Rescues*, 46.

12 Sitter File for Katherine Parr, Heinz Archive and Library, National Portrait Gallery.

13 *The Catalogue and Description of King Charles I's Capital Collection* (London: W. Bathoe, 1752), 3.

14 See Appendix Two for a detailed discussion of the likely route of acquisition for that portrait.

15 Search of the Getty Research Institute's Provenance Index Database, Christie's sale of 18 June 1785, Sale Catalog Br-A4197; Christie's sale of 8-11 August 1785, Sale Catalog Br-A4205; Thomas Dawson auction house, sale of 2-7 November 1807, Sale Catalog Br-532 and sale of 16-19 December 1807, Sale Catalog Br-538. No portraits potentially identifiable as either Jane Grey or Katherine Parr are held today in the Scarbrough Collection at Sandbeck Park, Maltby, South Yorkshire. Electronic communication, the Earl of Scarbrough, 27 March 2014.

6   The Norris Portrait

Called Lady Jane Grey

Unknown artist

Oil on wood panel; dimensions unknown

Undated

Provenance:

    Herbert Norris by 1931;

    Lillian Norris Everett (*d.*1979);

    Current whereabouts unknown.

Less is currently discoverable about the Norris Portrait than perhaps any other picture in this study. Notes on the back of two black and white photographs held in the Heinz Archive and Library at the National Portrait Gallery in London indicate that it was acquired in or before 1931 by the costume historian and designer Herbert Norris. The notes state that the portrait was a gift from an unnamed friend who had in turn purchased the painting in 1870 from an also-unnamed picture shop.[1] The portrait vanished from the historical record in about 1940 after the second photograph was taken, and Norris died in 1950. The painting has not been seen since, though recent extensive investigation has revealed that it is no longer held by the heirs of Norris's sole child and heir, Lillian Norris Everett, who died without issue in 1979.[2] The two photographs have apparently never before been published, and none of the major modern studies of Tudor-era portraiture refer to the painting in any significant way.[3] Yet it is an excellent example of how a portrait of one individual might sometimes be copied repeatedly and even used arbitrarily to represent a succession of sometimes vastly different individuals.

The two photographs of the painting reveal the presence of a series of inscriptions that read, "LADYE JANE GRAY, DIED 1553, AET[atis] 17." The inscription pre-dates 1752, the year in which the beginning of the calendar year was moved from 25 March to 1 January. In the absence of technical study, however, it is not possible to know whether the inscription is original to the painting or was added at some point after the image was created. But the fact that the portrait is inscribed in this specific manner implies that the sitter would not otherwise have been readily known to the painting's early owners. Portraits specially commissioned by a sitter or by the sitter's family or friends would not have needed any inscription to identify the sitter. Individually commissioned portraits were more likely to have included only an inscription identifying the age of the sitter at the time the portrait was created, and/or an inscription indicating the year in which the portrait was painted. Less commonly, they sometimes included the heraldic arms of the individual or his/her

CATHARINA REGINA VXOR HENRICI VIII

Fig. 5: *Queen Katherine Parr, by unknown artist*

family. It is therefore likely that the Norris Portrait was created well after Jane's death for inclusion in a portrait set produced by one or more artists for speculative sale on the open commercial market. The relatively inferior quality of workmanship seen in this portrait is also typical of most portrait sets from the late-sixteenth and early-seventeenth centuries.[4]

The assertion that the Norris Portrait was created posthumously for inclusion in a portrait set is further supported through comparison to a particular portrait of Katherine Parr specifically, and one that is known to have been produced posthumously (Fig.5). Dendrochronological analysis of the wood panel on which the Parr portrait was painted revealed that it dates to the late sixteenth century, though Parr died in 1548.[5] Like the Norris Portrait, the Parr portrait is inscribed to identify the sitter, "Catharine Regina Uxor Henrici VIII" (Katherine the Queen, Wife of Henry VIII), indicating that it was produced for a buyer/owner who could not otherwise recognize the lady depicted.

Direct comparison of the two images reveals so many similarities that the two portraits must have been based on a single reference image and thus depict the same sitter. Though the rendering of the face is considerably cruder in the Norris Portrait, it is essentially identical in appearance to the face in the inscribed Parr portrait. Differences in both the shape and the ornamentation of the French hoods are evident, but may perhaps be ascribed to "re-dressing" or deliberate costume adaptation on the part of the artist, as seen previously in the Hastings and Jersey Portraits. The necklaces, both comprised of festoons of pearls, are very nearly virtually identical, the Norris sitter's necklace having one fewer festoon visible. The pendants suspended from each necklace appear quite similar, except for a difference in relative scale. The same is true of the bodice jewel: both consist of a small quatrefoil upper portion set with a single rectangular stone, a larger portion also in the form of a quatrefoil but surrounded by scrollwork and centrally set with a square stone, and a pendant pearl suspended from the whole. Only the relative scale of the bodice jewel differs between the two paintings. The gowns too are similar but not identical, the yoke of the partlet worn by the Norris lady featuring added embroidery. The lining of both partlets are embellished with blackwork in floral patterns, however. Though the respective costumes display slight variation, reasonably attributable to aesthetic choices made by the respective artists, the sitters in the Norris and Parr portraits are certainly the same woman, and that woman is Katherine Parr. In all likelihood, artists or owners of the Norris Portrait utilized a portrait of Parr to represent her friend, ward, and co-religionist Jane Grey in the absence of any readily available authentic image of Jane herself.

The use of an image of one person to depict another was not limited to Jane Grey and Katherine Parr, however, even in relation to the Norris Portrait specifically. The same reference image or one of its several derivatives (discussed below) was used early in the eighteenth century to depict a lady of considerably less admirable character: Jane Shore, mistress of King Edward IV of the fifteenth century (Fig.6). The watercolored engraving has been credited to Sylvester Harding but was reportedly copied by Harding from an anonymous engraving previously published in 1714. That earlier version had been included in a brief historical pamphlet entitled *The life and character of Jane Shore*, intended to inform playgoers of 1714 regarding the central character of the play they were attending, *The Tragedy of Jane Shore*.[6] The author of the play was Nicholas Rowe, the same playwright who wrote *The Tragedy of Jane Grey* in advocacy of the Hanoverian succession in 1714. And as with Jane Grey, Rowe advocated through Jane Shore for a succession as established by law, in support of the Act of Settlement of 1701.[7] But whereas the historical Jane Shore is elsewhere best remembered as the infamous mistress of Edward IV, Rowe depicts her as an innocent victim

Fig. 6: *Called Jane Shore, watercolored engraving attributed to Sylvester Harding, 1790.*

of Richard of Gloucester's tyrannical efforts to alter the succession in 1483, directly comparable to Jane Grey's reputed victimization by John Dudley in 1553. This obvious adaptation by a succession of artists of one portrait of the religiously-reformist Katherine Parr to depict both her reportedly virtuous and pious co-religionist Jane Grey and the scandalous "fallen woman" Jane Shore requires us to refrain from the too-common reflexive assumption that any given posthumous portrait was necessarily based upon some "lost original."

The Norris lady conspicuously holds a small book in her right hand. As noted in the introduction to this study, Jane Grey's sixteenth-century hagiographers sought to define her in large part by her intellect and learning. The book was certainly included in this portrait specifically to denote that intellect. Its presence also visually distinguished Jane from Katherine Parr, even as the image was adapted from portraits of Parr, since books do not appear in any fully authenticated portraits of Parr. Further, later copyists eliminated the book as they adapted the Norris image for the engraving of Jane Shore, a person known for qualities other than her intellect. Books became a key compositional element in paintings newly produced at or after the end of the sixteenth century as depictions of Jane Grey. Conversely, as will be seen, the presence of a book in any portraits of unidentified women of the sixteenth century often led in later years to identifying those women as Jane Grey. Inclusion of a book thus became a crucial symbolic element on the inconography of Jane Grey.

[1]   Folder marked "ID Doubtful," Sitter File for Lady Jane Grey, Heinz Archive and Library, National Portrait Gallery, London.

[2]   My sincere thanks to Mrs. Helen Steele of Gloucestershire and Mr Lewis Chapman of West Lothian, Scotland for their generous assistance in my efforts to locate the Norris Portrait.

[3]   For example, Roy Strong completely omitted the Norris Portrait from his important studies of Tudor portraiture, *Tudor and Jacobean Portraits* (London: HMSO, 1969) and *English Icon: Elizabethan and Jacobean Portraiture* (New Haven: Yale University Press, 1987).

[4]   Cf. the Streatham and Houghton Portraits, also of relatively crude artistic quality and also thought to have originated from portrait sets.

[5]   *Portrait of Katherine Parr, Queen of England*, Sixteenth Century School, late sixteenth century, oil on wood panel, 21 ¼ in. x 15 ³/₅ in., Philip Mould Ltd. <http://www.historicalportraits.com/Gallery.asp?Page=Item&ItemID=1200&Desc=Katherine-Parr-%7C--English-Sixteenth-Century-School> Accessed 1 May 2014.

[6]   *Called Jane Shore*, Sylvester Harding, 1790, engraving printed on paper and watercoloured, Folger Shakespeare Library, Washington, DC. See Folger cataloguing data for discussion of the origins of the engraved image.

[7]   Rowe was himself named Poet Laureate in 1715 by the new King George I, in part on account of his dramatic public support for the Hanoverian succession.

LA N [...]

7   The Streatham Portrait

Called Lady Jane Grey

Unknown artist

Oil on wood panel; 33 ¾ in. x 23 ¾ in.

Undated

Provenance:

    Anonymous resident of Streatham, South London;

    Lane Fine Art, London, 2006;

    National Portrait Gallery, London, acc. no. NPG6804, 2007.

The Streatham Portrait, like the Norris Portrait discussed above, notably includes a book in the sitter's hand, denoting the sitter's learning. And like the Norris Portrait, the Streatham was inscribed further to identify the sitter as "Lady Jayne" [sic]. The inscription here survives in only fragmentary form, but examination in 2007 by Dr Libby Sheldon using various scientific techniques, including spectroscopy and Raman laser microscopy, led her to conclude that the inscription is exactly contemporaneous with the painted image rather than having been added later.[1] Christopher Foley of Lane Fine Art (London) and curators at the NPG agreed after careful research that Jane Grey was the lady specified. Dendrochronological analysis of the boards on which the painting was executed revealed that the tree from which the wood was harvested was felled no earlier than 1594, so that the portrait must have been created after that year, perhaps as late as the first decade of the 1600s. That timeframe neatly includes, of course, the period during which the Elizabethan succession was being most vigorously debated and even challenged and in which Jane Grey was being brought forward as a vehicle both for conduct of that debate and to symbolize individual affinities among the debaters.

The NPG has argued that the portrait may once have been included in a larger portrait set, perhaps of Protestant religious heroes.[2] Fine lines were incised across the eyes and mouth of the lady at some point early in the painting's history, perhaps as a symbolic act of "silencing" Jane Grey as an advocate for a particular strain of Protestantism. Little else is known about the painting, which after a brief period of exhibition in the Tudor rooms at the National Portrait Gallery following its acquisition was removed to Montacute House, South Somerset.

There is no documentation available at the time of this writing (March 2014) to confirm that the curators at the NPG directly compared the Streatham Portrait to either the Norris Portrait or the related inscribed portrait of Katherine Parr discussed previously, yet the similarities between the three are nonetheless compelling, even if perhaps not quite definitive for identifying a source or reference image (Fig.7). The Streatham Portrait is very naive in its execution, but the overall facial

Fig. 7: *Face and jewel details from (left to right) the Streatham, Norris, and Parr Portraits.*

shape is all but identical to that of the inscribed portrait of Parr. The Streatham lady's eyes do appear darker, the tip of the nose more rounded, and the mouth narrower, yet some of those differences may be a product of the lesser skill of the Streatham's artist in comparison to the artist who painted the inscribed Parr. The hood worn by the Streatham lady is remarkably comparable to that seen in the inscribed Parr, the only obvious difference being in the nether billiment with pyramidal pointed gemstones added to the Streatham. Yet precisely the same type of nether billiment is notable in the Norris Portrait, the stones being more prominent in the latter.

But the most obvious elements of commonality across the three portraits lie once again in the other jewels. The repetition across all three paintings of the necklace of festooned pearls cannot be mere coincidence, but must instead indicate some common reference image. The pendant suspended from the necklace of the lady in the inscribed Parr portrait is circular with at least four stones visible, which does differentiate it from the Norris and Streatham Portraits. Yet the pendants in the latter two are essentially identical: quatrefoils set with a central square dark stone, a teardrop pearl suspended from each. As noted in the preceding discussion of the Norris Portrait, the bodice brooch worn by that sitter is exceedingly similar to the same element seen in the inscribed Parr, though the Parr jewel is much more finely rendered. The bodice brooch worn by the Streatham lady is larger in relative scale and the middle element is more nearly round and set with five stones, so that it is admittedly different from the others, yet the overall form remains the same in all three: a small quatrefoil above a larger central piece set with one or more gemstones, with a large pearl suspended from the whole. Taken together, the similarities of the principal jewels depicted in the three portraits strongly suggest a single common reference image or pattern from which three separate artists created their own unique and individualized interpretations.

The gowns worn by the Streatham and Norris ladies are also very similar, though that in the inscribed portrait of Parr is noticeably different. The Streatham lady is attired in deep red, with embroidery and brocading confined to the oversleeves, undersleeves, and under-skirt.[3] The Norris lady is likewise dressed in red velvet, according to a handwritten note on a photograph of the painting, though only the yoke of her partlet and her undersleeves are embroidered in a large floral pattern. In contrast, Parr wears solid black and the gown is entirely unembellished, except for a band of pearls and gem-set goldwork quaterfoils across the breast. All three costumes include a partlet with a standing collar and blackwork embellishment, however. The slight variation in the

Streatham and Norris costumes can again be reasonably attributed to discretionary variation on the part of the respective artists seeking to produce unique portrayals of their subjects. On the whole, it seems entirely likely that the Streatham Portrait was based upon some earlier reference image that depicted Katherine Parr but, like the Norris Portrait, was adapted to "become" Jane Grey in the absence of an accessible authentic portrait of Jane.

[1] Object File on NPG6804, Heinz Archive and Library, National Portrait Gallery, London.

[2] Cataloguing data for *Lady Jane Dudley (née Grey)*, NPG6804, National Portrait Gallery Online Collection Database.
<http://www.npg.org.uk/collections/search/portrait/mw113910/Lady-Jane-Dudley-nee-Grey>Accessed 28 March 2014;
Charlotte Boland and Tarnya Cooper, *The Real Tudors: Kings and Queens Rediscovered* (London: National Portrait Gallery Publications, 2014), 99.

[3] While it may be tempting to interpret the color of the Streatham lady's gown as the same red commonly used to symbolize martyrdom, red and crimson were also regarded as popular "secular" colors throughout the sixteenth century. The color of her gown may therefore be nothing more than a "fashion choice."

8   The Houghton Portrait

Called Princess Elizabeth Tudor

Unknown artist

Oil on wood panel; 30 in. x 25 in.

Undated

Provenance:

    Richard Monckton Milnes, 1ˢᵗ Baron Houghton of Fryston Hall, Yorkshire, 1866;

    By descent to Lady Helen Cynthia Crewe-Milnes Colville, 1945-1968;

    Private collection.

This portrait is clearly a duplicate of the Streatham Portrait discussed previously. The Houghton Portrait is in poor condition, however, showing separation of the boards, large areas of botched restoration attempts, degradation of the varnish, and significant dirt. And instead of bearing an incorporated name inscription like the Streatham Portrait, the lady in the Houghton Portrait is identified only by means of a small brass label attached to the frame that names her as Princess Elizabeth Tudor. There is indeed a superficial similarity between the Streatham and Houghton Portraits and a portrait of Princess Elizabeth (Fig.8) formerly attributed to William Scrots and dated to ca.1546/7.[1] Yet the dendrochronological dating of the Streatham Portrait to the very end of Elizabeth's reign as queen implies that it, and quite probably the Houghton as well, was never intended to depict a young Elizabeth Tudor. The similarities to the early portrait of Elizabeth are likely the result of artistic compositional tropes repeated across many years. The many significant differences between the costume and jewels worn by Elizabeth and corresponding items worn by the Streatham and Houghton lady indicates that the latter two were not copied from the former.

The painting has on occasion been said to have originated in a house called Houghton, though that is a relatively common place-name in England, with at least five Houghton Halls, Houses, or Lodges known today.[2] Yet Christopher Foley, the London art dealer who handled the sale of the Streatham Portrait late in 2006, found evidence of a portrait of Jane Grey owned late in the sixteenth century by Frances Rodes of Barlborough Hall, Derbyshire.[3] Rodes is best known today for having been a Justice in the Court of Common Pleas and for having participated in a secondary role in the trial of Mary, Queen of Scots at Fotheringhay in 1586. He was also sympathetic to the emerging Puritan religious agenda.[4] He was probably a supporter, therefore, of the faction that advocated for a succession to Queen Elizabeth's throne based on the last will and testament of Henry VIII and the Succession Act of 1543. In other words, he was likely a "Jane-ist."

Frances Rode's fourth son, Godfrey, inherited a Houghton Hall in the manor of Great (or Long

Fig. 8: *Elizabeth I when Princess, ca.1546/7*

Houghton, near Darfield, South Yorkshire early in the seventeenth century. Foley found evidence that the Rodeses owned an entire collection of portraits of Protestant heroes, especially of those heroes of a more radical persuasion like themselves. Intriguingly, Godfrey's distant lineal descendant and heir, Marta Rodes Busk, was herself the great-grandmother of the 1st Baron Houghton of Fryston Hall.[5] When Marta Busk died in 1789, Houghton Hall passed to her daughter Rachel and Rachel's husband Richard Slater Milnes. An attempt was made to update the house, but Richard soon abandoned the effort and removed its contents to Fryston Hall.[6] Richard Slater Milnes's grandson Baron Houghton inherited Fryston in 1858. It is therefore possible, though as yet unproven, that the provenance of the Houghton Portrait can be traced back to the anti-Jacobean, radical Protestant Frances Rodes in the 1580s. It is entirely conceivable that Frances Rodes acquired the Houghton Portrait as an expression of his own anti-Jacobean stance during the Elizabethan succession debate.

As noted, the Houghton Portrait bears sufficient similarities to the Streatham to merit an assumption that one was copied from the other. The two sitters are depicted in virtually identical positions and overall attire. The two heads, including the headgear, are virtually identical, as is the embroidered pattern on the lining of the two partlets. But as noted previously when comparing the Streatham and Norris Portraits, there are subtle differences between the Streatham and the Houghton Portraits confirming that neither is a completely faithful copy of the other. Most obviously, there are no festoons on the necklace in the Houghton Portrait. Similarly, the central portion of the Houghton lady's bodice jewel contains only a single stone; the surrounding colored stones seen in the Streatham are absent. Nonetheless, pearls are situated at each of the four corners of the stone in the Houghton Portrait, just as in the Streatham, giving the appearance that the artist who created the former deliberately elected to reduce the complexity of the Houghton jewel. That reduction is seen again in the depiction of the girdle chain, with the chain in the Houghton containing half as many pearls between each goldwork quatrefoil as seen in the Streatham Portrait, and the hanging portion held in the sitter's proper right hand being noticeably shorter. Lastly, the pearl trim along the edges of the over-skirt in the Streatham Portrait is not present in the Houghton. In simplest terms, the Houghton Portrait contains far fewer pearls that does the Streatham, and the Houghton jewels are rendered with a much less refined technique than is evident in the Streatham. It therefore seems likely that the Houghton Portrait was actually derived from the Streatham by an artist having significantly less skill, especially in the depiction of jewels.

One element conspicuously *present* in the Houghton, Streatham, and Norris Portraits, and equally conspicuously *absent* from the Glendon Hall Portrait, the Hastings Portrait, and the Jersey Portrait, is the small book held by the sitter. The book supplements the inscriptions on the Streatham and Norris Portraits in identifying their sitters as Jane Grey. In all likelihood, the Houghton was also identified as Jane Grey early in its existence, and the frame label reflects a re-identification not arrived at until the nineteenth century or later.

As discussed in the Introduction to this volume, those who sought to utilize Jane in the first decades following her death as a vehicle through which a particular agenda might be advanced had to justify conferring on any woman the authority to speak in the male-dominated public sphere of theology. They cited Jane's exceptional intellect as their basis for according her a public voice. Though women were held to be generally inferior intellectually to men, Jane was revered as equal in intellect to nothing less than the degreed men of the universities. Rather than symbolizing personal piety, as is usually assumed today in the specific context of Jane Grey, the books depicted in her hands in this cluster of three portraits far more probably symbolized her intellect, education, and resultant superior capacity for reason and judgment. It is noteworthy that no book is present in any of the first five portraits, all of which were produced as portraits of Katherine Parr and only later became relabeled as Jane Grey. To the extent that Parr required, as a woman, legitimation of any authority to speak in a patriarchal culture, she derived that authority inherently through her publicly-recognized role as queen-consort. Jane had no such obviously inherent authority. Writers were thus compelled to offer some evidence of her superior intellect in order to justify granting to her the authority to speak. And artists creating portraits of Jane that were adapted from reference images of Parr felt equally compelled to add a book to the image as visual evidence of the same. It is worth noting at this juncture that books are similarly present in numerous other portraits of Jane Grey discussed later in this volume, further indication that books were an important identifying visual symbol in her iconography, though the symbolism attached to those books shifted over time from intellect to piety as the prevailing mythology surrounding Jane similarly shifted to emphasize personal piety over exceptional intellect.

[1] *Elizabeth I when a Princess*, attributed to William Scrots, ca.1546, oil on wood panel, 71 in. x 32 $\frac{1}{5}$ in., Royal Collection, RCIN 404444.

[2] These include Houghton Hall near King's Lynn, Norfolk, home of Sir Robert Walpole in the 18th Century (extant); Houghton Hall in Sancton, East Yorkshire, built ca.1760 for Philip Langdale (extant); Houghton House near Ampthill, Bedfordshire, home of the Earl of Ailesbury in the 17th Century (a ruin since 1800); Houghton Lodge, Stockbridge, Hampshire, built ca.1800 as a rental property (extant); and Great Houghton Hall, Darfield, South Yorkshire, built for Sir Godfrey Rodes early in the 17th Century (burned 1960).

[3] Electronic correspondence, Christopher Foley, 28 February 2012. See also William Betham, *The Baronetage of England* (London: E. Lloyd, 1805), V:457.

[4] The descendants of Frances Rodes would become non-conformist Quakers in the seventeenth century. Betham, *Baronetage*, 457.

[5] Joseph Wilkinson, *Worthies, Families, and Celebrities of Barnsley and the District* (London: Bemrose and Son, 1883), 137-164.

[6] Wilkinson, *Worthies*, 163.

The Lady
Jane Grey

9   The Wrest Park Portrait

Mary Nevill Fiennes, Lady Dacre (1524-1576)

Unknown artist

Oil on wood panel; 29 in. x 21 ¼ in.

Undated, ca.1550

Provenance:

    By descent with the Barons Dacre of the South;

    Thomas Lennard, 15ᵗʰ Baron Dacre, by whom sold 1701;

    Henry Grey, 12ᵗʰ Earl and 1st Duke of Kent;

    Lady Jemima Campbell, 4ᵗʰ Baroness Lucas of Crudwell, by inheritance;

    thence by descent with the Barons Lucas of Crudwell, Wrest Park, Bedfordshire, to 1917;

    Private collection.

As has been the case with others of the portraits discussed previously, the sitter in the Wrest Park Portrait displays a book held in her hands, her index finger inserted between the pages as though marking her place after being interrupted in the act of reading. The presence of the book visually reiterates the literary theme established within weeks of Jane's death that sought to legitimize her as a female voice in the male-dominated sphere of theology. This particular portrait gained wide notice, however, only after it was engraved in 1681 by Robert White for use as a depiction of Jane in Gilbert Burnet's extremely popular *History of the Reformation of the Church of England* (Fig. 9).[1] The engraving was also sold separately throughout the following century as the collecting of engravings became a popular pursuit among the leisure classes, and at least three eighteenth-century versions are known.[2]

    How and why White came to use this particular painting depicting Mary Nevill Fiennes, Lady Dacre, as a reference source for his engraved image of Jane Grey is unknown, though the presence of the book was quite probably a significant contributing factor.[3] But White clearly found the original likeness inadequate for his purpose, since he significantly embellished it when producing the engraving. He added pearls and embroidery to the headdress, supplemented the bodice and sleeves with fur accents decorated with ouches set with gemstones, and rendered the necklace more prominently than what was depicted in the original painting. The most likely explanation for these changes is that the unaltered portrait was deemed insufficiently regal to depict any Queen of England, even an uncrowned and executed one.[4] It is not known whether this portrait had already been rechristened as Jane Grey by the time White produced his engraving,

Fig. 9: *Called Lady Jane Dudley, line engraving by Robert White, 1681.*

or whether the popularity of the engraving itself prompted a new label for an ancestral portrait that had somehow lost its identity.

At the time of White's work in 1681, the original painting was in the collection of Dorothy North Lennard, second wife and widow of Richard Lennard, 13th Baron Dacre. Many of the ancestral portraits then in the Dacre collection bore no name inscriptions, so that the family must necessarily have relied instead on oral transmission and collective memory for the identifications of the sitters in those paintings.[5] Even written inventories of the Lennard family's possessions spread across multiple residences failed to itemize by name any but the most contemporary of the family's portraits, perhaps because no one then living could still identify the sitters in the earlier ones.[6] In specific regard to this portrait, for example, virtually all of Mary Lady Dacre's descendants through the second generation were deceased by 1638, leaving only distant great-grandchildren to name her as the subject depicted. Even her principal lineal heir in the third generation, Dorothy's husband Richard Lennard, had died in 1630, leaving as his own heir from a previous marriage an eleven-year-old child. That heir died in 1662, fully two decades before White created the engraving, and the portrait passed in the fifth generation into the hands of another child-heir. Only sixty-eight-year-old Dorothy remained alive in 1681 to bear witness for those earlier generations of her first husband's family. Whether she could correctly identify this portrait as being of her great-grandmother-in-law and do so as late as 1681 seems at best doubtful, especially given that she had been married to Richard Lennard for just five brief years more than a half-century earlier.

At least one other of the Dacre ancestral portraits had also been rechristened at some point in the seventeenth century, and that circumstance has considerable significance for this painting. That second portrait depicted the same individual as seen here, though at a more advanced age, together with her surviving son Gregory, yet the sitters were re-identified sometime before 1700 as Frances Brandon Grey, mother of Jane Grey, and her second husband Adrian Stokes.[7] The re-labeling of two separate portraits of a single Lennard ancestor as instead one a mother and the other a daughter from the Grey family indicates a strong affinity by the Lennards of the seventeenth century for the Greys of the sixteenth century.

The affinity was familial, social, and political. Mary Lady Dacre's daughter and heir, Margaret Fiennes Lennard, 11th Baroness Dacre, was a maternal great-aunt to Henry Grey, 1st Earl of Stamford and senior heir in the seventeenth century of the Greys of Bradgate.[8] The Lennard Barons Dacre were thus cousins, albeit distant ones, to the Grey Earls of Stamford. The two families are known to have socialized together and to have passed time at each other's residences. One of the Earl of Stamford's younger sons was even christened Leonard in apparent tribute to his Dacre relations.[9] And at the outset of the Civil Wars of the 1630s and 1640s, both the Greys and the Lennards became active supporters of the Parliamentary party.[10] Subsequently, the 2nd Earl of Stamford was implicated in the failed Rye Plot of 1683 intended to prevent a Roman Catholic royal accession through assassinations of both Charles II and his Catholic brother James, Duke of York. Stamford actively supported William of Orange in his bid to replace James II as King of England in 1688 by raising troops to aid William's invasion. Simultaneously, the 15th Baron Dacre, Thomas Lennard, staunchly supported the Exclusion Bill of 1679 and was among the twenty-three members of the House of Lords who ordered the English navy not to resist the invasion fleet of William of Orange in December 1688.[11]

The re-labeling of the Wrest Park Portrait, as well as of the companion portrait said to depict Francis Brandon Grey and Adrian Stokes, may have occurred as a deliberate, conscious action undertaken by Thomas Lennard in the 1670s as a symbolic visual confirmation of his Protestant loyalties. There was, after all, some basis among his contemporaries for suspicion of those loyalties. Thomas Lennard's wife was Anne Fitzroy, an acknowledged illegitimate daughter of King Charles II. The couple had wed in August 1674 with the King in attendance, and Lennard was elevated to the Earldom of Sussex two months later. In sharp contrast to her new husband, Anne strongly opposed the Exclusion Bill and supported James of York as heir to the throne, a fact that eventually contributed to the couple's scandalous separation in the 1680s.[12] Further, Lennard's younger brother Francis converted to Roman Catholicism in the 1680s and would eventually fight in James II's favor at the Battle of the Boyne early in 1689.[13] With his immediate family so publicly divided in its loyalties throughout the succession dispute of the last quarter of the seventeenth century, conspicuously owning and displaying a portrait said to depict Jane Grey, an icon of the anti-Catholic cause, undoubtedly afforded Lennard far greater political, religious, and social capital than did any portrait of an unremarkable and long-dead ancestor. In that regard, it is noteworthy that the identifying inscription on the painted surface of the Wrest Park portrait is in a later hand rather than a sixteenth-century hand, clear indication that the inscription was added long after the work was created. It may well have been added in the 1680s at Thomas Lennard's behest.

Three early copies of the Wrest Park Portrait are documented, though the locations of only two are known today. Of the two known, the first and presumed earliest was produced in the middle of the eighteenth century for Harry Grey, 4th Earl of Stamford and a distant cousin of the same Henry Grey who purchased the Wrest Park Portrait from Thomas Lennard in 1701. That first copy was held at Enville Hall until the beginning of the twentieth century, when it was removed to Dunham Massey by Roger Grey, 10th Earl of Stamford.[14] The second surviving copy, also now at Dunham Massey, is believed to date to late in the eighteenth century.[15] A third apparent copy was sold through Christie's in 1931 by Sir John Foley Grey, 8th Baronet and owner of Enville Hall from 1914 until his death in 1938.[16] The current whereabouts of the third copy are unknown, but all three copies were engraved by a variety of artists of the nineteenth century, both for use as illustrations and for sale as individual images. The later engravings all reproduced the original image more faithfully, without embellishment of the sitter's costume, reflecting the transformation of Jane in the popular mythology from a learned scholar who dressed much like her peers to an exceptionally pious maiden of uncommonly modest habits (Fig.10).[17] The book held by the sitter in this and several other portraits yet to be discussed thus became emblematic in the eighteenth and later centuries of Jane's presumed personal piety rather than of her exceptional intellect.

Lady Jane Grey.

From the original, in the Collection of

The Right Hon.ble The Earl of Stamford and Warrington.

Drawn by W.m Derby, and Engraved (with Permission) by R. Cooper.

Published July 1, 1824, by Harding, Triphook, & Lepard, Finsbury Square, London.

Fig. 10: *Called Lady Jane Grey, stipple and line engraving by Robert Cooper, 1824.*

1 Burnet, *History of the Reformation*, II:172; *Called Lady Jane Dudley (née Grey)*, Robert White, 1681, line engraving, 10 in. x 6 ⅜ in., National Portrait Gallery, NPG D24991 and D10931.

2 *Called Lady Jane Dudley (née Grey)*, unknown engravers, eighteenth century, line engravings, various sizes, National Portrait Gallery, NPG D24996, D244997, and D24998.

3 On correctly identifying the sitter in this portrait, see J. Stephan Edwards, "Framing a Life in Portraits: A 'New' Portrait of Mary Nevill Fiennes, Lady Dacre," *British Art Journal* XIV:2, 14-20.

4 Bendor Grosvenor and David Starkey, *Lost Faces: Identity and Discovery in Tudor Royal Portraiture* (London: Philip Mould Ltd, 2007), 85, caption to fig. 55. Grosvenor and Starkey argued that the Wrest Park Portrait is a "consciously historical portrait" of Lady Jane Grey but "perhaps posthumous."

5 See, for example, *Mary Nevill, Lady Dacre*, Hans Eworth, ca.1555-58, oil on wood panel, 29 in. x 22 ¾ in., National Gallery of Canada, Ottawa; *Mary Nevill, Lady Dacre and Gregory Fiennes, 10ᵗʰ Baron Dacre*, Hans Eworth, 1559, oil on wood panel, 19 ¾ in. x 28 ⅛ in., National Portrait Gallery, London, NPG 6855.

6 Essex Record Office, Chelmsford, D/DL/E8/1, ff. 1r–3v, D/DL/E8/2, f. 1r–v, D/DL/F156, f. 1-10; Society of Antiquaries (London) Manuscript 706A.

7 *Mary Nevill, Lady Dacre and Gregory Fiennes, 10ᵗʰ Baron Dacre, Hans Eworth*, 1559, oil on wood panel, 19 ¾ x 28 ⅛ in., National Portrait Gallery, NPG6855; Susan Foister, "Nobility Reclaimed," *The Antique Collector* (UK) 57:4 (April 1986), 58-60.

8 Margaret Fiennes (*d.*1612), suo jure 11ᵗʰ Baroness Dacre, married Sampson Lennard in 1564, and it is from them that the Barons Dacre descended. Lennard's sister Rachel married Edward Nevill (*d.*1622), Baron Bergavenny, and their daughter Elizabeth subsequently married Sir John Grey, grandson of Sir John Grey of Pirgo, the latter being the younger brother of Henry Grey, 3ʳᵈ Marquess of Dorset, 1ˢᵗ Duke of Suffolk, and father of Jane Grey. John and Elizabeth Grey's son Henry (1599–1673) was created 1ˢᵗ Earl of Stamford in 1628.

9 Thomas Barrett-Lennard, *An Account of the families of Barrett and Lennard* (privately printed, 1908), 286.

10 Barrett-Lennard, *Account*, 279-284 and 292-293. Though a Parliamentarian, Francis Lennard, 14ᵗʰ Baron Dacre, was one of the twelve Peers who opposed the trial and execution of Charles I in 1649. Francis was pardoned and restored in 1661 but thereafter maintained a state of self-imposed domestic exile at his principal estate, Herstmonceux Castle.

11 Barrett-Lennard, *Account*, 328; Lords Temporal and Spiritual to Lord Dartmouth, 11 December 1688, *Eleventh Report of the Historical Manuscripts Commission*, Appendix, Part V: *The Manuscripts of the Earl of Dartmouth* (London: HMSO, 1889), 229.

12 Barrett-Lennard, *Account*, 328.

13 Barrett-Lennard, *Account*, 301-302.

14 Christie, Manson & Woods, Ltd., *The Estate of the Late Lord Stamford, Dunham Massey, Altrincham, Cheshire. Valuation at Current Market Prices* (1977), 10; *A lady called Lady Jane Grey*, English School, mid eighteenth century, oil on canvas, 29 ½ in. x 23 in., National Trust Collection, Dunham Massey, DUN.P.31.

15 Christie, *Estate of the Late Lord Stamford*, p.37: "[In] The Staircase Hall Outside the Stone Parlour. Eworth. [£]200. Portrait of a Lady, half length, wearing a brown dress and white cap; holding a half open book - 29 in by 24 in.", ? Lady Jane Grey, English School, late eighteenth century, oil on canvas, 29 in. x 24 in, National Trust, Dunham Massey, DUN.P.12.

16 Christie, Manson & Woods, Ltd., *Catalogue of pictures by old masters: the property of Sir John Foley Grey, Bart*, 27 February 1931, Lot 114.

17 See, for example, *Called Lady Jane Grey (née Dudley)*, Robert Cooper, 1824, stipple and line engraving, 14 ⅞ in. x 10 ⅞ in., National Portrait Gallery, NPG D36349, derived from the copy owned by Harry Grey, 4ᵗʰ Earl of Stamford.

10   The Fulbeck Portrait

Anne of Bohemia and Hungary (1503-1547)

Unknown artist, after Hans Maler

Oil on canvas; 13 ¼ in. x 10 in.

Undated, after 1519

Provenance:

Col. John Stanford-Elliot (*d.*1823), Gedling House, Carlton, Nottinghamshire.;

Thence by descent to Walter Hugh Rawnsley (*d.*1936), Well Vale House, Alford, Lincolnshire;

By descent to Mary Fane Fry (*d.*2000), Fulbeck Hall, Leadenham, Lincolnshire;

Sotheby's, 8 October 2002;

Private collection.

Richard Davey included this picture in his inventory of portraits attached as an appendix to his *Nine Days Queen: Lady Jane Grey and her Times*, written in 1909.[1] Davey referred to it as being "formerly in the possession of Colonel Elliot; said to be now in one of the Colleges at Oxford." It had in fact remained with the descendants of Colonel John Stanford-Elliot, formerly of Gedling House (Nottinghamshire), a wealthy stocking-manufacturing heir. Those descendants moved it about over the generations, until it came to rest at Fulbeck Hall, Lincolnshire, late in the twentieth century. It was ultimately sold at auction in 2002 when the contents of Fulbeck Hall were liquidated.[2]

Davey dismissed the existing identification of the sitter as Jane Grey based on the costume, noting rather sharply that "Lady Jane could no more have worn such a hat and costume than a lady [of today] could be painted as wearing the crinoline and spoon-shaped bonnet of the mid-Victorian days." Davey did not propose any alternative name for the sitter, however. The identification as Jane Grey therefore remained intact until the Fulbeck auction in 2002.

The Fulbeck Portrait was reasonably popular early in the nineteenth century as a depiction of Jane Grey. It was repeatedly reproduced in both lithographs and engravings beginning as early as 1822, all with identifications as Jane (Fig.11).[3] Later in the same decade, the English portrait artist Charles Linsell created a painted copy for the Reverend Robert James Carr, Anglican Bishop of Worcester after 1831. Carr was vehemently opposed to the Roman Catholic Relief Act of 1829 and had voted against it in the House of Lords while Bishop of Chichester. The Linsell copy was no doubt intended by Carr as a tangible expression of his anti-Catholic sentiments. The copy has remained since at Hartlebury Castle, residence of the bishops of Worcester from the thirteenth century until 2007.

Fig. 11: *Called Lady Jane Grey, engraving by Antoine Maurin, 1820s.*

Fig. 12: *Anna of Bohemia and Hungary, by Hans Maler, 1519.*

The correct identification of this portrait is remarkably straightforward. One of my German correspondents with a keen eye for portraiture, Marianne Steinbauer, immediately recognized the portrait as a copy from an original in the Museo Thyssen-Bornemisza in Madrid.[4] The original depicts Anne, daughter of Wladislav, King of Hungary and Bohemia, as she appeared in 1519 before her marriage to Ferdinand, Archduke of Austria (Fig.12).[5] The original was painted by Hans Maler (*d.*1529), a German-born artist who worked extensively for Archduke Ferdinand of Austria, younger brother of the Holy Roman Emperor Charles V. Several of Maler's portraits of Anne survive, as do portraits of her by other artists and now in the Gemäldegalerie (Berlin) and the Landes-museum Ferdinandeum (Innsbruck).

The Fulbeck copy of Maler's original is on canvas and thus dates to no earlier than the seventeenth century, but more probably to late in the eighteenth century. It is perhaps the work of an English artist on the Grand Tour, since Maler's portrait of Anne was formerly part of the Barberini Collection in Rome, a favorite stop on the Tour. It is, however, a remarkably unusual source-model for rechristening as Jane Grey, and not just in terms of the decidedly Germanic costume. Through her marriage to Ferdinand, brother of the Holy Roman Emperor Charles V, Anne was a niece to Katherine of Aragon and cousin to Mary Tudor. And although she was therefore also a distant cousin to Jane Grey, her Roman Catholic faith gave her a natural affinity to Katherine of Aragon's cause and at least a presumed loyalty to Princess Mary's right to inherit the throne. How or why the artist of the Fulbeck Hall Portrait chose a known portrait of Catholic Anne of Bohemia and Hungary to copy and rechristen as Jane Grey is an unsolvable mystery.

[1] Davey, *The Nine Days Queen*, 359-362.

[2] *The Contents of Fulbeck Hall, Lincolnshire*, Sotheby's, London, 8 October 2002, Lot 372, 158.

[3] *Lady Jane Grey*, Antoine Maurin, printed by Francois Le Villain, published by Edward Bull and Edward Churton, 1820s, lithograph printed on paper, 19 in. x 13 ¼ in., National Portrait Gallery, NPG D32036; *Lady Jane Grey*, Antoine Maurin et al., 1830s, hand-colored lithograph printed on paper, 19 ¼ in. x 14 ⅛ in., National Portrait Gallery, NPG D34620; *Lady Jane Grey*, Robert William Sievier, published by John Brydone, 1822, stipple engraving printed on paper, 18 in. x 14 in., National Portrait Gallery, NPG D24992 and NPG D32037.

[4] Electronic correspondence, Marianne Stienbauer, 17 February 2012. I am very grateful to Ms Steinbauer for alerting me to the proper identification of this painting.

[5] *Anna of Bohemia and Hungary*, by Hans Maler, 1519, oil on wood panel, 17 ⅓ in. x 13 in., Museo Thyssen-Bornemisza, Madrid, 275 (1937.2).

11   The Fitzwilliam Portrait

Unknown Lady

Hans Eworth (or Ewouts)

Oil on wood panel; 43 ⅛ in. x 31 ½ in.

Undated, 1550s

Provenance:

> Francis Barchard (*d.*1856), Horstead Place, Uckfield, Sussex, by whom purchased 1854;
>
> By descent to Mrs Maude Barchard, by whom sold;
>
> P. and D. Colnaghi & Co. Ltd, London, 1949;
>
> Sir Bruce Ingram (*d.*1963);
>
> Bequeathed to the Fitzwilliam Museum, Cambridge, acc. no. PD.1-1963.

Research in 2005 on this portrait by Hans Eworth represented my first foray into the iconography of Jane Grey, emerging out of my coursework as a graduate student at the University of Colorado. The principal points of my evidence and argument included, first, the known patronage links between the artist who created the portrait, Hans Eworth, and the circle of John Dudley, Jane's father-in-law. Secondly, I argued that the brooch worn by the sitter, which depicts the Old Testament story of Esther who sacrificed herself in marriage to save her Jewish co-religionists from persecution, may have symbolized Protestant Jane's own "sacrifice" in an attempt to prevent the accession of the Roman Catholic Mary Tudor. Lastly, the leather cover of the book suspended on a chain from the lady's waist appears to be embossed with the letter D, which might signify the Greys' longstanding title Marquess of Dorset. But as with many first efforts in a new field of study, I did make mistakes. Most notably, I utilized the Spinola letter cited by Richard Davey as a reliable description of Jane's physical appearance, not yet realizing that the letter was certainly a fabrication (see Appendix One, p.177). And I attempted to account for the lady's very adult appearance, which contrasts sharply with Jane's young age at her death, by citing a serious illness Jane is said to have suffered in 1553, though my later readers found that argument unconvincing. Nonetheless, my assessment of the painting was published in the popular British magazine *History Today* in December 2005 and received minor attention from the British news media.[1] The Fitzwilliam Museum subsequently amended the labeling of the painting to "Perhaps Lady Jane Grey."

Less than 18 months later, Hope Walker, a student at London's Courtauld Institute of Art, published a reasonable challenge to my conclusion, doing so in association with an exhibition held in March 2007 by the London galleries of Philip Mould Ltd. Ms Walker argued that the sitter might instead be Jane Dormer, a close friend of Queen Mary. The D on the book could easily have corresponded to Dormer, Walker argued. Dormer was a cousin of Mary Nevill Fiennes, Lady Dacre, and the latter was a repeated patron of Eworth, a link very similar to my own proposed Dudley-Eworth link. Lastly, Walker argued that the formal structure of the painting, especially the positioning of the sitter, was similar to a portrait of Dormer's friend Queen Mary now held by the Society of Antiquaries.[2] The lady bears little resemblance to Jane Dormer as she appears in an authenticated portrait of her, however.[3]

Ironically, the portrait had been identified as Queen Mary herself when it was purchased in 1854 by its first documented owner, Frances Barchard. That identification went unchallenged until late in the twentieth century. The noted art historian Ellis Waterhouse, for example, interpreted the Esther brooch as confirmatory evidence that the sitter was indeed Queen Mary on the grounds that Esther was herself a queen.[4] J.W. Goodison, curator of the Fitzwilliam Museum early in the 1960s, considered that "it seems absurd that the identity of the woman [as Queen Mary] should be questioned."[5] But in 1985, Hugh Tait suggested that the sitter might be Lady Anne Penruddocke, based on his perception of a facial resemblance to that lady in a well-documented Eworth portrait of Lady Anne dated 1557.[6] The jewels worn by the sitter in the Fitzwilliam Portrait are far more costly than would ordinarily be expected for a person of Lady Anne's socio-economic standing, however. Indeed, the jewels Anne wears in the comparison portrait are decidedly modest, consisting primarily of a single gold chain without gemstones.

Most recently, Christopher Wickham, formerly of Bridgeman Art Library, has proposed Jane Guildford Dudley, wife of John Dudley (and thus Jane Grey's mother-in-law) as the sitter. The proposal has certain merits, though it has yet to be confirmed. As the wife of John Dudley, the patronage link to Hans Eworth remains valid. Jane Dudley died in January 1555 while in her late 40s, a not-impossible age for the sitter seen here. Jane Dudley is also known to have had a personal fondness for the story of Esther, having possessed two multi-panel sets of tapestries depicting that particular story. At least one of those sets was returned to her in August 1553 after having been previously seized in the wake of her husband's attainder for treason.[7] The D on the prayerbook might have been a monogram for Dudley, though John Dudley himself preferred monograms derived from his successive titles rather than from his surname.[8] Lastly, Jane Dudley made an unusual and explicit mention in her will of a girdle-book of the type seen in this portrait, which she called an "Almanack" and which she bequeathed to her friend Don Diego de Acevedo.[9]

Absent any documented provenance for this painting prior to its acquisition in 1854 by Francis Barchard, and despite extensive research efforts, there are too few clues to enable a reliable identification for the sitter. Evidence contained within the painted image, including the D on the girdle pendant book, is too sparse and too readily subject to a variety of interpretations. It is not even certain, for example, that the shape perceived on the cover of the book is in fact a letter D. Therefore, as with the sitters in several other putative portraits of Jane Grey discussed in this volume, the lady may be any one of hundreds or even thousands of women who lived in England during the 1550s. But having gained over a decade of experience and knowledge since first studying this portrait, I am now convinced that she is not Lady Jane Grey.

[1] "A New Face for the Lady," *History Today* 55:12 (December 2005): 44-45; "Portrait may be only image of Lady Jane Grey," *Sunday Times*, 13 November 2005.

[2] Hope Walker, "A Portrait of Lady Jane Dormer, Later Duchess of Feria?," *Lost Faces: Identity and Discovery in Tudor Portraiture*, edited by Bendor Grosvenor (London: Philip Mould, 2007), 86-87.

[3] *Lady Jane Dormer, Duchess of Feria*, after Antonio Sanchez Coello, ca.1563, oil on wood panel, 61 ½ in. x 42 in., Burton Constable Hall, Skirlaugh, Yorkshire.

[4] Ellis Waterhouse, *Catalogue of the exhibition of works by Holbein and other masters* (London: Royal Academy of Arts, 1950-51), 25.

[5] J.W. Goodison to R. Thesiger, Colnaghi &Co., Ltd., 1 February 1963, Fitzwilliam Museum file PD.1-1963.

[6] Hugh Tait: "The girdle-prayerbook or 'tablett': an important class of Renaissance jewellery at the court of Henry VIII," *Jewellery Studies* 2 (1985), 54-55, n.8.

[7] National Archives (Kew), Public Record Office, LR 2/120, "Inventory of the Goods & Chattels of John Duke of Northumberland taken 23 & 24 July 1553," ff. 88v and 99v; LR 2/118, f. 93r, "Certen stuff Delyvered for the furnyture of the Duches of NorthumberLande;" E 101/631/44, loose leaves.

[8] Paul Needham, *Twelve Centuries of Book- bindings, 400–1600* (New York: Pierpont Morgan Library, 1979), 184; see also the well-known Dudley armorial carvings in the Beauchamp Tower at the Tower of London.

[9] National Archives, PROB 11/37, f.194v.

12   The Somerley Portrait

Unknown Lady

Early-Sixteenth-Century Franco-Italian School

Oil on wood panel; 28 in. x 21 in.

Undated, early sixteenth century

Provenance:

John Boykett Jarman (*d*.1864), by whom sold 1833;

Stanley Auction House, London, 4 July 1833, Lot 74, as Lady Jane Grey by Luca Penni;

Welbore Ellis Agar (*d*.1868), 2nd Earl of Normanton;

thence by descent, Somerley House, Hampshire.

Once again, the presence both of a book held in the sitter's hand and of what may be a personal initial or monogram D figure in the rechristening as Jane Grey of a sixteenth-century portrait of an otherwise unknown lady. Art historian Gustav Waagen noted in 1857 that the sitter in this portrait had been identified as Jane Grey specifically on the basis of the D that appears on the lady's cuff button, it being associated with Jane's surname following her marriage to Guildford Dudley.[1] The presence of the book, consistent with several other putative portraits of Jane Grey, made the correlation of the button's D to Dudley all the more compelling. The sitter had already been identified as Jane Grey by the time the Somerley Portrait first entered the written historical record two decades prior to Waagen's observations, when it was offered at auction in 1833 by the London firm of Stanley.[2] The absence of an extended documentary provenance makes it impossible to know precisely when the rechristening occurred, however. But circumstantial evidence suggests that the seller, the collector-dealer John Boykett Jarman, may have fabricated the identification in an effort to increase the sale price.[3] The identification as Jane Grey would have literally capitalized on the controversy surrounding the passage of the Roman Catholic Relief Act just four years previously. The identification stood, despite occasional challenges, until 2010.

In addition to the presence of the book in the hands and the D on the cuff buttons, the overall aesthetics of the costume are consistent with eighteenth- and nineteenth-century mythologized interpretations of Jane Grey. Though not as overtly austere as the Puritan-like attire implied by John Strype and popularized by the Wrest Park Portrait, it is nonetheless relatively simple and unembellished. The French hood has a single upper billiment of goldwork without gemstones. The gown is constructed of a dark fabric without embroidery or brocading, showing only simple gold edging across the bodice and sleeve edges. The jewels are limited to a thin gold necklace with no apparent gemstones plus a girdle chain of gold balls interspersed with beads of what may be carved rock crystal, and at least four simple gold rings on her fingers. The only costume elements indicating significant wealth and status are the furred oversleeves, which have usually been assumed to be ermine, a fur commonly associated with royalty.[4] The costume therefore readily lends itself to association with a woman of status but who was otherwise quite modest and unassuming in her attire.

The costume does appear to be consistent with English fashions of the first half of the sixteenth century, but it is also entirely consistent with French designs from the same period. The widely squared neckline of the gown, leaving the shoulders bare, is seen in both English and French portraits reliably datable to the period between about 1520 and 1550, for example.[5] The headgear is known as a French hood specifically because the style originated in France. It became popular in England during the ascendancy at the royal court of Anne Boleyn, who had spent much of her youth in France and who reportedly continued to wear French fashion rather than the angular gabled Spanish hood favored by her rival, Katherine of Aragon. But the shape of the hood, following the natural curvature of the crown of the head, indicates a date prior to about 1540, the upper edge of hoods of the 1540s and 1550s becoming more nearly horizontal across the crown.[6] The red pleated undersleeves are likewise seen in both French and English costume early in the sixteenth century, but they had disappeared from English costume in particular by about 1540.[7] Whether the costume and the sitter are English or French, they certainly date to a period well before Jane Grey was even out of infancy.

Determining whether the lady is English or French can best be accomplished by reference to the artistic technique employed to create the image. The small number of art historians who have previously studied this picture largely agree that the work displays a strong Italian influence, both in subject composition and in the linear execution. In particular, the positioning of the sitter appears to have been inspired by the works of Raphael, so that attribution for this painting has typically centered on his students and followers.[8] The work was first attributed to Luca Penni, whom the sale catalogue of 1833 claimed had resided briefly in England and was known to have painted a portrait of Jane Grey specifically.[9]

Any identification of the sitter as Jane Grey necessarily depended, of course, upon attribution to an Italian artist who could plausibly be represented as having been present in England early in the 1550s, and at least one Italian surnamed "Penn" had indeed been recorded at the court of Henry VIII. A manuscript of "The King's Payments" now in the British Library reveals payments in March 1540 totaling 12*l*. 10*s*. made to "Anth. Toto and Bartill Penn, painters."[10] Those two men are usually identified as Antonio Toto del Nunziata (*d*.1554) and Bartolomeo Penni. Toto worked regularly for the Crown and court from about 1530 until the early 1550s, though few surviving works are today attributed to him.[11] Bartolomeo Penni has frequently been conflated with Luca Penni, yet modern scholarship reveals that the two were distinct individuals.[12] Other than Antonio Toto and Bartolomeo Penni, only a mere handful of Italian artists are known to have worked in England in the 1540s and 1550s, and no "Luca Penni" is found among them. The attribution to Luca Penni was, therefore, one of convenience and made to suit a pre-determined sitter identification that was itself invented in response to a political and cultural (and perhaps even financial) agenda.

Since the middle of the twentieth century, several other attributions to Italian or Italian-trained artists have been proposed. Charles Sterling, alternately curator of paintings at the Louvre and at New York's Metropolitan Museum of Art throughout the 1940s and 1950s, assigned the work to Andrea Sguazella (*fl*.1520s), while John Sherman asserted in 1960 that the sitter's costume was specifically French and thus attributed the painting to an unknown French artist working under the influence of the Italian Andrea del Sarto (*d*.1530), who had himself visited France briefly in 1518-1519.[13] More recently, Giuliano Bugiardini (*d*.1555) has been proposed, though this seems unlikely given that Bugiardini is not known ever to have traveled out of Italy, yet the costume seen here is decidedly non-Italian.[14] It is noteworthy that all but Bugiardini were deceased long before Jane Grey wed Guildford Dudley in May of 1553, effectively eliminating Jane as the sitter in every case except that of the earliest too-convenient attribution to Luca Penni. The greater likelihood is that the sitter is an unknown French woman, that the artist was either Italian or Italian-trained and working in France in the second quarter of the sixteenth century, and that the painting was simply imported to England sometime between the late-sixteenth and the early-nineteenth centuries. The sitter must for now remain unidentified.

[1] Gustav Friedrich Waagen, *Galleries and Cabinets of Art in Great Britain* (London: John Murray, 1857), 364.

[2] Stanley Auction House (London), sale of 4 July 1833, Lot 74 as *Lady Jane Grey* by Luca Penni, Lugt Number 13367, Getty Research Institute Sale Catalog Br-13857.

[3] Jarman is known to have been less than honest in his dealings. In about 1851, Jarman had the faces of two figures in *Adoration of the Magi* altered to resemble those of Sir Thomas More and his wife so that he could more readily sell the painting to Charles Winn of Nostell Priory (Wakefield, Yorkshire), who claimed descent from More. See "Nostell Priory 'mystery' painting on display," *Yorkshire Evening Post*, 1 April 2010.

[4] The fur is more probably leopard, which was popular in Europe in the sixteenth century.

[5] See for example, *Portrait of a French Lady*, Circle of Andrea del Sarto, ca.1518, oil on wood panel, 42 ½ in. x 34 in., Cleveland Museum of Art, 1944.92; *Mary Tudor when Princess*, Master John, 1544, oil on wood panel, 28 in. x 20 in., National Portrait Gallery, London, NPG428).

[6] Melanie Schuessler, "French Hoods: Development of a Sixteenth-Century Court Fashion," *Medieval Clothing and Textiles*, ed. Robin Netherton and Gale R. Owen-Crocker (Woodbridge: Boydell and Brewer, 2009), V:129-160.

[7] See for example, *Portrait of a French Lady*, Circle of Andrea del Sarto, circa 1518, oil on wood panel, 42 ½ in. x 34 in., Cleveland Museum of Art, 1944.92; *Portrait of Mary Wooten, Lady Guildford*, Hans Holbein, 1527, oil and tempra on wood panel, 34 ¼ in. x 27 ¹³/₁₆ in., St Louis Art Museum, 1:1943; *Margaret More Roper*, Hans Holbein, 1535/6, gouache on vellum laid on playing card, 1 ¾ in diameter, Metropolitan Museum of Art, 50.69.2.

[8] See, for example, *Portrait of a Gentlewoman (The Silent One)*, Raphael, 1505-1507, oil on canvas, 25 in. x 19 in., Museo Galleria Borghese, Rome; *Portrait of Maddalena Doni*, ca.1506, oil on wood panel, 25 in. x 18 in., Palazzo Pitti, Florence; *Woman with a veil*, 1514/15, oil on canvas, 32 in. x 23 ⁴/₅ in., Palazzo Pitti.

[9] See note 2 above. The limited modern scholarship on Luca Penni indicates that he was born in Rome in about 1500 and emigrated to France in about 1530, worked at Fontainebleau from 1538, and finally settled in Paris in 1550. He died in Paris in 1556/7. No documentation survives to indicate that Luca Penni was ever in England.

[10] British Library, Arundel MSS 97, f. 123v.

[11] See Bendor Grosvenor, "A Rare Tudor Survival," *Art History News*, 15 March 2012, <http://arthistorynews.com/articles/1149_A_rare_Tudor_survival> Accessed 23 May 2014.

[12] Kathleen Wilson-Chevalier, "Sebastian Brant: The Key to Understanding Luca Penni's Justice and the Seven Deadly Sins," *The Art Bulletin* 78:2 (June 1996), 236–237; M. Digby Wyatt, "On the Foreign Artists Employed in England in the Sixteenth Century, and Their Influence on British Art," in *Papers Read at the Royal Institute of British Architects* (London, 1867), 226; George T. Robinson, "Decorative Plaster Work," *Journal of the Society of Arts* 2005:39 (24 April 1891), 446; James Lees-Milne, *Tudor Renaissance* (London: T. Batsford Ltd, 1951), 47.

[13] John Sherman, "Three Portraits by Andrea del Sarto and his circle," *The Burlington Magazine* 102:683 (February 1960), 62.

[14] Personal communication, The Earl of Normanton, 11 April 2012. Lord Normanton was unable to recall who made the re-attribution or the specific basis on which it was made.

13   The Rotherwas Portrait   (co-authored with Hope Walker)

Portrait of a Noblewoman

Unknown artist

Oil on wood panel; 30 ⅛ in. x 22 ¹¹/₁₆ in.

Undated, *ca.*1550–1555

Provenance:
The Bodenhams of Rotherwas House, Herefordshire, until 1913;

   Ayerst Hooker Buttery and Horace Buttery, London, until 1950s;

   H.E.M. Benn, Haslemere, Sussex, until about 1960;

   The Hon. Clive Pearson, Parham Park, Sussex, until 1965;

   Agnew and Sons, London;

   Gifted by an anonymous donor to Minneapolis Institute of Art, acc. no. 87.6, 1987.

An employee of the Minneapolis Institute of Art (MIA), the current repository for this painting, contacted art history student Hope Walker in January 2010 seeking attribution of the work to Hans Eworth. Ms. Walker, whose graduate work focused on Eworth, ultimately determined that the artistry was not consistent with Eworth's technique. But since the MIA employee was simultaneously investigating the possibility that the sitter might be Lady Jane Grey Dudley, Ms. Walker contacted me in that regard. The suspicion by MIA personnel that the sitter might be Jane Grey was entirely new as of 2009. The portrait had never previously been proposed, exhibited, or published as a portrait of Jane.

The portrait contains several elements that might potentially recommend it as a depiction of Jane. The lady does appear to be young, certainly less than 30 years of age. The details of the costume, especially the horizontal line of the crown of the French hood and the standing collar of the partlet with its extensive blackwork embroidery, date the painting to the 1550s. The positioning of the sitter, standing squared to the viewer and gazing directly ahead, is often associated with royal sitters, though certainly women of much lower rank were sometimes also positioned in this manner.[1] The lady could perhaps have been an early Protestant, judging by the subject matter depicted in the figural pendant brooch affixed to her bodice. As discussed below, it appears to represent Mary Magdalene, one of only two saints retained from the previous Roman Catholic tradition by the reformist First Book of Common Prayer of 1549.[2] Further, like so many other portraits said to depict Jane and included in this study, the lady holds a small book in her hands, perhaps a prayerbook or other devotional text. Lady Jane Grey is famously known to have owned a near-identical book, which has survived and is sometimes exhibited at the British Library.[3]

The portrait has borne other identifications over the years, however, as well as other artist attributions. From the eighteenth century until the beginning of the twentieth, the sitter was said to be Margaret Tudor, Queen Consort to James IV of Scotland and elder sister of Henry VIII. Though that labeling was supported by an inscription in an eighteenth-century hand painted across the left sleeve, since removed, Margaret died in 1541, before this painting was created.[4] The auction house of Puttick and Simpson, in handling the first recorded sale of the painting in 1913, suggested that the sitter was instead Margaret's granddaughter, Mary, Queen of Scots, though their evidence to support the suggestion was not recorded.[5] Mary was dismissed as the sitter soon after the sale. By early 1915, it was proposed that the woman might be Cecilia (or Cecily) Bodenham, a well-known lady of the sixteenth-century Bodenhams of Rotherwas, the family and house from which the picture originated.[6] Yet that too is contradicted by the fact that Cecilia Bodenham died in 1545, before this painting was probably produced, and at almost sixty years of age, far too old to be the lady seen here.

Similarly, the painting was attributed very generically to "English School" at the time of its first sale in 1913 but was re-assigned to Hans Holbein literally within days of the sale.[7] Though the work does bear the same startlingly realistic rendering of the face as is seen in genuine pictures by Holbein, it was dismissed as his work in 1985.[8] Holbein died in 1543, but the sitter's costume dates to no earlier than about 1550.[9] There are also certain technical differences that eliminate Holbein as the creator. The attribution is now given as "Unknown artist," but John Bettes the Elder, Gerlack Flicke, Guillim Scrots, and Hans Eworth have each been proposed. None have yet been confirmed.

The book is an important element in this portrait, as MIA personnel suggested, and potentially posed the most definitive means for confirming whether the sitter was indeed Jane Grey. Such small books were relatively common in the early and mid sixteenth century among both Roman Catholics and Protestants. And the book seen here is indeed roughly identical in size to the prayerbook that Jane Grey is known to have possessed, inscribed, and carried with her to the scaffold in February 1554.[10] Yet other women of the era are known to have possessed similar small books, most notably Katherine Parr, so the presence of the book is not itself definitive evidence that the sitter is Jane Grey.[11]

The pattern of the remnants of script still visible on the open pages of the book indicate that the writing was certainly fully legible when the painting was first produced, but cleaning and re-varnishing carried out by Ayerst Buttery in 1913 removed most of it. Nonetheless, an ambitious

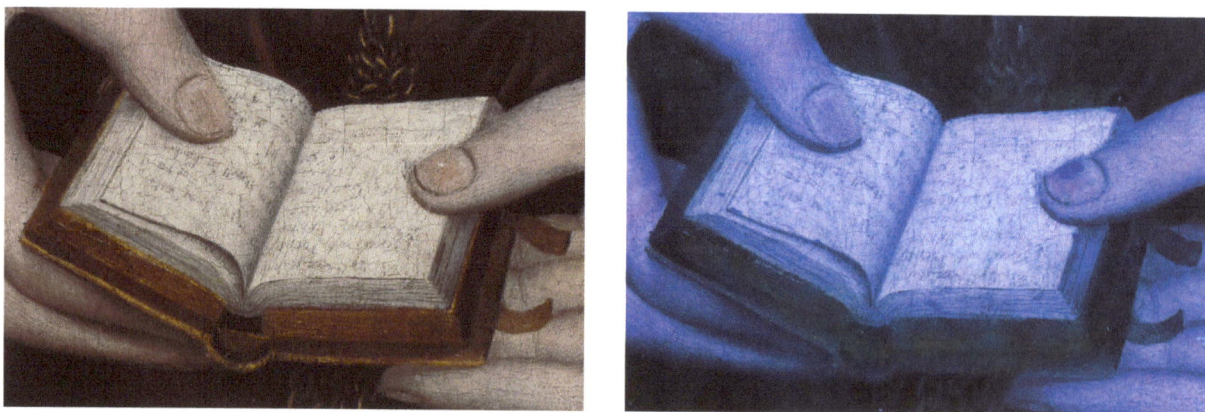

Fig. 13: *Rotherwas Portrait, book detail, under normal light (left) and near-UV light (right).*

effort was undertaken to recover enough of the script to make the text legible, so as to compare it to the text of Jane's surviving prayerbook.

Super-high-resolution digital photographs of the book were obtained under 370-400 nanometer near-ultra-violet light (Fig.13) and the resulting images were sent to a colleague at NASA's Jet Propulsion Laboratory (JPL) for specialized processing. The JPL has developed sophisticated proprietary computer software for analyzing digital ultra-violet photographs taken by its various Mars Rover missions, software that can elicit from those photographs microscopic evidence of fluorescence not readily discernible with the naked eye. It was hoped that the pigment used to paint the text of the book might either be composed of a substance that would fluoresce under UV light or contain contaminates that would similarly fluoresce. If fluorescence could be detected in sufficient amounts, even microscopically, the text might be able to be reconstructed. Unfortunately, the most common substances used in the sixteenth century to produce black pigment were lamp black and bone black, both carbon-based and thus non-fluorescent. No fluorescence was detected in any of the nineteen UV images taken of the book.

We concluded that the book was probably painted in two stages: the white pages were painted first and the paint was allowed to cure long enough to produce an impermeable surface. The text was then painted in on top of the cured white surface, which prevented the formation of a strong bond between the two layers. Then, when the painting was cleaned in 1913, the weak bond between the layers was broken and most of the black pigment was carried away with the cleaning solvents. The text could not be reconstructed and remains totally illegible. The book was ultimately not useful in identifying the sitter, therefore.

Only the figured brooch remained to provide a clue to the sitter's identity (Fig.14). In the past, the lady depicted in the brooch playing a lute was identified as Saint Cecilia, patron saint of music, leading to identification of the sitter as Cecilia Bodenham.[12] Yet the lutenist more probably represents Mary Magdalene. Though musical instruments, especially organs and violins, are often associated with Saint Cecilia, the lute is rare in Cecilian iconography.[13] The lute is far more commonly associated with the Magdalene.[14] Further, imagery of Mary Magdalene often portrays her in a garden or grove of trees, as seen here, in reference to her period of penitence in the wilderness. The Magdalene is also often identifiable by the presence of a small jar or pot placed close to the figure, in reference to the jar of ointment with which Mary anointed Christ's feet. Just such a jar is discernible beneath the right-hand tree on the brooch, though it is quite indistinct in photographs. The Magdalene was an exceedingly popular saint in England in the sixteenth century, so that the brooch may have no correlation with the name of the sitter. But if in fact the sitter used the brooch to convey her own identity through association with the name of a particular saint, the sitter was most likely to have been named Mary.

Fig. 14: *Rotherwas Portrait, details of bodice pendant brooch depicting Mary Magdalene.*

A search of numerous surviving jewel inventories, especially those of Queen Mary as the reigning monarch in the decade when this portrait was most probably produced, revealed a significant number of brooches containing the image of "a woman luting" and a "saile" or banderole with a scriptural text. None of the inventories offered sufficiently specific detail to make a firm match possible, however. A typical entry read simply "A brooch with a gentlewoman luting, and a scripture about it."[15] From this it could be surmised only that the design motif was a popular one reproduced in such quantity that it is unlikely that the brooch in this painting can be linked to a particular individual.

The text on the banderole above the lutenist's head was also considered for any significance it may possibly have for identifying the sitter. The text is in English, indication that the sitter was herself English and that the portrait was not imported from the continent. It is tempting to interpret the usage of English, rather than Latin, as a marker of Protestant affiliation, but such an interpretation is contradicted by pre-Reformation inventories describing similar religiously-themed jewels with English texts. The phrase itself, "Praise the Lord for ever more," is not sufficiently unique to be useful for identifying the sitter. It appears in several Old Testament writings and in hymns composed in the sixteenth century.[16] Although the jewel and its text may well have had personal symbolic meaning for the lady depicted wearing it, that meaning is now lost and seemingly unrecoverable.

In the narrow context of evaluating the suggestion that the sitter could potentially be Jane Grey, it is useful to examine the reported early provenance of the painting. At the time of the dispersal of the collection from Rotherwas in 1913, the Bodenham heirs claimed that the painting had always been in the family's possession. Family traditions are too often erroneous, but assuming the Bodenham tradition is accurate, it seems highly unlikely that they would have acquired a costly painting of Jane Grey, whether through gift or purchase. In the first instance, the sixteenth-century Bodenhams of Rotherwas had no demonstrable connection to the Greys of Bradgate. The closest discoverable link is a friendship between the Abbess Cecilia Bodenham and Christian Willoughby, a female cousin of Katherine Willoughby Brandon, much-younger second wife of Jane Grey's maternal grandfather Charles Brandon, Duke of Suffolk.[17] But since only Katherine Willoughby remained alive by the time Jane was even ten years old, that relationship is insufficient to explain any gift to the Bodenhams after 1550 by either Jane or her family, especially the gift of a portrait of such obvious quality and concomitant cost.

In the second instance, the Bodenhams of the sixteenth century were exceedingly unlikely to have knowingly purchased a portrait of the Protestant challenger to the throne of the Roman Catholic Mary Tudor, since the Bodenhams were themselves staunch Catholics. Roger Bodenham (d.1579), lord of the manor of Rotherwas after 1538, was twice arrested and interrogated for unspecified offenses during the reign of the Protestant Edward VI. Both events occurred within days of each promulgation of the Book of Common Prayer, the first in 1549 and the second late in 1552.[18] It is likely that his offenses were actually protests against the Book. So strong was Roger Bodenham's Catholic faith that he entered voluntary exile, first as a merchant-explorer between 1550 and 1552, and then as a permanent resident in Spain following the accession of Elizabeth in 1558.[19] He remained in Spain until the summer of 1575, amassing a fortune as a representative for English goods and commerce. His son, also named Roger, remained in Spain even after his elderly father's return to England. It is therefore difficult to imagine the Bodenhams purchasing at high cost and lovingly preserving a fine portrait of a woman who was their religious, if not political, enemy. Further, it seems almost impossible that such a purchase of a specifically English portrait could have been made after 1558, when the family was in exile in Spain. If the Bodenham family tradition asserting that the painting was always at Rotherwas is correct, it is thus highly improbable that the sitter depicted in the portrait is Jane Grey.

It is equally unlikely that the sitter is a member of the Bodenham family. She is very unlikely to be Roger Bodenham Sr's wife, Jane Whyttington (*b.ca.*1518), for example, since that lady was well over 30 years of age by the time this painting was created, after 1550. Bridget Baskerville, first wife of Roger Jr, can also be eliminated since the couple did not marry until 1582 (Roger Jr was a mature 37 years old at the time). Roger Sr and Jane Whyttington Bodenham did have two daughters who survived infancy: Elizabeth and Margaret. Online genealogical websites generally agree that Margaret was born after her brothers Thomas (*b.*1544) and Roger (*b.*1545), making her too young to be the lady in this painting, even if it dates to as late as 1560. Elizabeth, however, seems to have been born before her brothers, perhaps as early as 1538.[20] But because the elder generation of Bodenhams lived largely in exile between 1550 and 1575, and the second generation remained in exile until the early 1580s, it seems altogether unlikely that in those turbulent circumstances the family would have commissioned a costly portrait of any of its members, even daughter Elizabeth. Significantly, the Bodenham sale of 1913 included only one portrait identified as a member of the Bodenham family out of a total of 122 lots, and that portrait was a late-nineteenth-century copy of a lost seventeenth-century original.[21]

More probably, the painting entered the Bodenham collection long after it was created and thus depicts some other, as yet unknown lady. Indeed, the history of Rotherwas House itself almost requires this to be the case. The first significant house on the manor was not built until the first years of the seventeenth century. It was seized by Parliamentary forces during the Civil Wars of the 1640s and fell completely into ruin, making it unlikely that any artworks contained within survived that period. Rotherwas was re-built in 1731 and required furnishing entirely anew, from carpets to chandeliers. In all likelihood, the painting was purchased in or after 1731 to aid in decorating the new house. Because the inscription removed from the sleeve in 1913 appeared to date to the eighteenth century, it seems probable that the painting was actually purchased in the mistaken belief that it was an authentic portrait of Margaret Tudor, Queen Consort of Scotland. As Catholics, the Bodenhams of the early Hanoverian period were quite probably Jacobite sympathizers, and Margaret Tudor was the progenitor of the Jacobite Stuart heirs to the English throne. Yet the lady depicted is certainly not Margaret Tudor Douglas. Neither is she Mary Stuart, as was briefly claimed, nor Cecilia Bodenham or Lady Jane Grey. And she is also very unlikely to be any member of the Bodenham family. The identity of the lady in the portrait must remain a mystery, at least for the time being.

[1] See, for example, the drawings by Hans Holbein now in the Royal Collection. Among thirty three women who sat to Holbein, eight (25%) are positioned squared front.

[2] The other retained saint was the Virgin Mary.

[3] British Library, Harley Manuscript 2342.

[4] Chamberlain, *Hans Holbein*, I:353. The inscription was deliberately removed when the painting was cleaned and revarnished by Ayerst Buttery in 1913.

[5] Puttick and Simpsons catalogue, 8 April 1913, Lot 17, page 5.

[6] M.H. Dodd, "Cecilia Bodenham: A Portrait by Holbein", *Notes and Queries* 2nd series XI (March 20, 1915), 231.

[7] Puttick and Simpsons, 5; "The Rotherwas Holbein," *The Times of London*, 28 June 1913; "A Picture's Romantic History," *The Morning Post* (London), 28 June 1913; "New Holbein Is Found," *New York Times*, 28 June 1913; Chamberlain, *Hans Holbein the Younger*, I:353-358.

[8] John Rowlands, *Holbein: The Paintings of Hans Holbein the Younger* (Boston: David R. Godine, 1985), 237 and 269, plate 248.

[9] Until this study, it was believed that the portrait dated to as early as the 1520s, based on a dendrochronology report dated 1974 plus accompanying correspondence from Dr. John M. Fletcher, a pioneer in the science of dendrochronology. Muddled provenances, a profusion of dates, and Dr. Fletcher's confusing discussion of multiple portraits within a single dendrochronology report, coupled with the changing identifications for this portrait (Margaret Tudor, Mary Stuart, etc.), led to the belief that he was primarily describing the Rotherwas Portrait. In fact, he was discussing a portrait owned in 1974 by Mrs Eyre-Huddleston and subsequently passed to her heir, Canon Father Timothy Russ. In short, the Fletcher correspondence in the MIA's object file has no direct bearing on this painting, and no dendrochronology report for the Rotherwas portrait currently exists.

[10] British Library, Harley Manuscript 2342. The book measures 2 ¾ in. x 2 in. The original binding is no longer preserved.

[11] Janel Mueller, *Katherine Parr: Complete Works and Correspondence* (Chicago: University of Chicago Press, 2011).

[12] Dodd, "Cecilia Bodenham."

[13] Albert P. de Mirimonde, *Sainte-Cécilie: Métamorphoses d'un thème musical* (Geneva: Minkoff, 1974), 7.

[14] H. Colin Slim, "Mary Magdalene, Musician and Dancer," *Early Music* 8:4 (October 1980), 460-473.

[15] *Letters and Papers, Foreign and Domestic, of Henry VIII*, ed. J.S. Brewer (London: Longmans and HMSO, 1875), IV:3070. It must be noted that the early jewelry historian Joan Evans assumed that the jewel in this painting was indeed the same as that listed in the royal inventory, despite the vagueness of the written inventory description. See Joan Evans, *English Jewelry from the fifth century A.D. to 1800* (London: Methuen and Co, 1921), 73.

[16] See Psalms 113 and 148, both of which were set to music for use in Protestant worship services, the first in 1542 at Strabourg and the second in 1562 at Geneva. See also Edward Hamilton, *The Sanctus: A Collection of Sacred Music, Full and Complete in Every Department; Adapted to the Worship of All Protestant Denominations* (Boston: Phillips, Sampson & Company, 1857), 15.

[17] National Archives, PROB 11/37, f.18, Will of Cecily Bodenham.

[18] *Acts of the Privy Council*, ed. John Roche Dasent (London: HMSO, 1892), IV:219 and 261.

[19] J. Theodore Bent, "The English in the Levant," *The English Historical Review* 5:20 (October 1890), 654–664. See also *Calendar of State Papers Foreign, Elizabeth, 1558-1589*, Volumes 7, 10 and 11 of which contain numerous letters from both Roger Sr and Roger Jr, endorsed at Seville and addressed to William Cecil and the Privy Council, on a variety of issues. Though living in religious exile, they were sufficiently loyal English subjects to report regularly on Spanish naval and military preparations.

[20] A survey of numerous online genealogical databases reveals a general agreement that Elizabeth Bodenham was born circa 1538. This data requires appropriate confirmation, however.

21 *John Bodenham*, copy of a contemporary picture, by A.M., 1879, oval cartouche, 36 in. x 29 in., Puttick and Simpson, 8 April 1913, Lot 18, 6.

14   The Bodleian Portrait

Called Lady Jane Grey

Unknown artist

Oil on wood panel; 14 in. x 11 ½ in.

Undated

Provenance:

    Dr Richard Rawlinson(*d*.1755), by whom;

    Gifted to Oxford University, acc. no. LP 32, 1751.

Though the bust-length Bodleian Portrait ends the succession of depictions of Jane Grey that include a book, it has nonetheless been thought for over two hundred years to represent her. Its provenance prior to 1751 is entirely undocumented, making it impossible to determine whether it was thus labeled prior to its acquisition by its last individual owner, Dr Richard Rawlinson, or whether it was instead rechristened by Rawlinson. But as a non-juring bishop in the Anglican Communion, Dr Rawlinson opposed the earlier recognition in 1688 of William and Mary as co-monarchs following the deposition of Mary's father, James II. Rawlinson was thus an anti-Hanoverian, pro-Stuart Jacobite. Since Jane Grey was an icon of the anti-Stuart, anti-Jacobite cause, Rawlinson's interest in Lady Jane was certainly of a non-political nature. His interest was instead likely purely historical, since Rawlinson was a very active antiquarian who collected all manner of books, manuscripts, and pictures, most of which he eventually donated to Oxford University along with this painting, forming the Rawlinson Collection of the Bodleian Library.

The labeling of the Bodleian Portrait as Jane Grey stood essentially unchallenged from 1751 until the end of the nineteenth century. Then in 1887 the National Portrait Gallery acquired a painting very similar to the Bodleian Portrait, NPG764, discussed next in this volume. Officials at the NPG immediately perceived a resemblance between the Bodleian and NPG paintings. In March of 1887, George Scharf, Director of the National Portrait Gallery, received a letter from his counterpart at the South Kensington Museum (now the Victoria and Albert Museum), George Wallis, in which Wallis expressed an aesthetic preference for NPG764 and dismissed the Bodleian Portrait as "a very ugly edition of the same person."[1] That early comparison led to additional suggestions that the two paintings depicted the same sitter, or that one was a copy of the other.[2]

There are, however, differences between the two that indicate they are probably separate images of two distinct individuals. Most obviously, the two sitters are positioned differently, clear confirmation that neither painting is a direct copy of the other. On closer inspection, differences appear in the costumes worn by the two sitters. The collar of the chemise worn by the Bodleian lady, for example, consists of a simple loose ruffle that is worn open, with two un-tied points hanging from the closure. In contrast, the collar of the lady in NPG764 includes a high, dense ruffle worn fully closed. Further, the coat worn by the Bodleian sitter lacks the vertical slash over each breast seen in NPG764. And where the Bodleian lady wears a corded necklace under her chemise, the NPG lady has no necklace, though there is an indistinct pattern at the margin between the chemise collar and the fur trim of the coat. While these differences may also represent deliberate variations made by what were clearly two separate artists, the more logical explanation in this instance is that the ladies were each unique persons.

Alternative identifications for the sitter in the Bodleian Portrait have been proposed in the past. In the first half of the twentieth century, historian Margaret Toynbee argued for Mary Tudor, though the sitter bears little physical resemblance to authenticated portraits of Henry VIII's first daughter.[3] Sir Roy Strong, in his published discussions of the iconography of Elizabeth I, initially postulated that NPG764 – and thus indirectly the Bodleian portrait as a supposed copy – might depict Henry VIII's second daughter.[4] He subsequently noted, however, that he eventually became "less inclined to support re-identification [of the sitter] as the young Elizabeth," stating that she was instead "likely to remain unidentified" since "identification as Lady Jane Grey cannot be sustained."[5]

Reliably and correctly identifying the sitter in the Bodleian Portrait is problematic, since no documentation on the painting survives that might support naming the lady. Nor is there any evidence to be derived through examination of the panel or the painted image that might shed reliable light on her identity. There are no marks or inscriptions naming the sitter or indicating the date at which the painting was created. Dating by means of costume analysis is not helpful in this case, since the style of headgear and coat are seen across a span of at least two decades.

Fig. 15: *Katherine Willoughby Brandon.*

Fig. 16: *Right, Lady Katherine Grey Seymour and son.*

Fig. 17: *Lady Katherine Grey Seymour.*

Katherine Willoughby Brandon, Duchess of Suffolk (and step-grandmother to Lady Jane Grey) wears a nearly identical outfit, for example, in a miniature portrait of her datable to before 1543 (Fig.15).[6] Likewise, Katherine Grey Seymour, Jane's younger sister, wears a very similar coat in a well-known portrait of her that can be reliably dated to about 1562 through its inclusion of her infant son, though she wears the coat with the front open and the sleeves detached (Fig.16).[7] Seymour again wears a black coat lined with white fur in a second portrait from the same period, but this time with the coat closed and the sleeves attached, though the entire coat is heavily embellished with gold aiglettes (Fig.17).[8]

Just as there is no reliable evidence to identify the sitter, so too evidence to name the artist is lacking. The painting is unsigned and there are no visible maker's marks or artist's monogram on either side of the panel. The overall execution of the work is somewhat two-dimensional and flat, lacking in careful use of highlighting and shadowing to produce realistic contours. The starkly geometric delineation of the margins of the face at the hairline and sides, as well as of the headgear, suggests a lesser degree of training and accomplishment on the part of the artist.

In the absence of virtually any substantive evidence to identify the sitter, the artist, or even a reasonably narrow timeframe during which the portrait was created, it is unwise to suggest possible identifications for the young lady, even tentatively. And while past identifications as Lady Jane Grey or Elizabeth Tudor may have been based in part on the supposition that she is wearing ermine, a fur often assumed to denote highest status, studies of Tudor-era sumptuary laws have shown that actual use of ermine was not confined to royalty or even to the highest nobility.[9] The lady may as easily be any one of hundreds, if not thousands, of young women at or above the gentry and wealthy-merchant level who lived in England in the middle of the sixteenth century. Her identity must therefore remain unknown.

[1] George Wallis to George Scharf, 4 March 1887, Heinz Archive and Library, National Portrait Gallery (London), file on NPG764.

[2] Sir Roy Strong, Director of the National Portrait Gallery, noted without citation in Reginald Lane Poole and Kenneth Garlick, *Catalogue of Portraits in the Bodleian Library* (Oxford: Oxford University Press, 2004), 157; National Portrait Gallery Collections Database, <http://www.npg.org.uk/collections/search/portrait/mw01958/Unknown-woman-formerly-known-as-Lady-Jane-Dudley-ne-Grey>. Accessed 19 October 2010.

[3] Noted without citation in Poole and Garlick, *Catalogue of Portraits in the Bodleian Library*, 157.

[4] Roy Strong, *Portraits of Queen Elizabeth I* (Oxford: Clarendon Press, 1963), 54. I find no record of Strong addressing directly the identity of the sitter in the Bodleian portrait.

[5] Strong, *Tudor and Jacobean Portraits*, I: 76 and 109.

[6] *Katherine Willoughby Brandon*, inscribed "H Holben fecit," before 1543, miniature, watercolor, Collection of 28th Baroness Willoughby de Eresby, Grimsthorpe and Drummond Castles.

[7] *Katherine Grey Seymour and son Edward, Lord Beauchamp of Hache*, unknown artist, ca.1562, oil on wood panel, 29 in. diameter, round, Collection of the Duke of Northumberland, Syon House. Sleeves were a separate article of clothing and not permanently attached to the torso of a jacket, doublet, coat, or gown. They could thus be removed at will. See Ann Rosalind Jones and Peter Stallybrass, *Renaissance Clothing and the Materials of Memory* (Cambridge: Cambridge University Press, 2000), 201–202.

[8] *Portrait of Lady Katherine Grey*, attrib. Levina Teerlinc, ca.1555-1560, watercolor on vellum stuck to pasteboard, 1 $^2/_5$ in. diameter, Victorian and Albert Museum, London, P.10-1979.

[9] See, for example, Maria Hayward, *Rich Apparel: Clothing and the Law in Henry VIII's England* (Farnham: Ashgate, 2009).

(shown actual size)

15 NPG764

Unknown Lady

Unknown artist

Oil on wood panel; 6 ½ in. diameter

Undated, circa 1555-1560

Provenance:

   Amelia A. Boulton, from whom;

   Purchased by National Portrait Gallery, acc. no. NPG764, 1887.

When this painting was acquired by the NPG in 1887, it was immediately compared to the Bodleian Portrait, as previously noted, and the sitter was promptly rechristened as Jane Grey based on perceived similarities between the two paintings. The rechristening was buttressed by a family tradition which stated that this painting had originated at Ashton Hall, Lancashire, a hunting lodge owned in the nineteenth century by George Grey, 7th Earl of Stamford and a descendant of Jane Grey's paternal uncle, Lord John Grey of Pirgo. Yet the Greys had inherited Ashton Hall from the Booths, Barons Delamer, in the eighteenth century, so that there was no direct connection linking the picture, the hall, the Greys of Pirgo, and Jane Grey herself. And while the seller in 1887, Amelia Boulton, acknowledged that her father had simply purchased the painting from a broker in nearby Stalybridge, she claimed that the painting had previously been stolen from Ashton Hall. Roger Grey, 10th and last Earl of Stamford, later denied that the painting had ever been at Ashton, suggesting that Ms Boulton's story was largely fabricated, perhaps to enhance the financial value of the painting at the time of sale.[1]

As noted in the discussion of the Bodleian Portrait, George Wallis of the South Kensington Museum expressed an aesthetic preference for NPG764 and dismissed the Bodleian as "a very ugly edition of the same person."[2] But even given that NPG764 may be an aesthetically more appealing image than the Bodleian Portrait, there is too little objective evidence to indicate reliably that the two sitters are indeed the same person, as has been noted. More significantly, since NPG764 was rechristened in 1887 in part on the basis of comparison to the Bodleian Portrait, any desire to continue comparing the two would seem to compel dismissal of NPG764 as being of Jane Grey in the wake of the conclusion above regarding the Bodleian Portrait.

NPG764 is actually far more comparable to a portrait of an unknown lady now in the collection at Trinity College, Oxford University (Fig.18).[3] The two sitters are positioned identically, the headgear is virtually identical, and the faces are exceedingly similar, though the varnish of the Trinity picture is severely discolored and thus partially obscures the image. And even though the costumes seen in NPG764 and the Trinity picture are not exactly identical, they are more similar than are those of the ladies in NPG764 and the Bodleian Portrait. Further, the image format is nearly identical, both panels being round in shape and of near-identical size: 6 ½ inches for NPG764 versus 6 $\frac{1}{7}$ inches for the Trinity. In other words, were NPG764 to be subjectively associated with any other similar portrait, the Trinity painting is a far better candidate than is the Bodleian, despite the presence in the former of darker fur trim on the coat and a small cluster of flowers pinned at the breast. The current absence of objective evidence prevents direct correlation of the two images, however.

As with the Bodleian Portrait and others in this study, there is simply too little evidence to support any identification whatsoever for the sitter in NPG764. Like the Bodleian (and the Trinity), she may be any one of thousands of relatively prosperous or wealthy women who lived in England in the middle of the sixteenth century. It is exceedingly doubtful that NPG764 was intended by its artist to depict or even to represent Jane Grey.

Fig. 18: *Portrait of an unknown lady, age 32*

[1] Earl of Stamford to Mr G.K. Adams, 15 Nov 1948, Object File for NPG 764, Heinz Archive and Library, National Portrait Gallery.

[2] George Wallis to George Scharf, 4 March 1887, Heinz Archive and Library, National Portrait Gallery, file on NPG 764.

[3] *Portrait of an Unknown Lady*, aged 32 (formerly identified as Queen Mary), circle of Hans Eworth, 1557, oil on round wood panel, 6 $\frac{1}{7}$ in. diameter, Trinity College, Oxford University. My sincere thanks to Lee Porritt for alerting me to the existence of the Trinity College picture.

16   The Tayler Portrait

Lady of the Valois, Perhaps Elizabeth of Austria

Follower of François Clouet

Oil on wood panel; 10 in. x 8 in.

Undated

Provenance:

  A.M. and B. Tayler;

  Sold Christie's, South Kensington, 12 November 1998, Sale OMP-8193, Lot 4.

This painting was presented at auction in 1998 with little attendant publicity and was previously unknown to either historians or the general public. The auction catalogue indicated that the lady depicted had at some point in the past been identified as Jane Grey, though at the sale of 1998 it was described as simply *Portrait of a Lady*. The scanty provenance offered in the sale catalogue contributed nothing useful towards a detailed study of the painting.

The style of the costume worn by the lady dates the portrait to a period well after Jane Grey's death in 1554. The slashed shoulder rolls and paned or pinked oversleeves were most common in the last quarter of the sixteenth century, for example.[1] The beaded and jewel-edged mesh Juliet cap atop her head was similarly popular in the last third of the sixteenth century.[2] The cross-hatched pattern on the under-bodice appears commonly in portraiture of the same period, in the form both of pinking (slashing) as seen here and of embroidery like that in the Portland Portrait discussed below. The hair arranged in rolls across the top of the forehead using hidden arcelets and imparting a heart-like shape to the entire face was a popular continental fashion during the last quarter of the sixteenth century.[3] That the painting dates to at least the latter third of the sixteenth century is further evidenced by the size and shape of the ruff, which is datable to no earlier than about 1565.[4] We must therefore look to someone other than Jane Grey for an identification of the lady depicted.

As with several other portraits sometimes said to represent Lady Jane Grey, the jewels seen in this painting are crucial. In particular, the lady wears a large necklace pendant of goldwork set with a pyramidal stone, probably a diamond.[5] Above the central stone are two pearls, each set in an eight-pointed star. On either side of the pendant is a lizard or salamander, their hanging tails entwined. The whole is surmounted by a dome-shaped element in red enamel, the base of which is encircled by two parallel rows of fine gold beading. Small blue stones or beads of enamel are set between the rows of beading, and three strips of goldwork extend from the top row of beading to the apex of the red dome. The dome-shaped element arguably depicts a crown, suggesting that the pendant is a royal jewel.

King Francis I of France (*d.*1547) and his son Henry II (*d.*1559) are both known to have utilized the salamander as a personal badge, usually in conjunction with a crown. The motif was put to wide use in association with the French royal family, from bas-relief carvings on the chimney-fronts of various royal chateaux to the tooled-leather covers of books in the royal library to the livery worn by Francis's guards in 1520 at the Field of Cloth of Gold.[6] Early-modern philosophers attributed to the salamander an ability to survive fire, to regenerate its scales when in contact with fire, even to spit water and to quench fire.[7] It was thus a symbol of purity and regeneration. Similarly, the eight-pointed star as used in Christian art also symbolized regeneration or resurrection and was associated quite specifically with Christ and baptism.[8] Such symbolism was reiterated by Francis's motto, *Nutrisco et extinguo*, "I nourish the good and extinguish the bad." The overall design of the pendant thus strongly links it to Francis I and his descendants. Assuming that link is valid, the jewel was almost certainly crafted during the second quarter of the sixteenth century and probably remained among the royal jewels for some considerable time thereafter.

The French royal family, the Valois, included more female members than did the Tudors of England, resulting in a larger number of candidates for the sitter depicted. Francis I had six daughters, for example, though only one survived to full maturity: Margaret, Duchess of Berry. But portraits of Margaret reveal a markedly aquiline nose, essentially eliminating her as the lady seen in the Tayler Portrait. Francis's successor, Henri II, married Catherine de Medici, but again there is little resemblance between portraits of Catherine and this sitter (see Fig.29, page 121). The same is true regarding Henri's three legitimate daughters, Elizabeth, Claude, and Margaret, and one illegitimate daughter, Diane. Yet Henri's son, Charles IX, took as his wife in 1570 Elizabeth of Austria, and there is an appreciable resemblance between Elizabeth as she was depicted by François Clouet in 1571 (Fig.19) and the Tayler lady.[9] Elizabeth of Austria is thus a likely candidate to be the lady seen here.

Yet the Tayler Portrait is also strikingly similar to a surviving depiction of Anna of Austria, Queen Consort after 1570 to the Spanish King Philip II (Fig.20).[10] Intriguingly, Anna was an elder sister of Elizabeth of Austria. In Anna's portrait, she wears a virtually identical Juliet cap with an equally identical central jewel. Anna's gown and surcoat are of precisely the same cut and style as Elizabeth's, though Anna's surcoat is red rather than tan and is much more heavily embellished.

Fig. 19: *Elizabeth of Austria, Queen of France*

Fig. 20: *Anna of Austria, Queen of Spain*

But perhaps the most telling comparison is found in the necklaces and pendants. The necklaces are identical but for the use of a pearl in the central link of Anna's necklace versus a red stone in Elizabeth's necklace. Similarly, the pendant attached to Anna's necklace repeats the large central pyramidal black-colored stone and the teardrop pearl suspended from the bottom. A crown again surmounts the whole, though the element is more obviously a crown in Anna's portrait. But the surrounding heraldic beast has been changed from the French Valois salamander in the portrait of Elizabeth to the double-headed Spanish Habsburg eagle in the depiction of Anna.

Since the portrait of Anna has been dated to at least a decade after her death and bears a large inscription to identify the sitter, it seems likely that that painting was created as part of a portrait set. The precise timeframe for the creation of the portrait of Elizabeth is not presently known, however, so that it is not possible to determine whether one preceded the other or whether the two are contemporaneous. This leaves unresolved the important question as to whether one was adapted from the other or whether the two were instead created independently. If the former, it cannot now be determined which of the two ladies the Tayler image actually depicts. If the latter, the similarities are all the more remarkable and much more difficult to explain. We cannot as yet know whom the Tayler Portrait depicts, but the two leading candidates are certainly Elizabeth of Austria, Queen of France and Anna of Austria, Queen of Spain.

[1] Anna Fischel et al., ed., *Fashion: The Definitive History of Costume and Style* (New York: Dorling Kindersley for the Smithsonian Institute, 2012), 95.

[2] R. Turner Wilcox, *The Mode in Hats and Headdress: A Historical Survey with 190 Plates* (New York: Dover Publications, 2008), 78.

[3] *Encyclopedia of Hair: A Cultural History*, ed. Victoria Sherrow (Greenwood Publishing Group, 2006), 329; Doreen Yarwood, *Illustrated History of World Costume* (London: Dover Publications, 2011), 18-19; Douglas A. Russell, *Period Style for the Theater* (Boston: Allyn and Bacon, 1987), 123.

[4] Jones and Stallybrass, *Renaissance Clothing*, 68.

[5] Though diamonds are ordinarily clear, they were usually rendered as black in sixteenth-century portraits, owing to the use by Tudor-era jewelers of black foil backings that increased the luster of the set stones. See Bolland and Cooper, *Real Tudors*, 63. Raw, uncut diamonds often have a pyramidal shape, and were referred to in early-modern inventories as "pointed" if set with the apex turned upward, "table" if set with the flat base turned upward.

[6] R.J. Knecht, *Francis I* (Cambridge: Cambridge University Press, 1982), 6.

[7] Knecht, *Francis I*, 6.

[8] Robin Jensen, *Living Waters: Images, Settings and Symbols of Early Christian Baptism* (Leiden: Brill, 2011), 245-247.

[9] *Elizabeth of Austria, Queen of France*, François Clouet, ca.1571, oil on wood panel, 14 1/5 in. x 10 1/4 in., Musée du Louvre Museum, Paris.

[10] *Portrait of Anna of Austria, Queen of Spain*, unknown artist, ca.1600, oil on wood panel, 11 2/5 in. x 8 1/4 in, private collection.

(shown actual size)

17   The Yale Miniature Portrait

Unknown Lady

Attributed to Lucas Horenbout (*d.*1544)

Gouache on thin card; 1 $^{7}/_{8}$ in.

ca.1535

Provenance:

> Paul Mellon (*d.*1999), by whom;
>
> Gifted to Yale Center for British Art, acc. no. B1974.2.59, 1966.

In an exhibition entitled *Lost Faces: Identity and Discovery in Tudor Royal Portraiture* held in 2007 at the London gallery of Philip Mould Ltd, guest curator David Starkey and others presented this sixteenth-century miniature painting from the collection of the Yale University Center for British Art as an authentic life portrait of Lady Jane Grey.[1] The "discovery" captured the imagination of various media outlets in both the UK and the US, giving the miniature and the exhibition considerable international publicity.[2] Starkey's identification was not without controversy, however, and many leading experts—including Scott Wilcox, the YCBA's own Curator of Prints and Drawings —questioned the surprising conclusion.[3]

Starkey and his colleagues argued that the miniature was created in 1553 either "to capture Jane's fleeting moment of glory" or to symbolize "the endurance of suffering and ... imprisonment" that she shared with her husband Guildford Dudley later in that year, following Queen Mary's accession. They marshaled numerous pieces of evidence to support their finding, beginning with the physical description of Jane taken from Richard Davey's The Nine Day's Queen.[4] Secondly, the *Lost Faces* curators noted the presence of oak leaves and gillyflowers worn at the sitter's breast, which they linked to a known use of those elements as rebus-like personal badges by Jane's brother-in-law Robert Dudley and her husband Guildford Dudley, respectively.[5] Starkey further argued that the brooch pinned to the lady's bodice was "of an uncommon design" and could be correlated with an item listed among jewels presented to Jane during her brief reign.[6] Lastly, the inscribed age of the sitter, "AN[N]O XVIII" ("in [her] 18th year"), was consistent with Jane's age at the time of her brief reign, or so they argued.[7]

Yet none of these critical pieces of evidence survive careful scrutiny. The physical description cited by Davey was almost certainly the product of that author's own imagination, carefully fabricated in an effort to fill a void in the surviving historical record (see Appendix One: The Spinola Letter, p.177). At present, no reliably authentic detailing of Jane's physical appearance is known, so that there is no written account to which this or any other of her putative portraits can be compared.

Additionally, the wearing by one married woman of the personal badges of two men, even brothers, is virtually undocumented elsewhere in English portraiture. If the flowers in this portrait were indeed intended as personal badges, it is more probable that they are arranged in heraldic fashion, since heraldry was a near-obsession among the Tudor elite. In a heraldic arrangement, the sitter's own gillyflowers are impaled by, or are placed to the viewer's right of, her husband's badge of oak leaves and acorns on the left.[8] Yet art historians have far more commonly argued that flowers worn by portrait sitters of the Tudor period were intended to be understood for their common symbolic meanings and to convey to the viewer certain character attributes of, or emotions held by, the sitter. In the instance of the Yale Miniature Portrait, the oak leaves and acorns might have symbolized personal strength or fortitude, while the gillyflowers typically symbolized love.[9] But because gillyflowers, also called pinks, appear relatively commonly in portraits of Tudor women, their presence here does little to aid in identifying this particular sitter.[10]

As for the jewel (Fig.21), brooches containing faces in enamel or carved in stone were not at all "uncommon," despite the curators' claim to the contrary. Referred to in Tudor-era terminology as "faces in agate," they were highly prized and appear with regularity in both portraits and jewel inventories from the period.[11] And because the inventory of goods presented to Jane in July 1553 did not describe the individual items in any distinctive detail, it is not possible to associate the "face in agate" seen here with any specific item from that inventory.[12] The jewel is thus insufficiently unique or specific to aid in identifying the sitter.

All that remains, therefore, is the inscription indicating that the sitter was in her eighteenth year, or seventeen years old by modern reckoning.[13] The *Lost Faces* catalogue rightly argued that Jane's traditional date of birth, early October 1537, is the product of myth and legend, but erred in asserting that she could have passed her seventeenth birthday before July 1553. While the surviving historical record does not offer a specific date or even year for her birth, evidence gleaned from several of those who knew Jane well indicates that she was born in the winter of 1536/7. She therefore would not have reached her seventeenth birthday until very late in 1553 or early 1554, quite close to the date of her death on 12 February 1554.[14]

The curators indicated two possible timeframes during which a portrait of Jane might have been created. The first was in the midst of her very brief reign, 10-19 July 1553, and the second was at any point during her subsequent seven-month imprisonment in the Tower.[15] Starkey and his colleagues readily conceded that the first would indeed have required "quick" work on the part of the artist. Jane's reign began calmly enough, but within four days Mary had raised her standard in resistance and John Dudley was being dispatched at the head of an army to capture her. It is exceedingly unlikely that time or even thought was devoted during this chaotic period to summoning an artist to take a likeness of the would-be queen, and even less likely that any such work was completed before the reign had ended. And though the *Lost Faces* catalogue contended that after becoming prisoners, Jane and Guildford "were allowed many freedoms," they were in fact held in relatively strict confinement. In December 1553, for example, an order from the Privy Council was required before Jane could be allowed out of doors under guard, even within the secure walls of the Tower.[16] Even visits from immediate family members required prior written approval from the Privy Council.[17] Since the Tudors monarchs, including Mary, were all cognizant of the potential for portraits to be utilized for propagandist purposes, it is very unlikely that Mary or her Council allowed any portraitist to visit Jane for a sitting while she was a prisoner in the Tower.[18]

For the present, the miniature portrait defies reliable identification owing to a lack of sufficiently distinctive evidence. The provenance for the portrait extends back less than a century, making it impossible to link the item to any specific family, for example. Even the artist attribution is uncertain, with both Lucas Horenbout (*d*.1544) and Levina Teerlinc (*d*.1576) having been proposed. All that can be said about the portrait must be derived from the image itself. The sitter's neck and shoulders are uncovered, indicating that the miniature was painted in the warmer months of summer. The crown of the French hood is more rounded than the angular hoods of the 1550s. It is more consistent with earlier styles of the 1530s and 1540s.[19] And while the inscription does make it clear that the sitter was about seventeen years old when the painting was created, the number of women who achieved their seventeenth birthday during the broad timeframe for this work—roughly 1535 to 1545—was enormous. The sitter could very easily have been any one of literally thousands of young women of the English gentry and nobility who lived during the second quarter of the sixteenth century. In the continuing absence of any objective documentary evidence, we will likely never have a reliable identity for the lady. But we can be quite certain that she is not Lady Jane Grey.

Fig. 21: *Detail of "face in agate" brooch and flowers from the Yale Miniature Portrait.*

[1] David Starkey, Bendor Grosvenor, and Alistair Hawkyard, "The Search for Lady Jane Grey, *Lost Faces*, 79-83.

[2] See, for example, Nigel Reynolds, "The true beauty of Lady Jane Grey," *The Telegraph* (London), 5 March 2007; "Saying it with flowers: Starkey unveils the face of Lady Jane Grey," *Antiques Trade Gazette*, 5 March 2007; Bruce Fellman, "Looking for Lady Jane," *Yale Alumni Magazine*, May/June 2007; Cynthia Zarin, "Teen Queen: Looking for Lady Jane Grey," *The New Yorker*, 15 October 2007, 46-55.

[3] Evangelia Podaras, "Identity Questioned in Painting of 'Lady Jane'," *Yale Daily News*, 2 November 2007.

[4] Davey, *The Nine Days' Queen*, 252-253 and note 2 .

[5] The Latin word for "oak" is "rubor," rendering oak leaves and acorns a visual pun on the name "Robert." The association between gillyflowers and the name "Guildford" should be apparent.

[6] Starkey et al., *Lost Faces*, 81-82.

[7] Starkey et al., *Lost Faces*, 83.

[8] My thanks to Christopher Foley for alerting me to this issue.

[9] The *Lost Faces* curators argued that the flowers are quite specifically *Cheiranthus cheiri,* or wallflowers, which were sometimes incorrectly called "pinks" or "gillyflowers" in the sixteenth century. True pinks and gillyflowers are of the genus *Dianthus*, however. Flowers of *Ch. chieri* grow with short flower stems, called pedicles, branched in an alternating fashion along opposites sides of a single central axis stem, a morphological pattern referred to in botanical terms as "raceme inflorescence." Yet the short pedicles of the middle of the three clusters in this portrait appear all to emanate from a single common stem-point, called "simple umbel inflorescence." Some species of true gillyflowers or pinks, genus *Dianthus*, do exhibit umbel inflorescence. In all likelihood, the flowers seen here are true pinks of the *Dianthus* type rather than wallflowers, *Ch. chieri*.

[10] See, for example, the Glendon Hall Portrait, in which Katherine Parr is depicted holding a pink in her left hand, or the Wrest Park Portrait, in which the sitter wears a pink at her breast.

[11] See Marie-Christine Graz, *Jewels in Painting* (Milan: Skira, 1999), 112; Yvonne Hackenbroch, *Renaissance Jewelry* (London: Sotheby Park Bernet, 1979).

[12] Oxford University, New College Manuscript 328/1, ff. 38r-40v.

[13] Age could be expressed in sixteenth-century England using either of two formulae. One was "anno" or "anno suæ," meaning "in [his/her] year." By this formula, a newborn infant was "in his first year," and upon the first anniversary of his birth entered his second year, and so on. The alternate formula expressed age as "ætatis suæ," or "at his/her age of," calculated according to the annual anniversary of birth most recently achieved. "Ætatis suæ" is therefore the same as modern Western European reckonings of age, while "anno suæ" equals that modern reckoning plus one year.

[14] Edwards, "On the Birth Date of Lady Jane Grey," 240-242; "A Further Note," 146-148.

[15] Starkey et al., *Lost Faces*, 83.

[16] *Acts of the Privy Council of England*, II: 379. "A lettre to the Lieutenant of the Towre, willing hym at convenient tymes by his discreacion to suffer ... to have the libertie of walke within the gardeyn of the Tower ... the Ladye Jane ... upon suggestion that [she] ... be and have byn evill at esae [sic] in thier [sic] bodyes for want of ayre."

[17] None of Jane's family are known to have visited her at any time during her imprisonment. John Dudley's wife did visit her family, however, but only after obtaining written permission. See British Library Additional Manuscripts 26748, Original Minutes of the Privy Council, 24 November 1553 to 9 March 1553/4.

[18] Roy Strong, T*he Tudor and Stuart Monarchy: Pageantry, Painting, and Iconography* (Woodbridge: Boydell Press, 1998).

[19] Schuessler, "French Hoods," 129-160. The Yale Center's collection catalogue continues to offer a date of "ca.1546" for the miniature, despite the assertions presented in *Lost Faces*.

18   The Huntington Portrait

Portrait of a Lady

Unknown Netherlandish artist

Oil on canvas; 40 in. x 28 ½ in.

Undated, second quarter of the seventeenth century

Provenance:

    Henry E. Huntington (*d*.1927), before 1919;

    The Huntington Library, Art Collections, and Botanical Gardens, acc. no. 7.13.

Few portraits sometimes called "Lady Jane Grey" are more obviously misidentified than the Huntington Portrait, despite the presence at the middle of the right margin of an undated inscription naming Jane as the subject.[1] The painting was acquired sometime prior to 1919 by the California railroad magnate and art collector Henry E. Huntington and remains today in the collection of the Huntington Library and Museum in San Marino, California. The details of the acquisition are not documented, and neither is the rationale for the early association of the portrait with Jane Grey known. Presumably, the presence of the book in the lady's right hand facilitated rechristening the portrait as Jane, in the same way that so many other falsely-identified portraits in this study similarly depict the sitter holding or reading a book.

Yet the costume worn by the lady is entirely inconsistent with English fashion of the early 1550s. The massive starched ruff with lace edging, made to stand behind the head by means of a wire "supportasse" or "pickadil," became popular in England only in the last decade or so of the sixteenth century and remained fashionable throughout the first decade of the seventeenth.[2] The same was true of the starched and pleated cuffs of lawn with lace embellishments. But the heavily jeweled wide cloth belt was simply not a feature of English costume at any point between 1500 and 1650. The specific style of headgear seen here, though never fashionable in England, does nonetheless reveal the regional origins of the sitter.

The head covering is comparable in overall style to similar headdresses seen in several portraits of Netherlandish origin and dating to the middle of the seventeenth century. Catrina Hooghsaet wears a hood of equivalent general design, for example, in her portrait by Rembrandt dated 1657 (Fig.22).[3] The folded lateral edges or "wings" of the headpiece worn by Aaltje Gerritsdr Shouten in *Portrait of Cornelius Claesz Anslo and his Wife* (Fig.23), also by Rembrandt, match precisely those in the Huntington Portrait.[4] Shouten also notably wears a wide starched ruff, still fashionable in the Low Countries long after they had been abandoned by the English. Even the starched, pleated, and lace-edged cuffs are repeated with near-exactitude in Jan Daemen Cool's *Portrait of*

Fig. 22: *Detail, Portrait of Catrina Hooghsaet.*

Fig. 23: *Detail, Portrait of ... Aaltje Gerritsdr Shouten.*

a Young Woman with Fan of 1636 and in Cornelis de Vos's *Self-portrait of the Artist with his Wife Suzanne Cock and their Children* of about 1630.[5] The Huntington sitter is therefore certainly a Netherlandish lady of the second quarter of the seventeenth century or later.

The extensive jeweling of the lady's costume, though frequently seen in portraiture of wealthy English women from the second half of the sixteenth century, was relatively uncommon among Dutch sitters of the seventeenth century. Costume historians have noted that wealth was typically exhibited in Dutch portraiture by means of clothing that was predominantly black in color, rather than by means of extensive jewels. Achieving a stable deep black color in fabric entailed a multi-step dying process that was not only labor intensive but that also required costly ingredients.[6] The result was an end-product with a market price beyond the means of any but the wealthiest, so that the wearing of black was itself a marker of high economic status. And though this lady's gown appears (through the heavily discolored varnish) to be mostly brown or gold in color, rather than black, both the color and the many applied jewels may actually have been deliberately fabricated by the original artist as a more visually-interesting alternative to black. Rosemarijn Hoekstra has noted that it became customary among the Dutch after about 1640 to be depicted in imaginary dress.[7] The unknown lady seen here well may have instructed the artist to invent for her a costume that was both suitably costly in appearance and simultaneously more stimulating to the eye than a large expanse of deep black.

The portrait medallion suspended from the sitter's necklace (Fig.24), though partially obscured by discoloration of the overlying varnish, appears to depict a man with shoulder-length hair and a short beard. He apparently wears a ruff, though it is much smaller in relative size than that worn by the lady. But most significantly, the pattern of highlights and shadows surrounding the man's head indicate the presence of a lettered inscription that perhaps identifies the man. Careful cleaning of this area may render the inscription more readily legible, leading to an identification of the man and thus of the main female sitter as well. But the overall appearance of the man portrayed in the portrait medallion confirms that the portrait dates to the seventeenth century and thus cannot be an authentic portrait of Jane Grey.

Fig. 24: *Detail of portrait medallion*

[1] The inscription is today entirely obscured by dirt and by severe discoloration of the varnish, but is faintly visible in black-and-white photographs taken more than fifty years ago. The script is all upper case Roman block letters and reads "LADY IANE GRAYE."

[2] Valerie Cumming, C. W. Cunnington, P. E. Cunnington, *Dictionary of Fashion History* (Oxford: Berg, 2010), s.v. "pickardil."

[3] Rembrandt van Rijn, *Portrait of Catrina Hooghsaet*, 1657, oil on canvas, 49 ³/₅ in. x 38 ⁴/₅ in., private collection, Penrhyn Castle, Wales.

[4] Rembrandt van Rijn, *Portrait of the Mennonite Preacher Cornelius Claesz Anslo and his Wife Aaltje Gerritsdr Shouten*, 1641, oil on canvas, 69 ¹/₃ in. x 82 ²/₃ in., Gemäldegalerie, Berlin.

[5] Jan Daemen Cool, *Portrait of a Young Woman with Fan*, 1636, oil on canvas, dimensions unknown, National Gallery of Prague; Cornelis de Vos, *Self-portrait of the Artist with his Wife Suzanne Cock and their Children*, ca.1630, oil on canvas, 73 ²/₅ in. x 87 in., Hermitage, St Petersburg.

[6] Bianca M. Du Mortier, "Features of Fashion in the Netherlands of the Seventeenth Century," *Netherlandish Fashion in the Seventeenth Century*, introduction by Johannes Pietsch (Riggisberg: Abegg-Stiftung, 2012), 33-34.

[7] Rosemarijn Hoekstra, "Images of Dress in the Golden Age of Dutch Painting," *Costume* 33 (1999), 36-45.

19   The Klabin Portrait

Unknown Lady (inscribed "Jane Grey")

Unknown artist

Oil on wood panel; 13 ³/₈ x 9 ⁷/₈ in.

Inscribed 1553

Provenance:

    Sotheby's sale 21 March 1945, Lot 55;

    Fundação Eva Klabin, Rio de Janeiro, Brazil, before 1991.

This portrait was virtually unknown to historians prior to 2014, when it was revealed through a narrowly-focused Internet search undertaken by this author. It has never before been studied or published. Curators at the Eva Klabin Museum do not even know when, how, or whence it entered their collection. The museum is owned and operated by the Fundação Eva Klabin, established in 1995 following the death four years previously of Eva Klabin of Rio de Janeiro. She was the eldest daughter of Mauricio Klabin, a Lithuanian immigrant who co-founded what is now the Klabin Group, S.A., the largest producer, exporter and recycler of paper in Brazil. Eva inherited a significant portion of her father's wealth at his death in 1923 and, herself a childless widow after 1931, embarked upon a lifetime of collecting. Her former home-turned- museum houses art and artifacts spanning fifty centuries and gathered from Europe, Asia, Africa, and South America. The British Collection includes paintings by Joshua Reynolds, Thomas Lawrence, Thomas Gainsborough, and George Romney. The painting called "Jane Grey" is said to be the oldest British painting in the collection.

The inclusion in the partially-obscured inscription in the upper left-hand corner, "Ano Dmn 1553," would ordinarily indicate that the work was created in 1553, yet details of the lady's costume do not support that date. The sitter's headgear is unusual for an English woman of the 1550s, during which time the French hood with an attached posterior fall for covering the hair was ubiquitous. The unstructured cap-like headgear of the type seen here did not become popular in England until after about 1560, though it was seen somewhat earlier in continental costume. Additionally, the lady's unembellished neck ruff is moderately wide and carefully arranged in symmetrical figure-of-eight folds. It was almost certainly starched. Ruffs first appeared in England well after Jane's death in February 1554, though they were already popular in continental fashions, especially among the French and Spanish.[1] They were brought to England during the second half of the 1550s with the entourage of Queen Mary's Spanish husband, Philip. The English were relatively slow to adopt the foreign style, however. Indeed, despite her own affinity for things Spanish, Mary was herself depicted wearing a much narrower—and notably free-form and unstarched—Spanish-style ruff only once.[2] She more commonly wore the standing-collared partlet seen in so many of the other portraits included in this study. Even in portraits that depict Mary wearing a chemise under her partlet, the collar usually has a loosely flowing and unstarched simple ruffle. Not until the subsequent reign of Elizabeth I did larger, carefully folded and starched ruffs become fashionable enough among the English to appear regularly in their portraiture. Starched ruffs of the width and meticulous folding pattern seen in this portrait typically date to the mid 1560s and later, though they became ever wider over the course of the next several decades.

The lady's gown includes sleeve caps that appear quite bulbous, but because the composition reveals only a small portion of those caps, it is difficult to determine whether they are rolled sleeves or gigot sleeves. Regardless of their precise design, however, the general style is not consistent with English costume of the early 1550s. English women's fashion of that period instead favored a natural shoulder silhouette. Significantly enlarged sleeves caps of the type seen here began to appear only after about 1560. As with unstructured headgear and ruffs, however, enlarged sleeve caps of both small roll and expansive gigot types had previously been fashionable primarily in French, Italian, and Spanish women's costume.

The jewels worn by the sitter are very fine and thus consistent with a person wishing to give the impression of some considerable wealth. It is very noteworthy that the lady wears a large pearl-drop earring in her pierced left earlobe. The jewelry historian Diana Scarisbrick identified earrings and pierced ears as emerging in England only in the second half of the reign of Elizabeth I.[3] Prior to that time, the English considered pierced ears to be a visual indicator that an individual was of foreign origin, since they were popular primarily among the Spanish and French.

Both inscriptions (Fig.25) are partially obscured by discoloration of the overlying varnish, but they read in full, "Iane Grey/ Anº Dom/ 1553" and "Ætatis/ 16." In addition to seemingly dating the work to 1553, they explicitly identify the sitter as Jane Grey and give her age as 16 at the time the portrait was supposedly painted. As with several other portraits in this study, the inscribed name suggests that an early owner either was not capable of recognizing the sitter on sight or consciously

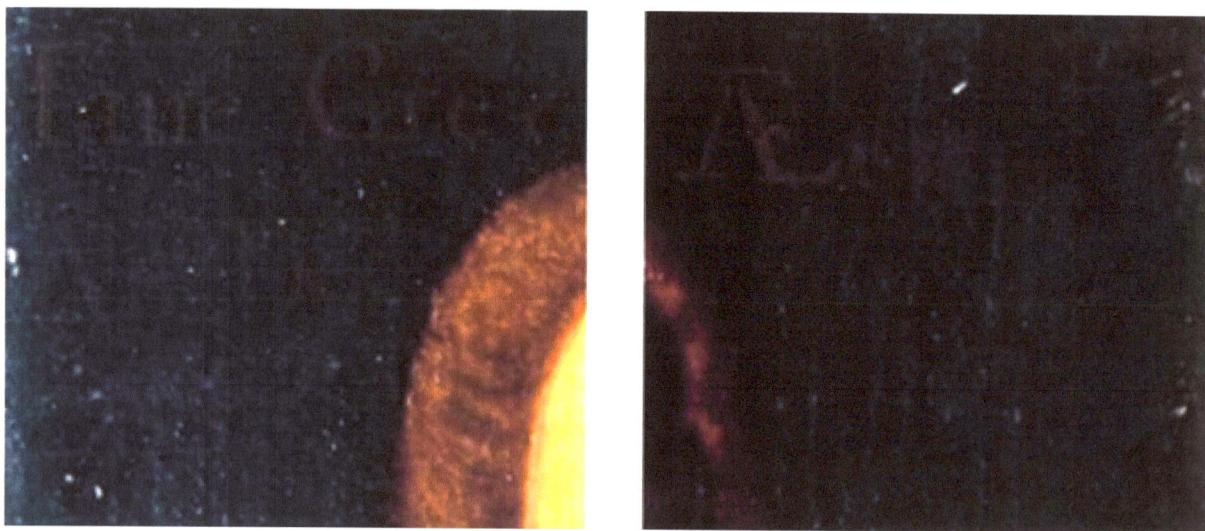

Fig. 25: *Klabin Portrait, inscription details. Left: "Iane Grey/ Anº Dmn/ 1553"; Right: "Ætatis/ 16."*

wished to newly rechristen the lady as Jane Grey. Whether the inscription was applied to the image at the time it was created or was instead a later addition can be determined with certainty only by careful examination using specialized scientific techniques. Circumstantial evidence, however, indicates that they are quite probably a later addition. The name of the sitter, for example, is given as simply "Iane Grey," without the inclusion of the honorific style "Lady." This is in striking contrast to virtually every other portrait of Jane. The inscription on the Streatham Portrait, for example, reads "Ladye Jane," while that on the Syon Portrait discussed below is "Queen Jane Grey." The absence of the honorific again suggests an owner who had no personal connection to the sitter, most probably because the sitter was long deceased.

The actual lettering style is itself unusual for English portraiture of the mid-sixteenth century. Through a decade of examining inscribed portraits, it would appear to this author that, in those instances in which English portraits were at all inscribed, the style used for inscriptions of sitters' names and ages, as well as for dates of creation of the works, were almost always entirely upper-case Roman letters. The use of minuscule in portrait inscriptions was limited to lengthy dedicatory or discursive texts. A portrait of the Cobham family, dated 1567 and now at Longleat House, bears a centrally-placed eight-line dedicatory inscription in both upper- and lower-case Roman letters, for example. The inscriptions stating the ages of each of the six children depicted in the portrait are, however, themselves entirely in upper-case letters. The use of minuscule within inscriptions of either age or date of creation did not become common in English portraiture until the end of the sixteenth century. The writing style used to create the lettering seen in this portrait suggests that it was added after the turn of the seventeenth century.

The available evidence overwhelmingly indicates that this portrait was actually created at some point well after the inscribed date of 1553. More probably, the painting itself dates to no earlier than the last quarter of the sixteenth century. Whether of English or continental origin, it was originally intended to depict some actual person who cannot today be readily identified. It was rechristened as Jane Grey, probably in the seventeenth century, and the inscribed date—'Anº Dom 1553'—was intended to refer to the year in which Jane entered historical prominence rather than the year in which the painting itself was created.[4]

[1] Jones and Stallybrass, *Renaissance Clothing*, 68.

[2] *Queen Mary I*, Hans Eworth, 1557, oil on wood panel, 8 in. x 6 ½ in., private collection.

[3] Diana Scarisbrick, *Jewellery in Britain 1066-1837: A Documentary, Social, Literary and Artistic Survey* (Wilby: Michael Russell, 2000) and *Tudor and Jacobean Jewellery* (London: Tate Publishing, 2000).

[4] Jane reigned briefly as Queen of England and Ireland from July 10 to July 19 of 1553, and she was executed on the following 12th of February, which in that era was still considered to be 1553. Prior to 1751, the beginning of the English calendar year fell on March 25, so that the days between January 1 and March 24 were considered the end of the old year rather than the beginning of the new.

20   The Grimsthorpe Portrait

Unknown Lady

Unknown artist

Oil on wood panel; 44 in. x 32 in.

Undated

Provenance:

> Sophia-Frances Chaplin Wright (d.1844), Upton Hall, Newark, Lincolnshire;
>
> Sophia Matilda Wright Heathcote (d.1880), North Luffenham Hall, Rutland, by whom bequeathed to;
>
> Clementina Drummond-Willoughby (d.1888), 24th Baroness Willoughby de Eresby, Grimsthorpe Castle, Lincolnshire;
>
> Thence by descent.

The Grimsthorpe Portrait, like the Klabin and Huntington Portraits, has been largely unknown to historians and has never been published as a depiction of Jane Grey. Unlike the latter two, however, the Grimsthorpe Portrait was never inscribed to identify the sitter as Jane. Nonetheless, a series of owners throughout the nineteenth century all understood the lady depicted to be Jane. A handwritten label on the reverse of the wood panel indicates that the painting was given in February 1844 to Sophia Wright Heathcote by her father, Thomas Wright of Upton Hall, Lincolnshire. The sitter was already identified as Jane Grey at the time of the gift.

The lady's costume is datable to the period between 1545 and 1555, the general period during which the Greys were most likely to have commissioned any life portrait of Jane. The standing collar on the partlet with its rich blackwork embroidery can be seen in numerous portraits firmly dated to that period, especially portraits of Queen Mary Tudor. Similarly, the voluminous russet undersleeves with openings along the inferior margin secured by "points" or ties that allow the sleeves of the chemise to protrude through appear frequently in portraits datable to both the 1540s and the 1550s.[1] The particular design of the French hood, with a crown exhibiting a more nearly horizontal silhouette than the rounded crowns of hoods of the 1530s and early 1540s, also dates the costume to 1545-1555. Thus the costume is essentially correct if the sitter is to be identified as Jane Grey.

Upon her death in 1880, Sophia Matilda Heathcote bequeathed the painting to her sister-in-law, Clementina Drummond Willoughby Heathcote, 24th Baroness Willoughby de Eresby, identifying it as a portrait of "Lady Jane Grey by Holbein".[2] Yet Holbein cannot be the artist of this picture since he had died in 1543, well before this picture was painted. Further, the sitter appears to be a woman of relatively mature age, older than Jane's seventeen years at the time of her death. The apparent age of the sitter, combined with the costume evidence, indicates that the sitter depicted is unlikely to have been Jane Grey.

Correctly identifying the lady is problematic owing to a complete absence of definitive evidence. Even the jewels, which have been so useful in identifying the sitters in other portraits in this study, are of little use here. The large round bodice brooch depicts the Judgment of Paris, a scene from classical mythology (Fig.26). The story of the Judgment was an exceedingly popular one in both continental Europe and England in the sixteenth century. The German artist Lucas Cranach the Elder painted more than a dozen images depicting the story, for example. In England during Elizabeth's reign, artists created versions in which Elizabeth I substituted for Paris, creating a visual allegory of Elizabeth as a fair and just monarch.[3] The story was sometimes reinterpreted in the sixteenth century in a reformist Christian context, with the Judgment of Paris presented as an allegory of God's gift to man of free will.[4] The brooch is therefore not sufficiently unique to enable association with a specific individual sitter.

Past assessors of the painting have on occasion questioned the age of the work. The authors of several handwritten notes affixed to the reverse of the panel reveal that each independently concluded that the painting technique seen in this picture was inconsistent with that of the sixteenth century. The consensus among those assessors dated the paintwork to the late eighteenth or early nineteenth century. Yet the technique exhibited in the jewels and costume are entirely consistent with that seen in other English paintings authentically dating to the middle of the sixteenth century. Only the face appears inconsistent with sixteenth-century technique, so that it is perhaps more likely that an early attempt to "restore" and to "improve" the paintwork of the face resulted in a confusing appearance. A definitive answer is impossible to achieve owing to the absence of any provenance for the painting prior to its possession by Thomas Wright. Two potential scenarios are possible, but both are necessarily speculative and cannot be proven true. They are nonetheless worth considering.

Sophia-Frances Chaplin Wright died 9 February 1844, making it is reasonable to conclude that Thomas Wright was merely fulfilling some final wish expressed by his dying wife when he gave the portrait to the younger Sophia in that same year.[5] In all likelihood, the painting was a cherished possession that the elder Sophia wished her daughter to have as a family heirloom. There is no direct evidence to document when or from where Sophia Chaplin Wright or her husband may have acquired the portrait, but three successive generations of Wrights are known to have been avid collectors of works of art.[6] Thomas Wright may have thus inherited the portrait from his father, also named Thomas Wright, or his grandfather Ichabod Wright.[7] It is also possible that the younger Thomas simply purchased the painting from some unknown source to decorate Upton Hall, newly built by him between 1828 and 1832.[8] Additionally, numerous members of the Wright family, in addition to being collectors, were also amateur artists of some repute. Sophia-Frances's husband Thomas Wright even exhibited repeatedly in the Royal Academy between 1801 and 1837.[9] It was a relatively common occurrence prior to the middle of the nineteenth century for non-specialists with little or no training to attempt to "restore" decayed or damaged works of art.[10] As successful artists themselves, it is entirely possible that a member of the Wright family felt compelled to lend his or her own hand to "improving" the Grimsthorpe Portrait, leaving behind a work that appears in some limited respects to be late-eighteenth or early-nineteenth century in origin.[11]

Alternatively, the painting may have been a Chaplin family possession that Sophia-Frances Chaplin brought with her upon her marriage to Thomas Wright. As part of her separate property ante-dating the marriage, she would have retained the legal right to dispose of it upon her death. If

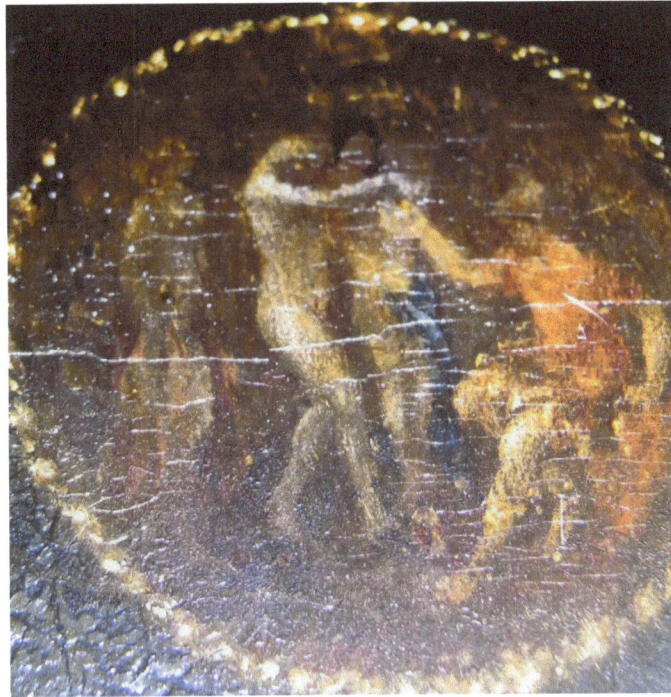

Fig. 26: *Brooch detail, Judgment of Paris*

the painting was indeed Sophia-Frances's separate property, it would account for Thomas's having given the portrait to his daughter so soon after Sophia-Frances's death. Further, Sophia-Francis Chaplin came from a family that was significantly wealthier and more socially prominent than the Wrights. She was herself the granddaughter of Lady Elizabeth Cecil, a direct lineal descendant of the Cecil Earls of Exeter and of William Cecil, Lord Burghley. Through her Cecil lineage, Sophia-Francis was related by both blood and marriage to the Dukes of Devonshire, the Dukes of Rutland, and the Earls of Salisbury.[12] Each of those families had historical links to Jane Grey, so that any of them might have possessed a putative portrait of Jane. The painting may therefore have been a Chaplin family heirloom, though it would have been rather unusual for it to have been alienated from the principal estates of the above-named families and to have passed instead into the female line represented by Sophia-Frances. But if this was the case, it is again possible that Thomas Wright or a relative "restored" the painting for Sophia-Frances, thereby imparting a more modern appearance to the paintwork. In any event, the painting does appear to date to the sixteenth century and to have perhaps been amateurishly restored in later years. The sitter is undoubtedly some reasonably wealthy lady of the Tudor period, though her identity is now hidden.

[1] Cf. the Glendon Hall, Hastings, Jersey, Fitzwilliam, and Rotherwas Portraits.

[2] Leeds Probate Registry, Will of Sophia Matilda Heathcote, Widow, dated 17 November 1874 with codicil of 1 November 1880, probated 15 March 1881.

[3] *Elizabeth and the Three Goddesses*, Hans Eworth, 1569, oil on wood panel, 24 3/4 x 33 1/5 in., Royal Collection, RCIN403446; *Elizabeth I and the Three Goddesses*, attrib. Isaac Oliver, ca.1590, watercolor and bodycolor on vellum, 4 ½ in. x 6 ⅛ in., National Portrait Gallery, NPG6947.

[4] Jane Kingsley-Smith, "Mythology," *A New Companion to English Renaissance Literature and Culture*, ed. Michael Hattaway (Chichester: Wiley-Blackwell, 2010), I: 134-149; Elizabeth Powers, "Choice/ Choosing," *Encyclopedia of Comparative Iconography: Themes Depicted in Works of Art*, ed. Helene E. Roberts (Chicago: Fitzroy Dearborn Publishers, 1998), 165-170.

[5] As a married woman with a living husband, Sophia-Frances Chaplin Wright was not eligible to devise an official last will and testament under the English common law principle of coverture as it existed at that time.

[6] *Catalogue of the more important part of the collection of Italian and English pictures, the property of Thomas Wright, Esq., of Upton Hall, Newark*, Christie and Manson, 7 June 1845; Leonard Jacks, *The Great Houses of Nottinghamshire and the county families* (Nottingham: W. and A.S. Bradshaw, 1881), 123-128.

[7] It is perhaps noteworthy that Thomas Wright's paternal uncle, John Wright of Butterley Park, Derbyshire, was a business partner of Francis Jessop, last known owner of the lost Harrington Portrait discussed in Appendix Two.

[8] A search of the Getty Research Institute's *Provenance Research Index Database* reveals nine portraits of female or non-gendered sitters purchased by "Wright," without forename or city of residence, between the five years between 1828 and 1833. This number includes two attributed to Holbein: one said to depict Mary Tudor as a Princess and the other said to depict Anne Boleyn. Others from the Tudor period include an non-gendered portrait attributed to Anthonis More and a portrait of Mary Queen of Scots attributed to Federico Zuccari.

[9] "Landscape paintings returned to hall," *The Newark Advertiser*, 1 November 2013. <http://www.newarkadvertiser.co.uk/articles/news/ Landscape-paintings-returned-to-hall> Accessed 23 January 2014.

[10] Aviva Briefel, *The Deceivers: Art Forgery and Identity in the Nineteenth Century* (Ithaca: Cornell University Press, 2006), 84-89.

[11] A recommendation has been made to the current owners of the painting that it be technologically assessed for evidence of any underlying image, whether the same or some other subject. That recommendation has yet to be acted upon.

[12] In contrast, the Wrights were descended from a line of ironmongers, albeit prosperous ones, late in the seventeenth century who became wealthy bankers by the middle of the eighteenth century.

21   The Pickering Portrait

Unknown Netherlandish Lady

Unknown Netherlandish artist

Oil on wood panel; 36 in. x 29 in.

Undated

Provenance:

    Percival Spencer Umfreville Pickering (*d*.1920);

    Sotheby's 21 July 1954, Lot 6;

    Probably Arthur Granville Soames, Sheffield Park, Sussex;

    Current location unknown.[1]

As with the Grimsthorpe Portrait just discussed, the Pickering Portrait bears no inscription to indicate that it is a depiction of Jane Grey, and neither has it ever been published in that capacity. It too has remained largely unknown to both scholars and the general public. And like the Norris Portrait, it is known solely by means of a single black and white photograph held in the Lady Jane Grey Sitter File in the archives of the National Portrait Gallery.[2] It gained very limited notice only once when the heirs of the English chemist and horticulturist P.S.U. Pickering offered it for sale in 1955 through Sotheby's of London. The painting disappeared following that sale.

The Pickering Portrait exhibits numerous similarities to the Wrest Park Portrait, and it is quite probably through comparison to the many popular engravings of that latter portrait that the Pickering was labeled as Jane Grey. Both portraits are three-quarter length with plain backgrounds. Each sitter wears a plain dark gown with a kerchief over the shoulders, though the kerchief worn by the Pickering lady is dark rather than white. A small cluster of flowers has been inserted at the openings of the partlets in both pictures, and the linings of those partlets are both heavily embellished with blackwork embroidery. A pair of enameled aiglettes are attached to the closures of each partlet.

Several differences between the two portraits allow for clearly distinguishing them as separate depictions of two unique individuals, however. Unlike the sitters in so many portraits said to depict Jane Grey, including the Wrest Park Portrait, the lady in the Pickering Portrait holds a pair of gloves with decorated cuffs rather than a book. The gloves mark the lady as a person of some wealth, since gloves were an expensive luxury item in the sixteenth century.[3] The Pickering lady also wears a choker-length necklace of pearls and goldwork set with colored gemstones, again a marker of wealth and status. But the differences in the headdresses offer the most significant means of distinguishing the two sitters as unique individuals. That of the Wrest Park lady consists of a "Paris head," a close-fitting wrap of plain white linen commonly worn by English widows in the middle of the sixteenth century.[4] In contrast, the Pickering lady's headdress is comparable to the jeweled one worn by the lady depicted in the Huntington Portrait. And based on the style of the headdress, we can conclude that the sitter in the Pickering Portrait is not Jane Grey, but is instead an unidentifiable Netherlandish lady of the middle of the sixteenth century.

[1] The black and white photograph of this painting held in the Lady Jane Grey Sitter File at the National Portrait Gallery's Heinz Archive and Library has on its reverse a penciled note indicating that the Pickering Portrait was auctioned by Sotheby's of London on 6 April 1955. The only Sotheby's sale of that date was devoted exclusively to rare books and manuscripts. No paintings were included.

[2] Sitter File for Lady Jane Grey, Heinz Archive and Library, National Portrait Gallery, London.

[3] Max von Boehn, *Modes & Manners: Ornaments; Lace, Fans, Gloves, Walking-sticks, Parasols, Jewelry and Trinkets* (J. M. Dent and Sons, 1929), 78-88.

[4] Lou Taylor, *Mourning Dress: A Costume and Social History* (Routledge, 2009), 52.

(shown actual size)

22   The Portland Miniature Portrait

Unknown Lady

Unknown artist

Watercolor on vellum; 2 in. x 1 ³/₅ in.

Undated, mid to late sixteenth century

Provenance:

    John Rushout (*d*.1859), 2ⁿᵈ Baron Northwick;

    William Cavendish-Scott-Bentinck (*d*.1879), 5ᵗʰ Duke of Portland;

    Private collection.

Like the Huntington, Klabin, Grimsthorpe, and Pickering Portraits, this miniature painting has largely escaped public notice and has never before been published or exhibited as a portrait of Jane Grey. Yet during its period of ownership by John Rushout, 2ⁿᵈ Baron Northwick early in the nineteenth century, it was said to depict Jane. Nothing is known of its prior provenance, leaving no indication as to when or why the miniature was thus labeled. Rushout owned at least one other miniature said to depict Jane, an enamel on copper by Henry Bone, enamel painter to King George III. But since Bone's only known depiction of Jane did not resemble this miniature in any way, this identification cannot have been made by means of comparison to the Bone miniature. The identification as Jane Grey most probably pre-dated its acquisition by Rushout.[1]

Rushout's collection was sold upon his death in 1859, at which time the Phillips auction house described the picture as an "exquisite miniature of Lady Jane Grey by Nicholas Hilliard."[2] The portrait was purchased by the 5ᵗʰ Duke of Portland on 4 August 1859 for 125 guineas, a quite substantial sum at the time. By 1889, however, the miniature had been re-identified as Jane's maternal grandmother, Mary Tudor Brandon, reportedly on the basis of a comparison to a double portrait of Mary and her husband Charles Brandon.[3] The workmanship was also re-assigned to Hans Holbein. Then in 1916, Richard Goulding produced an inventory catalogue of the Portland Collection in which he identified the sitter as Jane Grey's cousin Lady Elizabeth Fitzgerald Clinton, Countess of Lincoln. Goulding based his re-identification on his perception of a resemblance to Lady Elizabeth as she appeared in a portrait then at Carton House, County Kildare, Ireland and now in the National Gallery of Ireland (Fig.27).[4] Lady Elizabeth and Lady Jane were near-contemporaries, and both were descendants of Thomas Grey, 1ˢᵗ Marquess of Dorset, and his wife Cecily Bonville. Yet in the same Portland catalogue, Goulding noted that Sir Richard Holmes, Librarian for Windsor Castle, believed the lady to have been Margeurite de Valois and the artist to have been François Clouet (Fig.28).[5]

Fig. 27: *Elizabeth Fitzgerald*

Fig. 28: *Marguerite de Valois*

The style of the costume allows for the lady to be either English or French. The French hood worn on the head was popular in France throughout the first three quarters of the sixteenth century and in England during the middle two quarters. The only potential distinction might be in the tendency among English ladies after about 1550 to prefer hoods that assumed a more horizontal silhouette across the crown.[6] The specific design of the heavily embroidered and bejeweled partlet appears in both English and French portraits, as does the cut of the neckline of the gown and the slashing of the sleeves.[7] There are thus no clues within the painted image that might definitively denote the lady's regional origin.

Discovering the identity of the artist is similarly problematic. The original attribution to Hilliard is unsupportable owing to the inferior finish and detailing of this work in comparison to Hilliard's authentic miniatures. The same is equally true with regard to Hans Holbein. And Sir Richard Holmes's suggestion of François Clouet is likewise negated simply by comparing the workmanship of this portrait to that seen in Clouet's miniature of Catherine de Medici now in the Victoria and Albert Museum (Fig.29). The two portraits are nearly identical in scale and contain comparable elements, especially the extremely curly hair and the design of the partlet, yet the portrait of Catherine clearly exhibits a superior technical ability.[8] While both the identity of the artist who created the Portland Portrait and that of the lady depicted within it will perhaps continue to be debated, there is no evidence to support identifying her as Jane Grey. The sitter and the artist must each remain unknown pending the development of additional evidence.

Fig. 29 : *Catherine de Medici, by François Clouet*
(shown actual size)

[1] See *Lady Jane Grey after a portrait in the possession of Sir Jacob Astley, Bart.*, 1825, pencil drawing squared in ink for transfer, 9 ⁷/₈ in. x 7 ⁵/₈ in, National Portrait Gallery, NPG D17222. Bone's son, Henry Pierce Bone, also a noted miniaturist, used the Althorp Portrait as the model for his own version in 1844. See *Lady Jane Grey*, enamel on copper, 1844, 4 ¼ in. x 3 ¹/₃ in., Royal Collection, RCIN422351.

[2] *Catalogue of the late Lord Northwick's Extensive and Magnificent Collection of Ancient and Modern Pictures ... at Thirlestane House, Cheltenham* (London: J. Davy and Son, 1859), 64, Lot 63.

[3] *Exhibition of Portrait Miniatures* (London: Burlington Fine Arts Club, 1889), 91; electronic communication, Gareth Hughes, Collections Manager, Portland Collection, 2 November 2010.

[4] Richard Goulding, *The Welbeck Abbey Miniatures belonging to His Grace the Duke of Portland* (Oxford, 1916), 56-57. See also *Portrait of 'The Fair Geraldine' (Elizabeth Fitzgerald, Countess of Lincoln, c1528-1590)*, attrib. The Master of the Countess of Warwick, n.d., oil on wood panel, 18 ¹/₈ in. x 13 ²/₅ in., National Gallery of Ireland, NGI1195.

[5] Goulding, *Welbeck Abbey Miniatures*, 57. See also *Marguerite de Valois, Queen of Navarre*, Francois Clouet, n.d., sixteenth century, oil on wood, 11 ²/₅ in. x 8 ⁷/₈ in., Musée Condé, PE 589.

[6] Schuessler, "French Hoods," 129-160.

[7] See, for example: *Portrait of Elizabeth Fitzgerald*, n.4 above; two miniatures of Elizabeth I by Nicholas Hilliard (Royal Collection); *Marie de Montchenu, Lady d'Harcourt*, François Clouet, 1547 (Musée Condé); *Elizabeth of Austria*, Joris van der Straeten, 1570 (Monasterio de las Descalzas Reales, Madrid).

[8] *Catherine de Medici*, François Clouet, ca.1555, watercolour on vellum laid down on card, 2 ¹/₃ in. x 1 ¾ in., Victoria and Albert Museum, London, P.26-1954.

23   The eBay Portrait

Unknown Lady, called Lady Jane Grey

Attributed to Elizabethan English School

Oil on wood panel; estimated 10 in. x 12 in.

Undated, mid to late sixteenth century

Provenance:

  None available.

This portrait surfaced in a "Buy It Now" listing on the popular e-commerce site Ebay early in 2019. The price was set at £7500 (approximately $9700), though the seller also included a "Make An Offer" option. The listing described the portrait thus:

> Lady Jane Grey circa 1553 at the time Jane was made Queen of England for 9 days. It shows Jane in royal robes with a heavily embroidered dress and a magnificant [sic] aray [sic] of jewles [sic] and necklaces, [sic] she wears a bullion embroidered coif that holds her hair up and a wide brimmed hat with bird of paradise plumes[.] A rare survivor.

The seller attributed the work to "Elizabethan English School" despite the obvious contradiction that what we now refer to as the Elizabethan Period did not begin until the accession of Elizabeth Tudor in November 1558, almost five years after Jane Grey's death in February 1554. The painting probably does nonetheless date to the sixteenth century, based on the use of a single-board wood panel as the support.

There are three adhesive paper labels on the back of the board. The manufacture of the central label (Fig.31, top is consistent in style with auction house and sale gallery labels of the nineteenth century. It bears an inscription in French, "Jane Grey reine d' Angleterre 1554" (Jane Grey Queen of England 1554). The style of the handwriting is likewise consistent with that of the nineteenth and early twentieth centuries. The label in the upper right corner bears a different handwriting (Fig.31, bottom), the style of which is less readily datable but is nonetheless likely pre-twentieth century. That label is inscribed with a number, 6057, and two series of letters, JRR and UAR. These are probably inventory control identifiers used by an auction house or sale gallery that handled a sale of the painting at some point in its history.[1] The third label (not shown in detail) was applied much more recently and reads "660/6."

Fig. 30 : *Reverse of the board of the eBay portrait*

Fig. 31 : *Paper labels enlarged*

Despite the modern paper label indicating that the sitter is Lady Jane Grey, that identification is strongly contradicted by the subject matter of the painting. The pastoral or landscape background, for example, is very seldom encountered in female English portraiture dating from the first half of the sixteenth century. The overwhelming majority of portraits of English women of that period most commonly depict those women in an indoor and thus socio-culturally suitable domestic setting. This was particularly true of English women of royal rank similar to or greater than that of Jane Grey. Portraits of women in pastoral settings more commonly originate instead in southern and eastern Europe.[2] Additionally, the costume worn by the sitter is entirely incorrect for England in the middle of the sixteenth century. English women of high social status in that period wore French hoods almost exclusively, whereas this sitter is wearing a heavily decorated turban- or snood-like hair wrap similar to a coif or fall, and that wrap is overlaid with a rather enormous wide-brimmed hat augmented with numerous feathers resembling emu or ostrich feathers. Examples of high-status English women of the mid sixteenth century wearing wide-brimmed hats in their portraits are essentially unknown, and emu or ostrich feathers were exceedingly uncommon in English fashions of the same period.

The headgear seen in this painting is more consistent with fashions from the earliest decades of the sixteenth century in eastern and southeastern Europe, especially the Germanic states of the Holy Roman Empire and the Kingdoms of Bohemia and Hungary. Two particularly appropriate paintings illustrate the assertion. The first depicts Judith with the head of Holofernes, painted by

Fig. 32 : *Judith with the head of Holofernes,*
by Lucas Cranach the Elder

the German artist Lucas Cranach the Elder in about 1530, in which Judith's headgear is remarkably similar to that of the sitter in the eBay portrait (Fig.32, above).[3] Judith wears a nearly identical coif- or fall-like wrap for her hair that is again surmounted by a wide brimmed hat heavily decorated with ostrich-like feathers. The only apparent difference between the two hats lies in the slashing at each of the four quadrants of the folded-back brim of Judith's hat. Hints of more numerous slashes are faintly visible in the extended brim of the eBay sitter's hat, but they are partially obscured by a combination of discolored varnish, craquelure, and poor photography. And again like the sitter in the eBay portrait, Judith wears two heavily-jeweled and choker-like collars, the uppermost of which is very much like that of the lady in the eBay painting.

The second comparison example is the Fulbeck Portrait discussed previously (see p.66) and also once said to depict Jane Grey. That painting is now known to be a copy of a portrait of Anne of Bohemia and Hungary that was itself created in 1519 by Hans Maler. The Fulbeck sitter's headgear again consists of a wide brimmed hat overlying a turban-like coif, though no ostrich feathers are present there.

The rationale for identifying the sitter in the eBay Portrait as Jane Grey most probably stemmed from a past comparison to the Fulbeck Portrait. The latter was widely published as both lithographic and engraved prints beginning in 1822, all with the erroneous identification of the sitter as Jane Grey. The prints were produced in large numbers and widely circulated across Europe throughout the first half of the nineteenth century.[4] One was created by Robert William Sievier of Cavendish Square, London and printed by John Brydone, also of London (Fig.33). The inscription indicates

Fig. 33 : *Called Lady Jane Grey,*
by Robert William Sievier

Fig. 34 : *Called Lady Jane Grey,*
by Antoine Maurin

that it was first printed on 4 June 1822. The other engraving (Fig.34) was created at about the same time by Antoine Maurin, a Frenchman who resided in England in the 1820s. Scholarship on Maurin is sparse, but he is known to have produced engravings of numerous contemporary English persons as well as of other French citizens living in England. His non-contemporary subjects appear to be limited to just two female historical figures, however: Jane Grey and Marina Mniszech.[5] Another Frenchman, François Le Villain, printed Maurin's engravings in his own Paris workshop. They were then sold throughout Europe, either as individual sheets or leaves, or as one in a larger collection of engravings by several artists, all published by Edward Bull and Edward Churton of London.

It seems altogether likely that these prints, published so widely and authoritatively as authentic images of Jane Grey, served collectively to allow a former owner or past art dealer to identify the eBay portrait as likewise a depiction of Jane Grey. The style of the headgear is sufficiently similar between the Fulbeck and eBay Portraits and yet simultaneously so uncommon in English portraiture that one can concede a certain naive logic in concluding that the paintings depict the same woman. But in light of the confirmation in 2015 of the identity of the sitter in the Fulbeck Portrait as Anne of Bohemia and Hungary, that same logic would require identifying the lady in the eBay portrait as likewise Anne. Much more probably, however, the lady is some other person of status from the same geographic region as Anne (i.e., the region consisting of eastern Germany plus neighboring Bohemia and Hungary) and probably even from the same narrow chronological period, circa 1520-1530. She is certainly not Jane Grey, and it is all but impossible that the original artist intended her to represent Queen Jane. In actuality, the similarity of the costume in the eBay portrait to two paintings that both date to the third decade of the sixteenth century suggest the likelihood that the eBay Portrait was also created in that decade. The eBay Portrait may be as much as thirty years older than its seller believed at the time of the offering in 2019.

[1] The eBay seller did not provide any provenance for the painting in his listing or in my contact with him. A search of the Getty Museum's Sales Catalog Database for sales throughout Europe (particulary France) in the eighteenth and nineteenth centuries of portraits said to depict Lady Jane Grey reveals 44 separate recorded sales between the seventeenth and the twentieth centuries. Many can be eliminated based on the materials used (e.g.: enamel on copper, engraving) or size (e.g.: miniature, full length). A large number can also be excluded because their current whereabouts have already been reliably identified. Only a handful remain, but none of those are sufficiently well described in the corresponding sale catalogue to allow them to be identified with this painting.

[2] See, for example, the many confirmed portraits of Queen Katherine Parr, last wife of Henry VIII, of Queen Mary Tudor, and of Queen Elizabeth Tudor. An exception can be found in the Ditchley Portrait of Elizabeth, but that example is an allegorical painting in which the background is imaginary and serves a specific symbolic purpose. Perhaps the single most famous portrait of a woman in a pastoral setting is the *Mona Lisa* by Leonardo da Vinci, painted in northern Italy in the first decade of the sixteenth century. Intriguingly, a precise location of the Mona Lisa landscape was suggested by Italian researchers in 2012. See Rosetta Borchia and Olivia Nesci, *Code P. Atlante illustrato del reale paesaggio della Gioconda* (Mandadori Electa, 2012).

[3] My sincere thanks to Lee Porritt for alerting me to Cranach's depiction of Judith. The artist Lucas Cranach the Elder (*d.*1553) served as court painter to the Elector of Saxony, who was also Duke of Saxe-Wittenberg in eastern Germany.

[4] The late eighteenth and early nineteenth centuries witnessed something like a fad for collecting engraved prints of existing painted works of all kinds. Engraved prints were bought and sold both individually and bound together in volumes, and prices commonly reached or exceeded several shillings, or the equivalent of £75 ($100) or more if calculated in terms of earned wages.

[5] The story of Marina Mniszech (1588-1614), known in Russian folklore as Marinka the Witch, has certain parallels to that of Lady Jane Grey Dudley. Marina was the daughter of Jerzy Mniszech, a Polish nobleman with royal ambitions. Mniszech arranged in 1605 for Marina to wed the Russian Tsar Dmitriy I, known to history as False Dmitriy or Pseudo-Demetrius. Beginning in 1600, Dmitriy posed as the youngest son of Ivan the Terrible, Dmitriy Ivanovich, who had died nine years previously under suspicious circumstances. False Dmitriy claimed to have secretly escaped and to have remained in hiding until his "miraculous reappearance." He fled Russia and the authorities of Tsar Boris Godunov and gained the support of the Polish Crown, which was at that time often involved in armed conflict with Russia. He raised an army of sufficient size in 1605 to seize the Russian throne from Feodor II, the sixteen-year-old heir of Tsar Boris Godunov, who had himself died just six weeks earlier. Marina's father was a keen supporter of Dmitriy's claim to the Russian throne, facilitating the promotion of Marina as a bride for Dmitriy. The couple were soon wed in Kraków in November 1605, and she was crowned Tsarina in May 1606. Like Queen Jane Grey Dudley, Tsarina Marina reigned just nine days. Dmitriy was assassinated on 17 May 1606 and was succeeded by Tsar Vasili IV. Mary fled back to Poland in 1608, whereupon her father arranged for Marina to meet a second man claiming to be the deceased Dmitriy Ivanovich. This new Dmitriy had gained control over much of southern Russia by 1608 and had established a royal court and government at Tushino (now a suburb of Moscow). Marina publicly claimed that the second Dmitriy was one-and-the-same as her deceased husband, Tsar Dmitriy. But Dmitriy II never fully suceeded in replacing Vasili IV on the Russian throne and was instead murdered by one of his own followers in December 1610. Marina gave birth to a son, Ivan, one month later, at about the same time she married Ivan Martynovich Zarutsky, a Russian supporter of Dmitriy II living in exile in Poland. After unsuccessfully attempting to promote Marina's son Ivan as the "rightful" successor of Tsar Dmitriy (I and II), the couple fled to exile in Astrakhan, a town in southern Russia. The populace of Astrakhan quickly turned against the couple, however, and local Cossack soldiers turned them over to the Russian government. Zarutsky and Marina's three-year-old son Ivan were executed in Moscow in 1614, and Marina died in prison soon thereafter. The Russian national assembly resolved the disputed claims to the Russian crown in February 1613 by electing Michael Romanov, aged seventeen years, as Tsar Michael I of All Russia, initiating the Romanov Dynasty in Russia.

24   The South Carolina Portrait

Unknown Lady, called Lady Jane Grey

Attributed to Manner of Hans Holbein the Younger

Oil on canvas; 35 ½ in. x 41 ½ in.

Undated, first half of the seventeenth century.

Provenance:

    Unknown museum in South Carolina, de-accessioned 2014;

    Charlton Hall Auctioneers, Columbia, South Carolina, December 2014;

    Current whereabouts unknown.

This portrait first surfaced after an unnamed museum in South Carolina de-acessioned it in 2014. It was then offered for sale on 13 December 2014 through Charlton Hall Auctioneers of West Columbia, South Carolina. But widespread media notice came only in March 2015 through its inclusion in an article in the *Maine Antique Digest*.[1]

The painting itself is neither signed nor marked, but lettering added to the frame identifies the supposed sitter as Lady Jane Grey Dudley. Rendered in very ornate Gothic script, the lettering at the top reads "Beheaded 12th Feb[ruar]y 1554." That at the bottom gives the person's name as "Lady Jane Grey." Because the year is given as 1554, the inscription must post-date the implementation in 1582 by most continental European countries of the Gregorian calendar system.[2] The inscription may also post-date 1752, the year in which Great Britain finally switched from the Julian to the Gregorian calendar.

The costume worn by the sitter indicates that the painting dates to the first half of the seventeenth century. The wide brim and high crown of the hat are typical of that broad period. The style of the hat also suggests a sitter from the Low Countries, especially when worn by a woman. Likewise the ruff following the natural slope of the shoulders rather than being propped up to become more nearly horizontal is typical of the second and third quarters of the seventeenth century and again suggests the sitter is perhaps from the Low Countries. The round ornament suspended from a ribbon at the lady's waist is perhaps a pocket watch (Fig.35). Lockets were more commonly worn higher on the body, while this object lies below the hip. And unlike a spherical pomander, the item seen here, though round and thick, has a flat upper surface. Pocket watches of the relatively small size seen here were not available until the middle of the seventeenth century.

The most likely explanation for a portrait dating to the middle of the seventeenth century becoming erroneously identified as a depiction of Jane Grey lies in the presence of the book beneath the lady's left hand together with her seemingly severe costume. Many of the falsely-identified portraits discussed in this volume similarly include a book that early portrait-owners and viewers correlated with the prayerbook Lady Jane reportedly carried with her to the scaffold. The books in those portraits also symbolized Jane's renowned intellect. Many other women also owned books, however, and were educated. Similarly, the unembellished black dress is consistent with the mythology that Jane dressed in a proto-Puritan manner, yet the outfit depicted was a common one in the Netherlands and other areas, including England in the middle of the seventeenth (but not the sixteenth) century.

Though said to depict Lady Jane Grey, this painting is actually a portrait of some unidentified English or Netherlandish woman of the second quarter of the seventeenth century. Like so many others, it somehow lost its identity

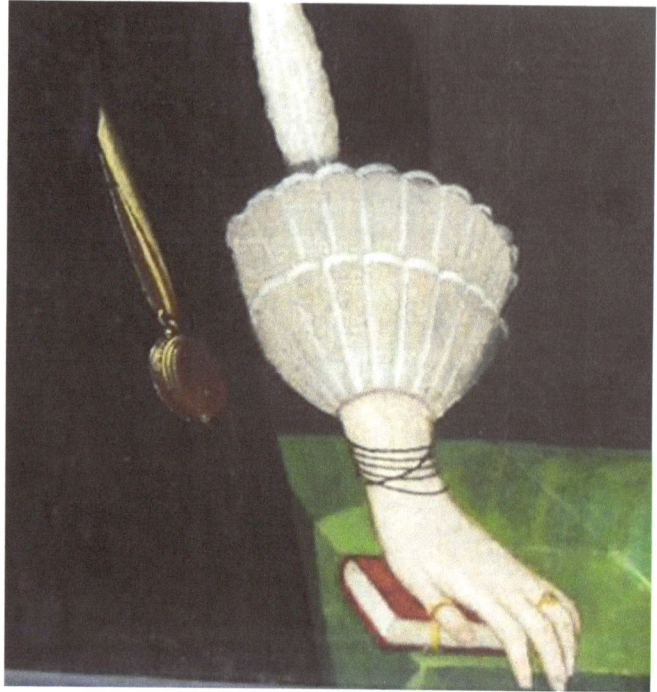

Fig. 35 : *Detail of pocketwatch*

and was relabeled, probably in the eighteenth or nineteenth century, to suit a past owner's personal biases.

Regarding the fanciful artist attribution, the Charlton Hall Auctioneers sale catalogue stated that this painting was created "in the manner of Hans Holbein the Younger." In all probability, the catalogue merely repeated whatever information had been made available by the unnamed museum that de-accessioned the painting. The basis for the attribution is otherwise entirely mysterious. The painting bears no resemblance whatsoever to genuine works by Holbein, whether in terms of depictional realism, artisitic technique, or compositional style. The attribution appears to have been 'wishful thinking' at best, perhaps in a misguided attempt to bolster the erroneous sitter identification through naming of an artist sometimes said to have painted a portrait of Jane.[3] The London art dealer Christopher Foley observed, "The 'Carolina' portrait is certainly English and of the 1620's. Roy Strong put together a group of similar portraits which he attributed to 'The Master of the Large Hands,' an anonymous primitive, who seems to have been working in the West Country, perhaps based in Exeter, at that date. He is truly a bad painter!"[4]

[1] Pete Prunkl, "Paintings and Jewelry Rule in Columbia," *Maine Antique Digest*, 13 December 2014.

[2] Under the older Julian calendar in use throughout Europe before 1582, the New Year began on 25 March. Thus in Jane Grey's own day, the date of death was correctly given as 12 February 155*3*. Great Britain adopted the Gregorian Calendar in 1752 and recognized 1 January as the beginning of the new calendar year thereafter, so that the date of Jane's death was subsequently correctly given as 12 February 155*4*.

[3] Hans Holbein died in 1543, when Jane was no more than seven years old. He did not, in fact, ever paint her portrait.

[4] Christopher Foley to J. Stephan Edwards, email correspondence, 24 November 2015.

25   The Althorp Portrait

Mary Magdalene in a Sixteenth-Century Setting

Master of the Female Half-Lengths, *fl.* before 1540

Oil on wood panel; 21 in. x 15 in.

First half of sixteenth century

Provenance:

Sarah Churchill, Duchess of Marlborough (*d.*1744);

Thence by descent with the Spencers of Althorp House.

One of the more heavily romanticized portraits sometimes identified as Lady Jane Grey is found in the collection of the Earl Spencer and held at Althorp House, Northamptonshire. It was engraved and reproduced often throughout the nineteenth century as an authentic portrait of Jane, first in 1817 as an illustration for Thomas F. Dibdin's *Bibliographical Decameron*.[1] Early in the twentieth century, the novelist-historian Richard Davey reproduced an engraving from the painting as the frontispiece illustration for his influential biography of Jane, *The Nine Days' Queen*. Davey argued for the authenticity of the image in an appendix to his volume and denounced a contradictory opinion previously expressed by Sir George Scharf, first director of the National Portrait Gallery. Davey characterized Scharf's findings as "prejudiced" and based upon "ludicrous errors of judgment" owing to Scharf's supposed "singular ignorance or rather disregard of the value of costume in determining the period of a picture."[2] Davey has thus far prevailed, so that the current *House Visitor Notes* pamphlet for Althorp states that the painting "represents Lady Jane Grey in her 16th year before her marriage when she still lived at her father's home Bradgate." The *Visitor Notes* go on to indicate that the townscape visible through the windows depicted behind the sitter is actually Leicester, though the town lies over six miles from Bradgate. The current website for Althorp House showcases the portrait as one of the Spencer treasures on display in the Great Room.[3]

The painting has been identified as Jane since at least the beginning of the eighteenth century. It enters the historical record through the Spencer ancestor Sarah Churchill, Duchess of Marlborough, a close confidant to Queen Anne and a devoted Whig supporter of the terms of the Act of Settlement of 1701. A paper label attached to the back of the panel and attributed by the Spencer family to the Duchess's own hand identifies the sitter as Jane Grey. The fifth Earl Spencer, a direct descendant of the Duchess, extended the longevity of the identification to "as far back as the seventeenth century."[4] And though Richard Davey attributed the work to Luca Penni, the portrait has usually been assigned to the Netherlandish artist Lucas de Heere. The painting has until now apparently not been critically assessed by any art historian since Scharf late in the nineteenth century. In light of the often-problematic nature of family traditions, it is necessary to set aside the Spencer tradition identifying the sitter as Jane Grey and to assess the painting anew.

The lady's costume offers several clues to both the date and the regional origin of the painting, and thus to the sitter's actual identity. The specific design of the French hood seen in this portrait, with its low profile, rounded crown and forward-swept sides, reached peak popularity in the 1520s and 1530s. In contrast, hoods from the late 1540s and early 1550s, when Jane Grey was only just entering young adulthood, assumed a flat crown with a higher profile.[5] Further, the bodices on English dresses in the first half of the sixteenth century were typically heavily boned and relatively rigid, so that the entire front of the bodice was flat on the vertical line. This largely concealed the shape of the covered breasts and produced a linear silhouette.[6] In contrast, women's costumes in paintings from the same period but produced in the Low Countries or the German states often exhibited bodices that followed the natural outline of the breasts. Importantly, a bodice construction nearly identical to that worn by the Althorp lady is seen in a picture of Saint Catherine by the Netherlandish artist known only as "The Master of the Female Half Lengths" (Fig.36).[7] Indeed, much of the work of that artist bears numerous striking similarities to this painting.

The identity of the unknown Master has been disputed since he was first identified in the nineteenth century as a distinct artist. At present, "he" is thought actually to have been a group or workshop of artists rather than one individual. Similarly, the location of that workshop is also a matter of debate, though most scholars agree that it was located in the Low Countries, perhaps Antwerp, Bruges, Ghent, or Mechelen. The artist or workshop was most active in the 1520s and 1530s. It was relatively prolific in its production of small panel paintings depicting individual women or small groups of women, usually aristocratic in appearance, and often engaged in either personal devotion or music-making.[8] Because the Master created so many paintings of such obvious resemblance to each other, it is usually assumed that he was working to meet the demands of an emerging consumer market calling for small-scale, affordable works of art for domestic decorative purposes.[9] Most of his works were therefore not commissioned portraits of actual people, but rather aesthetically appealing pictures of either Biblical subjects or imaginary persons and intended for speculative sale and quick profit.

Comparison of numerous elements depicted in the other works of the Master to corresponding elements in the Althorp painting is revealing. For example, the Althorp sitter's face and head are essentially identical to those of sitters in *Female Musician* (Fig.37) now at the Savoy Gallery in Turin and *Lady playing a lute in an interior* (not pictured), suggesting that the artist(s) worked from a pattern.[10] The headgear worn by the various sitters is likewise virtually identical. The *Musician* and the *Lady playing* each wear red gowns comparable in almost every respect to that worn by the Althorp lady, the only differences being in the gold embroidery added to the bodice trim of the latter and in the design of the various undersleeves. Further, the wide necklace worn high across the shoulders of the Althorp lady is indistinguishable from necklaces worn by sitters in at least three other paintings attributed to the Master: *St Mary Magdalene Writing* (Fig.38), *St Mary Magdalene Playing a Lute* (Fig.39), and *The Concert* (Fig.40).[11] Lastly, just as with the Althorp painting, many of the Master's works include a large and prominently placed lidded vessel, commonly associated in art with Mary Magdalene's ointment jar, leading art historians to identify that subset of his paintings as depictions specifically of the Magdalene.[12] The Althorp Portrait displays such extensive similarities, not only in terms of the sitter's physical appearance 8

Fig. 36: *St Catherine*

Fig. 37: *Female Musician*

Fig. 38: *St Mary Magdalene Writing*

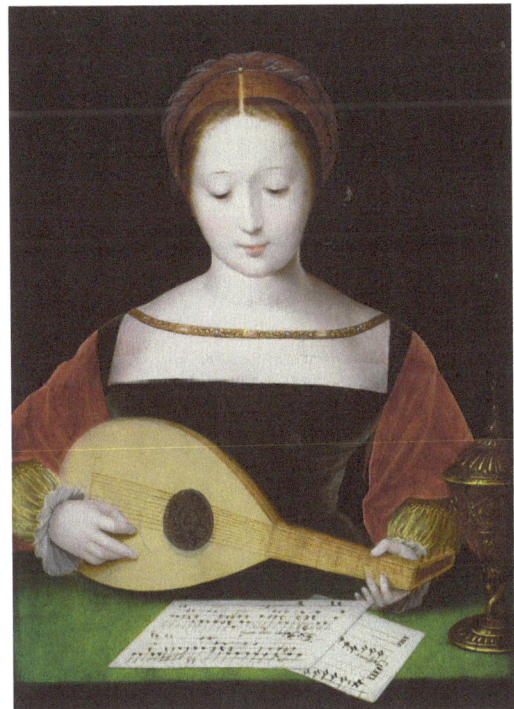

Fig. 39: *The Magdalene Playing the Lute*

Fig. 40: *The Concert*

and costume, but also in the inclusion in each of symbolic objects and the repetition across the group of a common domestic setting, to a large number of works firmly attributed to the Master that we are compelled to attribute the Althorp Portrait to him as well. And since approximately a half dozen of the most similar are each called Mary Magdalene, the conclusion that the Althorp Portrait also depicts Mary Magdalene is essentially inescapable.

The rationale in the seventeenth or eighteenth century for identifying the sitter in the Althorp Portrait as Jane Grey lay most probably in the nature of the domestic scene depicted. As with so many other portraits in this study, the image depicts the lady engaged in reading a book. In this instance, the visible illuminated pages of the book suggest a devotional text, consistent with the attachment to Jane Grey beginning early in the eighteenth century of a reputation for unusual personal piety. Simultaneously, the mythology that developed arounjd Jane's name included the notion that she lived most of her life in self-imposed isolation and devoted herself entirely to study, especially religious study. This particular aspect of the mythology was based on a single vignette recorded by Roger Ascham, tutor to Elizabeth I. Ascham visited the Grey's Leicestershire seat of Bradgate in 1550 and found Jane in her chamber reading Greek literature, yet the majority of the household were outdoors involved in a hunt. During Ascham's conversation with Jane, she described the great joy she obtained from study.[13] Historians and other writers have, since at least the turn of the eighteenth century, frequently extrapolated from this one episode to create a portrayal of Jane as eschewing any pursuits other than study.[14] Seemingly personifying that myth, the lady in the portrait sits alone at her desk engaged in study. As Jane became newly re-popularized through literature and drama in the late-seventeenth and early-eighteenth centuries, the Althorp Portrait lent itself well to service as a kind of "proxy" portrait of her.

1 Thomas Frognall Dibdin, *The Bibliographical Decameron; Or, Tens Days Pleasant Discourse Upon Illuminated Manuscripts, and Subjects Connected With Early Engraving, Typography, and Bibliography* (London: W. Bulmer and Company, 1817), III:249.

2 Davey, *The Nine Day's Queen*, 360-361.

3 "Portrait of Lady Jane Grey,"
<http://www.spencerofalthorp.com/heritage/object/portrait-of-lady-jane-grey>
Accessed 17 December 2013.

4 The 5th Earl Spencer as quoted in Davey, *Nine Day's Queen*, 360.

5 Schuessler, "French Hoods," 129-160.

6 Ninya Mikhaila and Jane Malcolm-Davies, *The Tudor Tailor: Reconstructing Sixteenth-Century Dress* (Hollywood: Costume and Fashion Press, 2006), 22-23.

7 *St Catherine*, Master of the Female Half-Lengths, n.d. 1530s, oil on wood panel; 17 ¾ in. x 14 ¼ in., Pinocateca di Brera, Milan.

8 "Circle of the Master of the Female Half Lengths," *The Collectors: Old Master Paintings*, ed. Roy Bolton, exh. cat., 2009, 124-125; *Grove Dictionary of Art*, s.v., "Master of the Female Half Lengths." Over sixty works attributable to the Master have survived in various public and private collections.

9 On the emergence in the Low Countries of a consumer-driven market in decorative art for the domestic setting, see Filip Vermeylen, "Exporting Art Across the Globe: The Antwerp Art Market in the Sixteenth Century," *Nederlands kunsthistorisch jaarboek* 50 (1999), 12-29; Neil De Marchi, "The Antwerp-Mechelen Production and Export Complex," *In His Milieu: Essays on Netherlandish Art in Memory of John Michael Montias*, ed. Amy Golhany, Mia Mochizuki, and Kisa Vergara (Amsterdam: Amsterdam University Press, 2007).

10 *Female Musician*, Master of the Female Half-Lengths, sixteenth century, materials unknown; size unknown, Galleria Sabauda (Turin); (not pictured) *A lady playing a lute in an interior*, Master of the Female Half-Lengths, n.d., oil on wood panel, 21 ½ in. x 16 ½ in., Christie's London, Sale 7782, 8 December 2009, Lot 2.

11 *St Mary Magdalene Writing*, Master of the Female Half-Lengths, sixteenth century, oil on wood panel; 21 2/3 in. x 16 ½ in., private collection; *The Magdalene Playing the Lute*, Master of the Female Half-Lengths, sixteenth century, oil on wood panel; 10 5/8 in. x 8 in., Christie's London, Sale 6604, 10 July 2002, Lot 16; *The Concert*, Master of the Female Half-Lengths, sixteenth century, oil on wood panel, 23 3/5 in. x 20 7/8 in., private collection.

12 George Ferguson, *Signs and Symbols in Christian Art (*Oxford: Oxford University Press, 1954), 135 and 171; Rosa Giorgi, *Saints in Art*, trans. Thomas Michael Hartmann (Los Angeles: Getty Publications, 2003), 257.

13 Roger Ascham, *The Scholemaster* (London: John Daye, 1570), 201.

14 Burnet, *History of the Reformation*, 290. See also Davey, T*he Nine Days Queen*, 173. Davey described Jane as a "poor isolated little girl" of whom "we ... can but feel more of pity than admiration, as down the long vista of four and half centuries we picture her sitting alone, poring over the Phaedon...." Chapman cites Jane's supposed "capacity for self-isolation." See Chapman, *Lady Jane Grey*, 56 and 76.

26   The Madresfield Portrait

Unknown Lady, perhaps Mary Magdalene

Follower of Ambrosius Benson

Oil on wood panel; 28 ¼ in, x 22 ¾ in.

Undated, second quarter of the sixteenth century

Provenance:

> By descent since the early nineteenth century with the Earls Beauchamp, Madresfield Court, Malvern, Worcesterhsire;

Elmley Foundation, 1989.

Richard Davey included this painting in his list of putative portraits of Jane Grey appended to his *Nine Days Queen* and rather optimistically suggested that the sitter's face bore a resemblance to the lady depicted in the van de Passe Engraved Portrait.[1] He further noted, more weakly, that the costume was "one that Jane might have worn." Though the portrait was commonly attributed to the artist Lucas de Heere, Davey instead suggested William Scrots, whom he called "Streete."[2] The artist has more recently been re-identified as an anonymous follower of the Flemish master Ambrosius Benson (*d*.1550), while the sitter is still described in the Madresfield Court visitors pamphlet as Jane Grey.[3] That notion is visually re-enforced today in the display of the painting next to a portrait labeled as Jane's husband Guildford Dudley.[4]

Madresfield Court has been owned by the Lygon family since the sixteenth century, but the family fortunes suffered to such an extent in the seventeenth century that a significant quantity of assets was sold to raise cash. It therefore seems more probable that the painting entered the Lygon collection early in the nineteenth century through an inheritance from the ancestors of Susannah Hanmer Lygon (*d*.1785), mother of the first Lygon Earl Beauchamp.[5] The inheritance is said to have "transformed the family fortune ... and the collections of the house were enormously increased" as a result.[6]

Susannah Lygon was one of several distant claimants to the estate of the immensely wealthy William "The Miser" Jennens (or Jennings) of Acton Place, Suffolk. Jennens was a godson of William III and was pro-Hanoverian and anti-Jacobite throughout his life, which spanned the whole of the eighteenth century. Jennens died unmarried, without legitimate issue, and intestate at the advanced age of 97 in 1798. The value of his estate, said at the time to have been greater than that of any other commoner in Great Britain, stimulated litigation on a massive scale filed by a multitude of claimants, both genuine and spurious. The descendants of Susannah Hanmer Lygon, Jennen's niece at a remove of several generations, found themselves in possession of one third of the Jennens estate in the first decade of the nineteenth century.[7]

The painting was probably rechristened as Jane Grey in the wake of the succession dispute resolved by the Act of Settlement of 1701, and that new identification made it appealing to Jennens. The rechristening was perhaps prompted in part by the presence in the lady's hands, once again, of a book that could be read as emblematic of Jane's perceived piety. Additionally, the veils worn by the sitter lend to the image an air of modesty and chastity, two virtues that began to be strongly associated with Jane early in the eighteenth century. The costume is not consistent with English fashion at any point in the sixteenth century, however. The extensive veiling, in particular, is more typical of the Low Countries. Likewise, the soft, non-boned bodice and wide rounded neckline of the gown suggest an origin in the Low Countries.[8]

It has been asserted in at least one instance that the portrait depicts a lady in the guise of Mary Magdalene.[9] The scarlet color of the gown is often associated in Christian art with sin and likewise often used in depictions of the Magdalene, in particular, as symbolic of her penitence (see, for example, the Althorp Portrait). Similarly, portraits of the Magdalene often show her reading a book, frequently identifiable as a religious text specifically. Further, the most common emblem of the Magdalene used in sixteenth-century art, a pot or jar denoting the pot of ointment she used to anoint Christ's feet, is visible in the lower left corner of the image. The Madresfield Portrait is also directly comparable to a painting by Ambrosius Benson now in the Louvre Museum, Paris (Fig. 41).[10] The two images are in fact so similar to each other and to so many others by Benson that it seems probable that they were produced in quantity to meet the needs of an emerging market for decorative art, as was the case with the Althorp Portrait and other works by the Master of the Female Half-Lengths. As such, the lady depicted here was almost certainly merely an artist's studio model standing in for Mary Magdalene.

Fig. 41: *Young Woman Reading a Book of Hours, by Ambrosius Benson*

[1] Davey, *Lady Jane Grey*, 361.

[2] William Lygon, *Catalogue of the Pictures, chiefly historical portraits, at Madresfield Court* (London: William Clowes and Sons, 1927), 17.

[3] John de la Cour, *Madresfield Court* (2010 visitors pamphlet), 7.

[4] The costume worn by the sitter in the portrait called Guildford Dudley dates to the end of the sixteenth century, long after the deaths of Jane and Guildford in 1554. The labeling is therefore similarly erroneous.

[5] William Lygon (1747-1816), created 1st Earl Beauchamp in 1806, was the son of Reginald Lygon (ne Pyndar) and Susannah Hanmer Lygon.

[6] Cour, *Madresfield Court*, 2.

[7] Messrs. Harrison and Willis, *The Great Jennens Case* (Sheffield: Pawson and Brailsford, 1879); Patrick Polden, "Stranger Than Fiction: The Jennens Inheritance in Fact and Fiction," *Common Law World Review* 32 (2003), 3:211-247 and 4:338-367.

[8] Mikhaila, *Tudor Tailor*, 22-23.

[9] Unpublished inventory of the collection at Madresfield Court prepared by Sotheby's in 1990.

[10] *Young Woman Reading a Book of Hours*, Ambrosius Benson, 1520s, oil on wood panel, 29 ½ in. x 21 ¾ in., Musée du Louvre, Paris.

27   The Anglesey Abbey Portrait

Ideal Female Head

Unknown Artist

Oil on wood panel; 20 in. x 17 ¾ in.

Undated

Provenance:

>Huttleston Rogers Broughton, 1st Lord Fairhaven, (*d*.1966);

>National Trust, Anglesey Abbey, Cambridgeshire.

The composition of this picture, a left full profile, is relatively rare in English portraiture of the sixteenth century. While a number of profile portraits are known, they almost invariably depict men rather than women, and the majority of even those were the work of just one artist, Hans Holbein.[1] Profile portraits of English women of the sixteenth century are instead limited almost exclusively to carved-stone cameos set in jewelry.[2] In contrast, sixteenth-century painted portraits of female sitters viewed in full profile far more commonly emerged from Northern Italy, especially Florence.[3] The profile nature of this portrait suggests at least an Italian-born or Italian-trained artist, but more probably an Italian sitter and an Italian origin for the painting itself.

The style of the costume is decidedly inconsistent with English fashion in general and that of Jane Grey's lifetime in particular. The headgear indicates a sitter from south-central Europe, perhaps southeastern France, the southern German-speaking states, or northern Italy. Additionally, the caul and low-profile hat are consistent with styles of those regions in the 1560s or 1570s, more than a decade after Jane Grey's death in February 1554. Based on the costume alone, Lady Jane Grey can reliably be eliminated as the sitter in this portrait.

The face appears on the whole too perfect, too obviously consistent with facial ratios and proportions long held by Western European artists as an aesthetic ideal. It is in many ways comparable to Michelangelo's *Ideal Head of a Woman* (Fig.42).[4] A straight line drawn from the forehead to the chin of the Anglesey image very neatly traces the plane of the face, and that plane is precisely ten degrees off vertical (Fig.43). Similarly, the line of the nose is precisely ten degrees off vertical and is unnaturally straight. The nares are perfectly horizontal from the tip of the nose to the face. The bottom of the nose rests precisely halfway between the eyes and the chin. The terminus of the cupid's bow of the upper lip aligns perfectly with the pupil of the eye. The horizontal line between the upper and lower lip is at the midpoint of the distance between the tip of the nose and the tip of the chin. The only discernible flaw in the ratios and proportions of the face is in the placement of the ear: the tip of the earlobe is higher than it should ideally be, i.e., on a horizontal line with the tip of the nose. In light of the too-perfect proportions of the lady's facial features, the painting is unlikely to be a depiction of any real person, but is instead most probably an imagined portrait of some non-

Fig. 42: *Michelangelo's* Ideal Head of a Woman.

Fig. 43: *Detail of the Anglesey Abbey Portrait with geometric graphic showing proportions.*

existent feminine ideal.

There is some evidence to suggest that this painting may have come to England at the turn of the nineteenth century in the collection of Joseph Franz Anton, Graf von Waldburg-Zeil-Wurzach. A member of a family of lesser Prussian nobility and himself a Grand Dean of the Cathedral of Strasburg and Canon of the Metropolitan Chapter of Cologne, Count Truchsess (as he was commonly known) reportedly lost the bulk of his fortune in the aftermath of the French Revolution. He immigrated to London at the turn of the century, bringing with him from Vienna a significant portion of his larger collection of over 700 paintings.[5] By 1803, he had built Truchsess Gallery in Portland Square to house the collection, which was then valued at 60,000 guineas and described as "one of the finest collections of pictures that ever adorned the British metropolis."[6] Count Truchsess's stated ambition was the bulk sale of his collection to 10,000 subscribers at six guineas each for the purpose of establishing the core of a national gallery of art.[7] Failing in that attempt and deeply indebted to multiple creditors, Truchsess offered the collection in pieces at public auctions in 1804, 1806, and 1810.

The catalogue for the sale of the Truchsess collection held in May 1804 described Lot 631 as "Profile of a woman, by Ciro Ferri, oil on wood panel."[8] The physical dimensions of the panel in that lot match precisely those of the central image of the Anglesey Abbey portrait, though the shape of the panel, whether rectangular or oval, is not explicitly stated in the catalogue. While the majority of the 907 lots in the Truchsessian sale of 1804 did not find a buyer, Lot 631 apparently did sell since it did not reappear in the subsequent sale attempts of 1806 and 1810.[9] The buyer was not identified, however.[10]

At the time of the first Truchsessian Gallery sale, Anglesey Abbey was owned by the Reverend

George Leonard Jenyns. He had inherited the estate, along with Bottisham Hall, in 1796 from the widow of his cousin Soame Jenyns, the wealthy writer and politician. Best remembered as the father of the naturalist Leonard Blomefield (né Jenyns),[11] Rev. Jenyns's new fortune was considerable, contrasting sharply with his modest occupation as vicar of Swaffham Prior, near Bottisham Hall, and prebendary of Ely Cathedral. It is quite possible that the newly enriched Anglican priest purchased the portrait in the Truchsessian Gallery sale and installed it in his imposing new residence of Anglesey Abbey. Rev. Jenyns may well have been tempted by the absence of any pre-existing identification for the sitter in the portrait and, as a faithful Anglican responding to the re-emergence during the first half of the nineteenth century of Jane Grey as a religious martyr-figure, simply decided—somewhat arbitrarily—that the portrait depicted Jane.

It is equally possible that the painting was acquired by any of the other subsequent nineteenth-century owners of Anglesey Abbey, whether from some interim owner following the Truchsessian Gallery sale or from some other as-yet-unidentified source. It is noteworthy that every owner of Anglesey Abbey between 1796 and 1912 was an Anglican cleric. John Hailstone, who purchased the Abbey from Rev. Jenyn's estate in 1849, was vicar of Bottisham from 1839 to 1861 and Rural Dean of North Cambridgeshire from 1863 until his death in 1871. Hailstone's successor in ownership of Anglesey Abbey, James George Clark, was ordained to the Anglican priesthood in 1872. Any of these men would have had a "natural" inclination toward identifying the otherwise unknown sitter in the portrait as one of the first martyrs of the Anglican Church and a national heroine who was all but idolized throughout the Victorian era.

[1] See, for example, *Portrait of Erasmus of Rotterdam writing*, Hans Holbein, 1523, oil and tempera on wood, 16 $9/10$ in x 13 in., Musée du Louvre, Paris; *Portrait of Simon George*, Hans Holbein, 1533, oil and tempera on oak, 12 $1/5$ in. diameter, Städelsches Kunstinstitut, Frankfurt; *Portrait of Edward VI* (anamorphosis), William Scrots, 1546, oil on wood panel, 16 ¾ in. x 63 in., National Portrait Gallery, NPG1299.

[2] Many such jewel cameo profiles of Elizabeth I are known, for example, including the Heneage Jewel (Victoria and Albert Museum, London, accession number M.81-1935) and the Barbor Jewel (V&A Museum, London, acc. no. 889-1894).

[3] See, for example, *Portrait of Barbara Pallavicino*, Alessandro Araldi, c.1510-1520, oil on wood panel, 18 $3/10$ in. x 13 $4/5$ in., Galleria degli Uffizi, Florence; *Profile Portrait of a Young Woman*, Sofonisba Anguissola, late sixteenth century, oil on canvas, 27 in. x 20 $2/3$ in., The Hermitage, St. Petersburg; *Portrait of Laura Battiferri*, Agnolo Bronzino, c.1555-1560, oil on canvas, 32 $2/3$ in. x 23 $3/5$ in. Palazzo Vecchio, Florence.

[4] *Ideal head of a woman*, Michelangelo, *ca*.1525-28, black chalk on paper, 11 ¼ in. x 9 ¼ in., British Museum, PD 1895-9-15-493.

[5] Alexander Gilchrist, *Life of William Blake* (London: MacMillan, 1880), I: 217.

[6] *The Monthly Magazine, or British Register* Vol. XVI, part II, no 105 (1 Sept 1803) (London: Richard Philips, 1803), 160. Adjusted for inflation, 60,000 guineas of 1803 would have a value today in excess of £5,000,000.

[7] *Supplementary Number to the Fourteenth Volume of the Monthly Magazine* 14: 96 (25 Jan 1803) (London: Richard Phillips, 1803), 602.

[8] Truchsessian Gallery Sale Catalogue (Getty Research Institute Catalogue Number Br-264), "Lot 631, Profile of a Woman, by Ciro Ferri, oil on wood, 1' 3"h x 1'w."

[9] See Description of Sale Catalogue Br-264 at the Getty Research Institute's *Provenance Index Database* online, <http://www.getty.edu/research/tools/provenance/> Accessed 14 July 2014.

[10] *Truchsess Gallery Sale Catalogue*, Getty Research Institute Catalogue Number Br-264.

[11] Leonard Jenyns was offered the post of ship's naturalist aboard the *H.M.S. Beagle* in 1831, but declined due to his obligations as vicar of Swafford Bulbeck. The post went instead to Charles Darwin.

28 The Berry Hill Portrait

Unknown Lady, likely Elizabeth Tudor or Katherine Grey Seymour

Unknown artist

Oil on wood panel; 12 $^5/_8$ in. x 9 in.

Undated

Provenance:

> John Lumsden Propert (*d.*1902);
>
> John Pierpont Morgan (*d.*1913);
>
> Metropolitan Museum of Art, New York;
>
> de-accessioned January 1956;
>
> Parke-Bernet Galleries, sold 25 October 1956;
>
> Berry Hill Galleries, New York until at least 1961;
>
> Private Collection, Scarsdale, New York;
>
> Butterscotch Auctioneers and Appraisers, Pound Ridge, NY, 21 November 2021, Lot 209;
>
> Private Collection.

At least four paintings of strikingly similar appearance can be grouped together under the single category 'Berry Hill Type.' The group centers on the Berry Hill Portrait discussed here, to which is added the Soule Portrait, the Chawton Portrait, and the Syon Portrait, each discussed separately below. Among the four, the Berry Hill Portrait itself evidences the greatest aesthetic artistry, technical skill, and depictional realism. Additionally, infrared reflectography studies conducted in August 2022 revealed a freehand underdrawing without any evidence of the use of a pattern, not even for the face. Changes in the underdrawing are also apparent, the most notable of which is elongation of the fourth and fifth fingers of the proper right hand and minor repositioning of those fingers to open the hand slightly. Cross-hatching indicating contours and shadows also appears on the face, fur collar, gloves, and hands.[1] The overall appearance of the underdrawing suggests that the portrait was executed *ad vivum*, or from a live sitter. Correlation of the visual evidence of greater artistic and aesthetic quality with the results of the IR studies confirms that the Berry Hill portrait is indeed the first produced from amongst the four known versions, there being little need or likelihood that the person depicted would have sat more than once for effectively identical additional portraits by the same or other artists. The Berry Hill

Portrait is therefore considered here to be the prototype for this group.

The Berry Hill Portrait appeared in the historical record for the first time late in the nineteenth century in the collection of John Lumsden Propert of London, founder in 1855 of the Royal Benevolent Medical College, Epsom.[2] Propert focused his leisure time on collecting portrait miniatures of all types. He developed sufficient expertise to enable him to write and to publish *The History of Miniature Art: With Notes on Collectors and Collections* in 1887.[3] He curated early exhibitions of miniatures for the Burlington Fine Arts Club and later exhibited his own extensive collection in 1897.[4] The catalogue for that later exhibition does not include any item that can today be associated with this portrait, however. Neither was the portrait listed in the earlier personal collection catalogue compiled by Propert in 1890.[5] It is therefore not possible to ascertain whom Propert understood the painting to depict nor from whence he acquired it.

Propert's collection was liquidated after his death in 1902, with ownership of this small image passing to the American financier J. Pierpont Morgan. By 1907, the sitter was identified as Lady Jane Grey, and the work was dated quite narrowly to the time of Jane's marriage in May of 1553, with attribution to François Clouet. The Morgan collection catalogue explicitly linked this picture to an engraving published in 1748 by George Vertue (Fig.44, below), though Vertue identified the Syon Portrait as his reference image for the engraving.[6]

Fig. 44: *Lady Jane Grey by George Vertue*

Morgan's son donated a large portion of his father's collection to the Metropolitan Museum of Art in New York City following the senior Morgan's death in 1913. This painting was among those donated. The MMA downgraded the identification of the sitter to *Said to be Lady Jane Grey* and entirely dismissed the attribution to Clouet, preferring instead the generic "British School." The painting was displayed in the MMA's galleries periodically over the next forty years under the new label. The MMA ultimately de-accessioned the portrait in January 1956, along with a significant number of other works that had similarly been re-attributed since their acquisition.[7] The picture was sold at auction in October 1956 by Parke-Bernet Galleries of New York as *Portrait of a Lady*. Berry Hill Galleries purchased it, and it remained with them for at least the next five years. The portrait vanished thereafter into a private collection until late in 2021, when a keen-eyed auction enthusiast spotted it in an online catalogue for Butterscotch Auctioneers and Appraisers in the affluent New York suburb of Westchester County. The consignor(s) identified the sitter as Mary, Queen of Scots, and Butterscotch assigned the lot a pre-sale estimate of USD 5000–10,000.[8] The painting ultimately sold for a total of $158,661 (£118,107) with premiums and with a revised identification as "Probably Elizabeth I."[9]

The multiplicity of identifications throughout the portrait's documented history (Unknown Lady, Jane Grey, Mary Stuart, Elizabeth Tudor) together with the work's status as a likely prototype or reference image of the larger group requires us to examine the evidence carefully in search of a more nearly definitive conclusion. Sir Roy Strong initiated the scholarly research on the Berry Hill Type as a whole in his foundational study *Portraits of Queen Elizabeth I* published in 1963. Strong considered only three of the four paintings from the Berry Hill Type, however: the Berry Hill, the Soule (see p.182), and the Syon Portraits (p.194). He characterized all three as "borderline cases." After adding NPG764 (discussed previously, p.94) to his group, he categorized the four somewhat ambivalently as "Princess Elizabeth: Perhaps Lady Jane Grey."[10] Strong again expressed uncertainty in 1987 when he reiterated that the three portraits "***may*** represent" Elizabeth [emphasis added].[11] He further declared that "no [early] picture remotely resembling an ad vivum likeness is known ... only mechanical workshop productions."[12] It can reasonably be inferred from Strong's statements that, although he considered the Berry Hill Portrait more probably to represent Elizabeth than Jane, he did not consider any of the pictures of the Berry Hill Type to be authentic likenesses of Elizabeth Tudor. That inference is supported by Strong's further assertion that a draft proclamation on portraiture of Elizabeth written in December 1563 was perhaps stimulated by inauthentic portraits of the Berry Hill Type, specifically, already in circulation as portraits of Elizabeth.[13]

A copy of the draft proclamation survives to attest to the concerns voiced by Elizabeth in relation to her portraiture. The proclamation suspended further production and sale of portraits of the Queen that "far erred" in "sufficiently express[ing] the natural representations of her Majesty's person." The moratorium was to last until such time as "some special person" could be appointed to produce an official portrait of which the Queen might herself approve.[14] Whether the errant portraits at issue were those of the Berry Hill Type is not at all clear, however, since the proclamation did not explicitly identify any offending single portrait, group of portraits, or artist(s). And since virtually none of the four surviving portraits of the Berry Hill Type are known to have been identified prior to the early twentieth century as depictions of Elizabeth, it is necessary to consider whether the portraits may depict some other lady of the Tudor period.

Before considering alternative sitters, however, we must first establish a reasonably narrow timeframe during which the Berry Hill Portrait was likely produced. Technological studies conducted following the painting's sale in November 2021 included a dendrochronological analysis of the wood panel support. The preliminary results of that unpublished study indicate a *terminus post quem*, or earliest possible date of panel usage, after about 1545.[15] With consideration given to such time-related variables as processing, shipping, marketing, and storage of the panel prior to use, the usage date could range from about 1550 to as late as 1565.

Further narrowing of this broad timeframe is possible through dating of the ruffs at the neck and wrists of the sitter in the portrait. The sitter wears a neck ruff comprised of two layers of carefully shaped white lawn or linen fabric edged with gold embroidery and that rises to the wearer's ears. Ruffs of this type did not appear in English portraits until about 1558, the last year of the reign of Mary I, though no portrait of Mary wearing a double ruff is known today. Yet ruffs had become sufficiently fashionable by the first months of the reign of Elizabeth I that she is depicted in a portrait commemorating her coronation on 15 January 1559 (Fig.45, below left) wearing one very similar to that seen in Berrry Hill Portrait. Though both the Portland Coronation Miniature and a full-sized version held by the NPG date to no earlier than the late 1580s, they are generally thought to have been derived from a lost original.[16] Evidence supporting the existence of a lost original includes the routine use beginning as early as January 1559 of an image very similar to that of the Coronation Portrait as *incipit* or initial portraits on numerous illuminated royal charters (Fig.46, below right).[17] Further, the wearing of double ruffs of the type seen in the Berry Hill Portrait had become sufficiently widespread by 1562 that the government issued a proclamation in

Fig. 45: Queen Elizabeth I,
Coronation Miniature,
The Portland Collection, Welbeck Abbey

Fig. 46: Incipit *illumination,*
Inspeximus *of Royal Charter, 13 May 1559*
Trinity Hall, Cambridge

May of that year addressing excess in their use.[18] We can therefore conclude, based on correlation of the results of the dendrochronological analysis of the board on which the portrait is painted with the evidence derived from costume dating, that the work dates to no earlier than *ca.*1558 and may have been created as late as the mid 1560s. Use of that timeframe as the principal limiting parameter consequently shortens any list of potential sitters.

The production of multiple copies from a single reference image and the distribution of those copies beyond the sitter's family circle implies that the sitter was a person of some prominence, or what might today be called "famous" or "a celebrity." But since women in sixteenth-century England were not afforded participation in most public spheres of endeavor, the opportunities for any one woman to gain widespread notice were quite limited. Women could not hold elected or appointed public office, for example, and they could not participate openly in the political process. Women were barred from the military and thus did not become military heroes. It was still very rare in the Tudor period for a woman to publish under her own name, so that women seldom gained fame as authors.[19] Neither could they participate in any official capacity in religion, though some did gain fame or notoriety in that sphere, usually through public scandal or martyrdom or both, such as Anne Askew. Yet female religious heroines and martyrs were seldom celebrated through portraiture, owing perhaps in part to the often iconoclastic leanings of religious reformers of the Edwardian and Elizabethan eras. As a result, those women of sixteenth-century England who were likely to merit multiple copies of a portrait intended for distribution beyond the natal family were usually women of royal lineage. The list of women of royal blood who were alive during the widest possible period for this portrait, about 1555 to about 1570 (based on dendrochronological and costume dating plus a generous margin of error), is limited to just eight women: Mary Tudor, Elizabeth Tudor, Mary Stuart, Margaret Douglas, Jane Grey, Katherine Grey, Mary Grey, and Margaret Clifford.

Five of those eight women fail to meet certain basic criteria for identifying them as the sitter. Mary Tudor died in 1558 at the age of 42 years and before ruffs of the type seen in the Berry Hill Portrait became fashionable. Similarly, Jane Grey predeceased Mary Tudor by over four years and well before ruffs made their first appearance in English portraiture. Margaret Douglas was a mature woman of 40 years in 1555 and thus too old to be the young woman depicted here. Conversely, Mary Grey was too young, being just ten years old in 1555 and having yet to gain widespread notice. The Greys' cousin Margaret Clifford can likely be eliminated as well since she did not acquire widespread prominence until she became Elizabeth's heir-presumptive following the deaths of Katherine Grey in 1568 and Mary Grey in 1578.

Mary Stuart can be tentatively eliminated, but not definitively so. The use of French oak in the fabrication of the Berry Hill's panel is unusual in the English context, Baltic oak being far more common. The presence of French oak requires considering a French artist as the creator of the image.[20] Mary Stuart resided in France from early childhood and did not return to the British Isles until August 1561, so it is not out of the realm of possibility that the painting was executed in France, transported to England, and the Soule and Chawton/Hever variants were then painted in England. Mary was, after all, Elizabeth's heir by feudal right and custom, and the two engaged in a long-running dispute over Mary's claim to the English crown. Mary also enjoyed significant support from among English Catholics who opposed Elizabeth's Protestantism.

Analysis of the surviving iconography of Mary Stuart reveals that artists did not depict her wearing ruffs until after about 1565, however.[21] Additionally, the unadorned presentation of the sitter in this portrait contrasts sharply with the more opulent presentations of Mary Stuart in her contemporaneous portraiture. It is nonetheless noteworthy that Mary wears an identical string of white beads knotted at the chest in a portrait dated to 1558-61 and attributed to the French artist François Clouet, the artist formerly associated with the Berry Hill Portrait.[22] But, if we tentatively eliminate Mary Stuart of Scotland as the sitter, the list of royal ladies potentially identifiable as the sitter depicted in the Berry Hill shortens to just Elizabeth Tudor and Katherine Grey.

Several factors impact differentiation between the two candidates. Roy Strong asserted in 1963, for example, that "the full frontal image is entirely consistent with the early Elizabeth iconography."[23] Strong based his assertion on a comparison of the sitter's position in the Berry Hill Portrait to the position of the sitter(s) in the Soule Portrait and the Syon Portrait, both of which he believed to date to *ca.*1559. The Soule Portrait is a copy of the Berry Hill Portrait (see p.172), however, and is therefore no longer useful as corroborating evidence. The Syon Portrait dates to no earlier than 1602 (see p.196) and is also a copy of the Berry Hill Portrait, rendering it similarly no longer useful as corroborating evidence. Strong also compared the sitter's position in the Berry Hill Portrait to Elizabeth's position in both the full-sized and the miniature versions of the Coronation Portrait, again believing each to date to *ca.*1559. Yet the full-sized version of the Coronation Portrait has since been reliably dated to no earlier than the 1590s, while the miniature version has been equally reliably dated to *ca.* 1600.[24]

The two versions of the Coronation Portrait exhibit numerous differences in detail, but both are nonetheless commonly believed to have been based on a single 'lost original.' Yet the only other images of Queen Elizabeth wearing full coronation attire known today are the large number of early *incipit* illuminations similar or identical to the illumination in Figure 40 (p.150), as well as Elizabeth's image on certain coinage of 1558-1561.[25] Given that the coronation miniature and the full-sized version both date to the end of Elizabeth's reign rather than the beginning, it is not out of the realm of possibility that each was based, at least in terms of overall composition, on the many *incipit* illuminations from the first years of the reign, each respective artist having created costuming details through reference to other portraits of Elizabeth. In other words, the two Coronation Portraits may simply have been derived directly from the *incipit* type, with the costume for each rendered through an exercise in artistic license. Regardless, the only images remaining from amongst the authentic "early Elizabeth iconography" known to Strong in 1963 for his comparison to the Berry Hill Portrait is the large body of *incipit* illuminations, all of which adhere to the ancient iconographic topos of 'monarch enthroned.'

Elizabeth Tudor does not appear "full frontal," or squared front, in any of her other painted portraiture, with one exception. Her body, her head, or both are instead turned a few degrees to the viewer's left in a portrait of 1546 (Fig.47, p.163, top left), the Clopton series (Fig.48, p.163, top right), and NPG4449 (Fig.49, p.163, bottom left), though the eyes do directly engage the viewer in those portraits. The only confirmed early portrait of Elizabeth I other than the *incipit* illuminations and in which she is truly squared front is the Philp Portrait (Fig.50, p.163, bottom right), but that image was not available to Strong in 1963.[26] Further, at least seven of the women included in Hans Holbein's series of drawings of Henrician courtiers of the 1530s and 1540s are depicted fully squared front, as are at least three of the male sitters. And Katherine Grey appears "full frontal" or squared front and with eyes engaging the viewer in the Belvoir miniature dateable to 1562 (Fig.54, p.164). The positioning of the sitter in the Berry Hill Portrait is therefore not conclusive in identifying the sitter.

The dark brown color of the eyes in the Berry Hill portrait might initially appear to support identifying the sitter as Elizabeth Tudor since her eyes appear dark brown in her portrait of *ca.*1546

Fig. 47: *Elizabeth when Princess, ca.1546*

Fig. 48: *The Clopton Portrait*

Fig. 49: *NPG 4449*

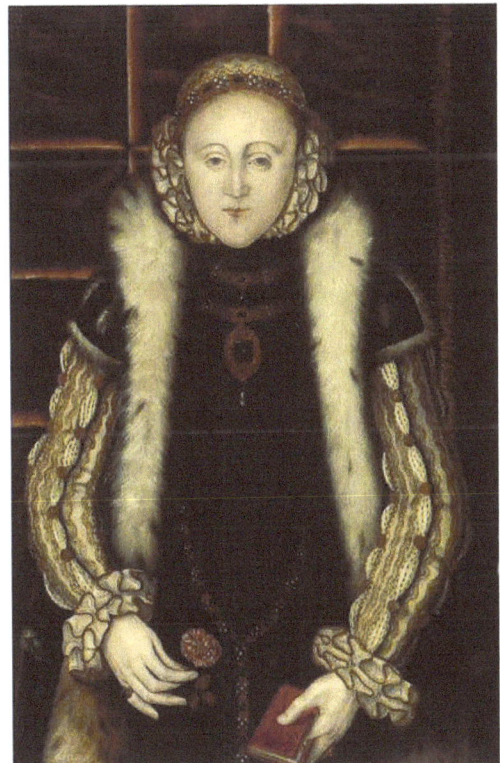

Fig. 50: *The Philp Portrait*

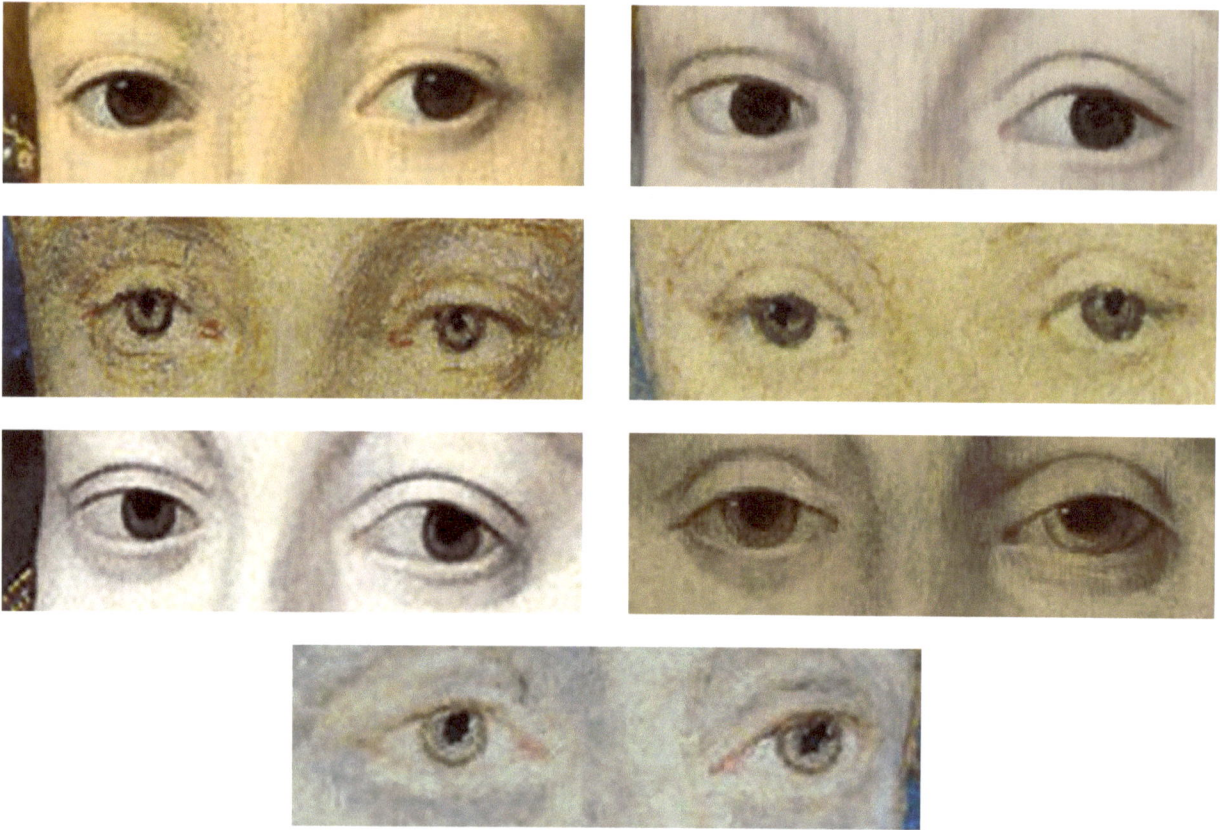

Figs. 51-57: *The eyes of Elizabeth I as depicted in (left to right and top to bottom) RCIN404444, NPG4449, RCIN420944, RCIN420987, the Clopton Portrait, the Philp Portrait, and a miniature by Hilliard.*

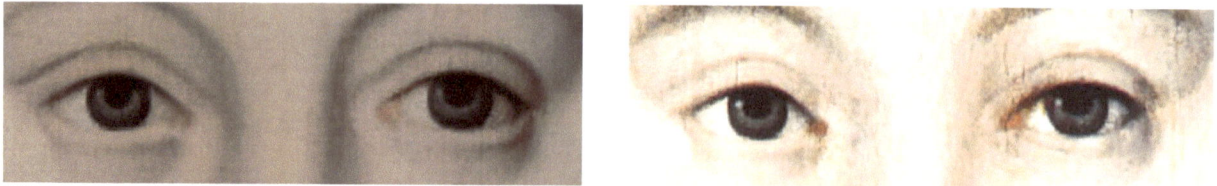

Fig. 58 and 59: *The eyes of the sitter(s) depicted in the Soule (left) and Chawton/Hever (right) Portraits.*

Fig. 60: *Katherine Grey Seymour and son Edward Seymour, Lord Beauchamp of Hache, ca.1562. (The Belvoir Miniature, shown actual size)*

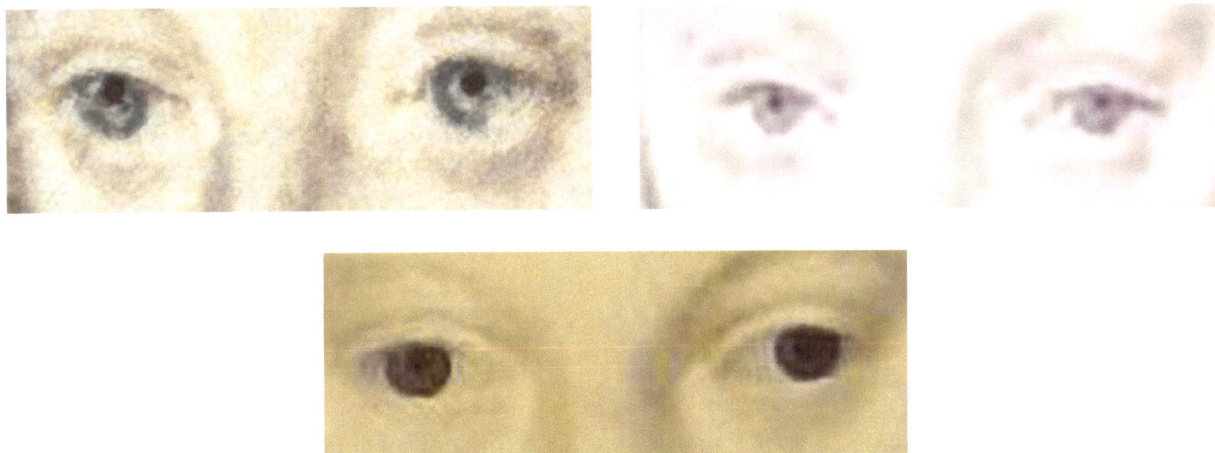

Figs. 61-63: *Katherine Grey Seymour's eyes depicted in the V&A miniature, the Belvoir miniature, and the Syon full-sized portrait.*

(Fig.47).[27] But as Strong noted in 1963, the color of Elizabeth's eyes is remarkably inconsistent in her portraiture, and no written documentation survives to attest to her eye color.[28] Though the eyes are dark brown in NPG4449, they are light gray-brown in two miniatures now in the Royal Collection, blue-gray in the Clopton portrait, an almost golden color in the Philp portrait, and a very pale, almost white color in a miniature by Nicholas Hilliard dated 1572 (Figs. 51-57, p.164).[29] And the eyes in the Soule and Chawton/Hever copies of the Berry Hill Portrait are a dark gray-blue rather than the brown of the original (Figs.58 and 59, p.164). When considered as a whole, the color of the sitter's eyes must be regarded as inconclusive for identifying the sitter as Elizabeth I, there being no reliable indication of the color of Elizabeth's eyes.

Neither is the color of the eyes useful in identifying the sitter as Katherine Grey. Her eyes are depicted as light blue in an early miniature now in the collection of the Victoria and Albert Museum (Fig.61, top left) as well as in the Belvoir miniature (Fig.62, top right). The eyes appear brown in color with specks of gray in the full-sized version of the Belvoir Miniature now at Syon House and on wood panel, however (Fig.63, above center), contrasting sharply with the light blue color in the two miniatures.[30] Thus, just as with the iconography of Elizabeth I, that of Katherine Grey offers only contradictory evidence for determining the authentic color of Katherine's eyes, limiting use of that physical characteristic when considering either woman as the sitter in the portrait.

The sitter in the Berry Hill Portrait wears a costume of remarkable simplicity for any Tudor English woman of high status, much less one of Tudor royal blood. The headgear consists of what appears to be a bonnet with a rigid or semi-rigid forward-facing brim and a non-rigid posterior portion, beneath all of which lies a coif with a ruffled edge embellished with gold embroidery. The bonnet contrasts with the French hoods customarily worn by almost all women of high status in English portraiture of the mid-Tudor period, including those worn by Elizabeth herself in two of her early portraits.[31] It is nonetheless roughly similar in appearance but not fully identical to the headgear worn by Elizabeth in NPG4449 and the Clopton series, though a posterior fall enshrouding the hair is brought forward and carefully folded atop the crown of the head in those images.[32] In contrast, Katherine wears only a coif in the Belvoir miniature and the Syon enlargement, and she wears a French hood in the V&A miniature. Thus the headgear, if considered in isolation, appears

Fig. 64: *Katherine Grey Seymour, the V&A miniature (shown actual size)*

to favor identifying Elizabeth as the sitter.

Other elements of the costume are either inconclusive or argue against Elizabeth as the sitter, however. The sitter clutches a pair of leather gloves, a common iconographic symbol denoting wealth and freedom from work or labor. Yet even though gloves do appear frequently in portraits of Elizabeth, they are certainly not exclusive to her iconography. Numerous other female sitters of the Tudor era similarly hold gloves in their hands.[33] Additionally, a two-layered ruff appears in each of the several portraits of Elizabeth discussed thus far, but Katherine also wears a two-layered ruff in all her confirmed portraits. Similarly, the white fur collar or stole appears in each of those many portraits, though the front of Katherine's coat is secured up to the neck in the V&A miniature (Fig.64, above left).[34]

Historians have consistently identified the fur collars or stoles in portraits of the Berry Hill Type as ermine, a fur commonly associated with royalty, but that identification does not bear up to close scrutiny.[35] The outer coarse hairs, or guard hairs, of ermine (*Mustela erminea*) seldom exceed 15mm (0.6 in.) in length while the soft fine underfur or pelage is seldom more than 10mm (0.4 in.) in length.[36] The individual hairs of the fur depicted in portraits of the Berry Hill Type are significantly longer. Additionally, ermine is a silky fur that lies close to the surface of the hide, whereas the fur seen here appears coarse and stands up from the surface. Lastly, any dark spots present on ermine garments are artificially created through attachment of ermine tail tips, which remain black even in winter. The resulting spots are small, entirely black, well defined, and often regularly spaced. In contrast, the spots on the Berry Hill sitter's garment are large relative to ermine tails, are variegated in color, exhibit diffuse margins, and are irregularly spaced. The fur seen here cannot be identified definitively but may be lynx belly fur. Sumptuary laws promulgated in 1533 notably limited the wearing of lynx fur to members of the royal family but failed to mention ermine.[37]

Only the jewels vary to any significant degree amongst the images under discussion. In the V&A miniature of Katherine, the ties at the front closure, at the shoulders, and along the sleeves are all embellished with almost two dozen pairs of gold aiglettes, visually supplementing the billiments of goldwork and gemstones adorning her French hood. None of these elements are present in the Belvoir miniature or the Syon enlargement, however. In comparison, Elizabeth wears in NPG4449, the Clopton series, and the Philp portrait not only numerous pairs of aiglettes, but an important royal jewel as well. The jewel takes the form of a necklace of clusters of pearls alternated with goldwork quatrefoils set with what are probably single-cut or 'pointed' diamonds. A large quatrefoil of goldwork hangs from the necklace and is set with a very large single-cut or 'pointed' diamond.[38] From that hangs a large teardrop-shaped pearl. The necklace and pendant are remarkably like Mary's neck jewel included in portraits of her by Hans Eworth and Antonis Mor.[39] In sharp contrast, the jewels in the Berry Hill portrait are limited to a single long strand of white beads, perhaps pearls, worn knotted over the breast. The absence of goldwork, colored stones, and/or diamonds is entirely anomalous in the iconography of Elizabeth Tudor specifically and of the Tudor royal family more generally. Such an anomaly requires explanation if the sitter is to be identified as Elizabeth I, yet no such explanation is readily apparent to this author.

Having considered the Berry Hill Portrait in the context of Elizabeth I's iconography, we must likewise consider it in the context of Katherine Grey's limited iconography. This facilitates further situating the portrait in a broader political, religious, social, cultural, and even familial context.

And within that broader set of contexts, it is important first to recognize Katherine Grey's status as heir-presumptive to Elizabeth I from November 1559 until Katherine's death in January 1568. The Third Act for the Succession (1543/4) together with the Last Will and Testament of Henry VIII stipulated that, should Mary and Elizabeth Tudor both fail to produce heirs of their own bodies, the crown should pass to the line descended from Henry VIII's younger sister Mary Tudor Brandon.[40] Katherine Grey was Mary Tudor's eldest surviving granddaughter after the death of her elder sister Jane Grey in 1554.

Elizabeth regarded both Katherine and her younger sister Mary Grey with suspicion owing to the treasonous events surrounding the royal succession of 1553, and the new queen initially demoted Katherine from Lady of the Privy Chamber to Lady of the Presence Chamber. That did little to limit the attention focused on Katherine, however, especially as long as Elizabeth refused to marry.[41] The Spanish ambassadors noted that Katherine herself even frequently reminded those around her of her claim to the throne and became visibly annoyed whenever that claim was minimized or overlooked.[42]

But more importantly, the Spanish communicated directly with Katherine in regard to a short-lived plot to smuggle Katherine out of England and to marry her to a Hapsburg prince. Then, should Elizabeth die without having married and were Katherine to accede successfully to the English crown, Spain would be assured of English support in its ongoing disputes with France.[43] The death of Francis II in December 1560 brought an end to that scheme, however, and Katherine soon found herself back in Elizabeth's good graces. The Spanish ambassador even reported that Elizabeth briefly suggested formally adopting Katherine, if only "in order to keep her quiet."[44] But in light of these Spanish aims, we must consider the Berry Hill Portrait in the context of courtship portraiture that customarily circulated throughout Europe.

In a related pre-marital context, but perhaps a more significant one, several members of the English Privy Council supported a marriage late in 1560 between Katherine Grey as Elizabeth's heir presumptive and James Hamilton, 3rd Earl of Arran as heir presumptive through a maternal line to Queen Mary Stuart of Scotland.[45] Hamilton carried the advantage of being a follower of the reformed ('Protestant') Scottish church and an opponent of Queen Mary Stuart. Such a marriage would not only ensure peace between England and Scotland and preserve a reformed religious settlement throughout Great Britain but would also have the important additional benefit of preventing a marriage between a future Queen Katherine and any Roman Catholic continental prince or monarch.[46] Support for a Grey-Hamilton marriage was sufficiently strong that the English diplomat Thomas Randolph, sent to Scotland in September 1560 to treat secretly with Hamilton regarding Hamilton's siege of the Scottish city of Leith, reported back to Elizabeth's chief minister, Sir William Cecil, that the match was all but certain.[47] If the Berry Hill Portrait depicts Katherine Grey, it was quite possibly created as a pre-marital portrait during the brief period late in 1560 when Katherine figured at the forefront of English foreign relations and just months before her relations with Elizabeth degenerated irreparably.

Katherine's status as Elizabeth's heir again became complicated when the queen declared late in 1560 her desire to marry Robert Dudley, son of the much-despised late John Dudley, Duke of Northumberland. Many blamed the elder Dudley for the alteration of the succession in 1553, and son Robert earned a scandalous reputation of his own in September 1560 following the death of his wife Amy Robsart in questionable circumstances. The queen's choice of consort thus carried little support, and even the queen's trusted advisor and chief minister William Cecil advised strongly against it lest it result in political instability.[48] But so long as the queen refused to marry, the realm faced a succession crisis, and many English Protestants looked to Katherine as the heir preferrable to Elizabeth's feudal heir or heir-in-blood, the Roman Catholic Mary Stuart, Queen of Scotland. That crisis took an unexpected turn, however, when Katherine Grey secretly married Edward Seymour, Earl of Hertford and the eldest son of Edward Seymour, Duke of Somerset and a man still much-loved in public memory as Lord Protector in the first years of the reign of Edward VI. Katherine and the Earl of Hertford wed late in 1560, and Katherine bore the first of two sons in September 1561. Upon learning of the clandestine marriage and Katherine's pregnancy, the queen committed Katherine to the Tower of London in August 1561.[49] Katherine remained there until 1563 when, following the birth of a second son by Seymour, she was removed to a succession of custodians at various estates well beyond London and far from Seymour.

Despite her imprisonment for the last seven years of her life, Katherine retained the support of a significant number of ranking political figures in her claim to the throne. When Elizabeth fell ill with smallpox in October 1562 and briefly became comatose, the Privy Council conducted emergency debates on the issue of the succession, and many councillors favored Katherine as successor to Elizabeth. Others supported Henry Hastings, Earl of Huntington as the sole adult male candidate, though his claim was tenuous at best, while still others supported Mary Stuart.[50] Katherine's marital status posed certain issues for her claim, however, since Elizabeth had commissioned an inquiry in 1562 that resulted in an official annulment of the marriage and that made her sons illegitimate and thus ineligible to succeed to the crown. Yet Katherine was the only heir to Elizabeth that had thus far produced issue, and that issue was conveniently male.[51]

It is likely in a context of personal rehabilitation to the succession that the Belvoir miniature was produced. In that miniature, as noted above, Katherine is positioned fully squared front, just as in the Berry Hill Portrait. Further, she holds up her infant son and heir as if assertively presenting him to the viewer, and she wears a visual memento of her husband Edward, son of the late Lord Protector. Martin Spies dates the Belvoir miniature to late 1562 or early 1563, at the time of or in the immediate wake of the succession crisis brought about by Elizabeth's near-fatal bout with smallpox.[52] Spies also argues that the miniature, currently in the collection of the Manners dukes of Rutland at Belvoir Castle, perhaps came to the Manners collection from Petworth House in about 1750, when Katherine's descendant Frances Seymour, daughter of the 6th Duke of Somerset, married John Manners, Marquess of Granby.[53] That transmittal provides an important link between the Seymours, the Belvoir miniature, and the iconography of Katherine Grey that survives today at Syon House, and that link will become relevant in a subsequent discussion of the Syon Portrait.

In summary, the evidence related to the Berry Hill Portrait indicates that it was likely created between 1558 and 1562 and that it is an *ad vivum* portrait. The squared front positioning of the sitter is consistent with both the Philp portrait of Elizabeth Tudor and the Belvoir miniature portrait of Katherine Grey, though it varies from the positioning of Elizabeth in NPG4449 and the Clopton series as well as from the positioning of Katherine in the V&A miniature. And while the color of the eyes matches that of Elizabeth's eyes in her portrait as a princess circa 1546 but not that of Katherine's eyes in the Belvoir miniature, the eye color of both women varies across a wide spectrum in their other portraits. The costume worn by the sitter is sufficiently plain to be anomalous when compared to the surviving iconography of Elizabeth, but consistent with Katherine's simple costume in both the Belvoir and the V&A miniatures. Lastly, no written records have yet been uncovered to enable conclusively identifying the sitter depicted in the Berry Hill Portrait. Therefore, in the absence of any evidence toward a definitive identification, the only label that can reasonably be applied to the portrait is "Unknown Lady circa 1558-1562, likely Elizabeth Tudor or Katherine Grey."

1 The owner(s) of the Berry Hill Portrait very kindly allowed this author access to the infrared reflectography images on the condition that they not be published without permission. That permission was ultimately not given.

2 Metropolitan Museum of Art, Object File for MMA 17.190.6.

3 John Lumsden Propert, *The History of Miniature Art: With Notes on Collectors and Collections* (London: MacMillan and Company, 1887).

4 "Obituary, John Lumsden Propert, M.B.Lond., M.R.C.S., L.S.A," *British Medical Journal* 1:2150 (15 March 1902), 638; *Catalogue of the Historical Collection of Miniatures formed by Mr J Lumsden Propert* (London: Burlington Fine Arts Society, 1897).

5 John Lumsden Propert, *Catalogues of Miniatures, Enamels, Pastels, and Waxes, at 112, Gloucester Place, Portman Square* (London: William Clowes and Sons, 1890).

6 *Pictures in the Collection of J. Pierpont Morgan at Princes Gate and Dover House, London*, intro. T. Humphry Ward (London: Privately Printed, 1907), f.64r-66r. *Lady Jane Grey*, George Vertue, 1748, line engraving, 18 ³/₈ in. x 22 ¼ in., National Portrait Gallery, NPG D32035; George Vertue, "Notebooks," *The Sixteenth Volume of the Walpole Society*, 1937-38 5 (1938), 50.

7 Katherine Baetjer, "Buying Pictures for New York: The Founding Purchase of 1871," *Metropolitan Museum Journal* 38 (2004), 161-190.

8 "The Lost 'Berry-Hill' portrait of Lady Jane Grey: An unrecognized gem at auction in the US," *The Auction Augur*, 14 November 2021. <https://auctionaugur.blogspot.com/2021/11/the-lost-berry-hill-portrait-of-lady.html> Accessed 19 January 2024.

9 "Early Portrait of Elizabeth I Sells for $158,661 at Butterscotch," *Antiques and the Arts Weekly*, 22 November 2021. < https://www.antiquesandthearts.com/early-portrait-of-elizabeth-i-sells-for-158661-at-butterscotch/> Accessed 19 January 2024.

10 Roy Strong, *Portraits of Queen Elizabeth I* (Clarendon Press, 1963), 53-54.

11 Roy Strong, *Gloriana: The Portraits of Queen Elizabeth I* (Thames and Hudson, 1983), 52.

12 Strong, *Gloriana*, 59.

13 Strong, *Gloriana*, 59. More probably, portraits of what Strong referred to as the Clopton Type were the inspiration for the proclamation.

14 National Archives, State Papers 12/31/25, f.46r-v.

15 "Tree Ring Analysis of a Panel Painting," December 2022, Daniel Miles, Oxford Dendrochronology Laboratory, Oxford University, with Ian Tyers, Dendrochronological Consultancy Ltd, UK.

16 *Queen Elizabeth I*, Nicholas Hilliard, ca.1600, 89mm x 56mm, Harley Foundation, Portland Collection, Welbeck Abbey. *Queen Elizabeth I*, Unknown English Artist, ca.1600, oil on panel, 50 ¹/₈ in. x 39 ¼ in., National Portarit Gallery, NPG 5175.

17 *Inspeximus* confirming the royal charter for Trinity Hall, Cambridge, dated 13 May 1559. <https://oldlibrarytrinityhall.files.wordpress.com/2020/11/68995e76-023f-444e-be1f-dc9b50578fc4_1_201_a.jpeg>Accessed 23 May 2023.

18 Susan Vincent, *Dressing the Elite: Clothes in Early Modern England* (Oxford: Berg, 2003), 128 and n.55.

19 Katherine Parr was the first woman to publish under her own name during her own lifetime, in the mid 1540s, and only after becoming queen-consort to Henry VIII and acquiring the power and prestige associated with that royal status.

20 My thanks to Bendor Grosvenor for suggesting the possibility of a French connection.

21 Mary Stuart wears a ruffle-edged under-partlet, for example, in a portrait dendrochronologically dated to no earlier than 1560. See *Mary, Queen of Scots*, Unknown Artist, ca.1560-1592, oil on panel, 9 ⁷/₈ in. x 7 ¹/₂ in., National Portrait Gallery, NPG1766.

22 *Mary, Queen of Scots*, François Clouet, ca.1558-1560, watercolour on vellum, 8.3 cm. x 5.7 cm., The Royal Collection (UK), RCIN 401229.

23 Strong, *Portraits of Queen Elizabeth I*, 53-54.

24 Charlotte Bolland, *Tudor and Jacobean Portraits* (London: NPG, 2018), 32; Fiona Clapperton, "Elizabeth:

The Coronation Miniature," The Harley Foundation, Welbeck Abbey. <https://harleyfoundation.org.uk/explore/entry/coronation-miniature/> Accessed 7 February 2024.

[25] Elizabeth I appears enthroned and wearing full coronation attire on the sovereign and ryal denominations of the coinage of 1558-1561.

[26] The Philp Portrait (Fig.44, p.153) was discovered in the early 1970s by the art dealer Richard Philp. See Richard Philp, "Defrocking a Flapper Girl," <http://antiques.richardphilp.com/stories/de-frocking-a-flapper-girl/> Accessed 23 May 2023. It does depict Elizabeth "full frontal" and was dendrochronologically dated in the mid 1970s by Dr. J.M. Fletcher, a pioneer in the field, to *ca.*1566. That finding has since been challenged, however. See Jennifer Hillam and Ian Tyers, "Reliability and repeatability in dendrochronological analysis: tests using the Fletcher archive of panel-painting data," *Archaeometry* 37:2 (August 2007), 395-405. The Philp Portrait sold through Sotheby's (London) on 4 December 2008 as Lot 2, with the buyer unknown.

[27] X-ray fluorescence demonstrates that the brown color of the eyes in the Berry Hill Portrait are original and not the result of pigment degradation, as can sometimes occur with the use of the blue pigment smalt, which often degrades to brown or golden brown over time. "Scientific Analysis Report 2206," Scientific Analysis of Fine Art LLC (New York), 20 August 2022, 14-15.

[28] Strong, *Portraits of Queen Elizabeth I*, 17.

[29] *Elizabeth I*, British School, watercolour on vellum laid on card, *ca.*1560-1565, Royal Collection Trust, RCIN420944; *Elizabeth I*, British School, watercolour on vellum laid on playing card, *ca.*1565, Royal Collection Trust, RCIN420987; *Queen Elizabeth I*, Nicholas Hilliard, watercolour on vellum, 1572, NPG108.

[30] The Belvoir miniature and the larger version on wood panel at Syon are likely roughly contemporaneous, though the larger has yet to undergo dendrochronological analysis. Another copy on canvas hangs in the Print Room at Syon and significantly post-dates the others.

[31] See, for example, the portrait of 1546 (Fig.42, p.153) now in the Royal Collection and a miniature said to depict Elizabeth *ca.*1565 and also in the Royal Collection (*Elizabeth I*, British School, watercolour on vellum on playing card, *ca.*1565, Royal Collection

Trust, RCIN420987).

[32] The headgear may represent a transitional form between the French hood popular from the 1530s through the reign of Mary I and the *atifet* popularized later in the reign of Elizabeth. Atifets have a heart-shaped or 'widow's peak' brim rather than the linear brim seen here. The headgear worn by Katherine Grey in the Belvoir miniature has the shape of an atifet but appears to be a linen coif rather than a bonnet.

[33] See, for example, the several portraits of Mary I by Hans Eworth and Antonis Mor, in many of which Mary holds a pair of gloves. See also *Portrait of a Woman, probably Mary, Lady Scudamore*, Marcus Gheerhaerts the Younger, 1601, Yale Center for British Art, New Haven, CT; *Portrait of a lady*, Unknown artist, 1576, The Tate, London; *Portrait of Elizabeth Fitzgerald, Countess of Lincoln*, Unknown artist, inscribed 1560, Agecroft Hall, Richmond, VA; or *Portrait of a Lady*, Attributed to William Scrots, undated mid sixteenth century, Christie's London, Lot 182 in sale of 7 December 2011.

[34] Katherine Grey removed the sleeves, a separate and distinct article of clothing in the Tudor era, for the Belvoir miniature and the Syon enlargement, consistent with her removal of a bonnet likely worn over the coif.

[35] See, for example, Elizabeth McFadden, "Fur Dress, Art, and Class Identity in Sixteenth- and Seventeenth-Century England and Holland," Unpublished PhD diss., University of California, Berkeley (2019), 378.

[36] Mária Tóth, "Identification of Hungarian Mustelidae and other small carnivores using guard hair analysis," *Acta Zoologica Academiae Scientiarum Hungaricae* 48:3 (January 2002), 242 and 248.

[37] 24 Henry VIII, c. 13: An Acte for Reformacyon of Excesse in Apparayle.

[38] Artists of the Tudor era sometimes rendered diamonds as black owing to their transparency and a resulting tendency to display the darkness of shadows usually present behind the setting. Silver metallic pigments might also be used, and silver metal usually oxidizes or tarnishes to black over time.

[39] The large pendant pearl has usually been identified as 'La Peregrina,' a pearl of 204 grains discovered in Panama in 1513. 'La Peregrina' was famously purchased by Richard Burton in 1969 and given to his wife, Elizabeth Taylor. Recent research, however,

suggests that the pearl worn by Mary Tudor and her sister Elizabeth Tudor was 'The Tudor Pearl,' also called 'The Mary Tudor Pearl' or 'The Pearl of Kuwait,' weighing 258 grains. See https://www.medieval.eu/the-tudor-pearl-owned-by-mary-tudor/. That pearl was auctioned at Christie's, London on 24 November 2004 as Lot 255, fetching £150,850. https://www.christies.com/lot/lot401819?ldp_

[40] 35 Henry VIII c.1; "Last Will and Testament of King Henry VIII," *Rymer's Foedera* Volume XV, edited by Thomas Rymer (London, 1726-1735), 110-117.

[41] Leanda de Lisle, *The Sisters Who Would Be Queen: The Tragedy of Mary, Katherine, and Lady Jane Grey* (London: Harper's Press, 2008), 181.

[42] Gómez Suárez de Figueroa y Córdoba, Count de Feria to King Philip II of Spain, 24 March 1559, *Calendar of State Papers, Spain* (Simancas), I:45-46.

[43] De Lisle, *Sisters Who Would Be Queen*, 188-189.

[44] Bishop Álvaro de la Quadra to the Count de Feria, undated January 1560, *CSPS*, I:122.

[45] De Lisle, *Sisters Who Would Be Queen*, 200-201.

[46] See Stephen Alford, *The Early Elizabethan Polity: William Cecil and the British Succession Crisis, 1558-1589* (Cambridge, 1998), 71-96 for a thorough discussion of Anglo-Scottish relations between 1560 and 1563 and the role played in amongst the English by James Hamilton.

[47] Thomas Randolph to William Cecil, 23 September 1560, *Calendar of State Papers Foreign: Elizabeth* (HMSO: 1865), III:309-327.

[48] De Lisle, *Sisters Who Would Be Queen*, 199-204.

[49] De Lisle, *Sisters Who Would Be Queen*, 214-15.

[50] Hastings was the son of Catherine Pole, herself a fourth-generation descendant of George, Duke of Clarence, younger brother of King Edward IV and King Richard III.

[51] Henry Hastings, though wed in 1553 to Katherine Dudley, daughter of John Dudley, Duke of Northumberland and sister of Robert Dudley, Earl of Leicester, died without issue in 1595. Mary Stuart, widowed in 1560, remained unmarried and childless until 1565, when she embarked upon her ill-fated marriage to Henry, Lord Darnley and in 1566 bore a son, the future King James VI & I of Scotland and England.

[52] Martin Spies, "The Portrait of Lady Katherine Grey and Her Son: Iconographic Medievalism as a Legitimation Strategy," *Early Modern Medievalisms: The Interplay Between Scholarly Reflection and Artistic Production*, edited by Alicia Montoya, Sophie van Romburgh, and Wim van Anrooij (Brill, 2010), 165-190.

[53] Frances Seymour was the daughter of Charles Seymour, 6th Duke of Somerset, who was in turn the great-grandson of Edward, Lord Beauchamp, depicted in Katherine's arms in the miniature.

29   The Soule Portrait

Called Elizabeth I, possibly Katherine Grey Seymour

Unknown artist

Oil on wood panel; 13 ¼ in. x 11 in.

Undated

Provenance:

Christie's London, 24 May 1937, Lot 131, A Young Lady by Clouet;

Annie Elizabeth Snowden Raworth, Madame de Saint Jean, Manoir de St Jean, Jersey;

Christie's, 12 February 1954, Lot 12, as "A Girl by Clouet";

Leger Galleries, London, as "Queen Elizabeth *ca*.1560 by unknown artist";

Gardner Bosworth Soule, Queens, New York (*d*.2000);

Private collection.

It should be apparent to even the most casual viewer that there is a strong iconographic relationship between the Berry Hill Portrait just discussed and the Soule Portrait seen here. It appears all but certain that the Soule Portrait was simply copied from the Berry Hill Portrait. But the Soule Portrait displays an inferior artistic quality, and the copyist made several alterations during the copying process. The Soule Portrait is only a bust length, for example, rather than a half length like the Berry Hill. Chamfering done long ago on the reverse of the panel suggests it was a deliberate compositional choice made by the copyist rather than the result of the panel having been cut down later. Additionally, the hands and gloves included in the Berry Hill Portrait lie beyond the compositional field of the Soule Portrait. The crown of the bonnet is likewise absent in the Soule Portrait. Further, the gold embellishment of the hat brim in the Berry Hill Portrait is here absent. The fur boa or coat collar is prominently spotted in the Soule Portrait, whereas spotting is only faintly detectable in the Berry Hill Portrait.[1] The ruff in the Soule Portrait is considerably larger in every dimension. And in regard to the physicality of the sitter, the forehead is wider in the Soule than in the Berry Hill, and the hairline is shaped like a wide inverted V, causing the face to appear more diamond-shaped in the Soule Portrait. Lastly, the eyes in the Soule Portrait are grey-blue rather than the medium brown of the Berry Hill Portrait.

The Soule Portrait is unusual in the context of the portraiture of Lady Jane Grey in that, despite its considerable similarity to the Berry Hill Portrait, it was not formally identified as a depiction of Jane until Strong suggested the possibility early in the 1960s. Instead, the lady remained entirely unidentified throughout the first decades of the painting's documented history, though the work was attributed to the French artist François Clouet, much like the Berry Hill Portrait.

In a first-effort to identify the sitter following acquisition of the portrait in 1954, Leger Galleries sought the opinion of David Piper, Assistant Keeper of the National Portrait Gallery. Piper noted that the image bore a resemblance to numerous portraits said to depict Jane Grey, including the Berry Hill and Syon Portraits, though none of those other portraits had ever been fully authenticated. But Piper determined that the sitter was unlikely to be Jane Grey based on the costume, which he dated to "the period 1555/65, probably about 1560." He further noted a similarity between the sitter depicted here and a miniature portrait of Elizabeth formerly in the collection of the Duke of Portland (Fig.45, p.160).[3] He found the correlation "not decisive," however, and judged his own conclusion as little more than "a reasonable likelihood."[4] Leger accepted Piper's very tentative assessment as definitive and subsequently exhibited the painting at the London Antiques Dealers Fair of 1954 as a portrait of Elizabeth I.[5] No evidence survives to indicate that either Mr Piper or Leger Galleries considered any other candidate-sitter beyond Jane Grey and Elizabeth Tudor.

Leger's ready acceptance of a "reasonable likelihood" as outright fact may perhaps have been motivated by financial considerations, even if only in part. Certainly a portrait identified as Queen Elizabeth I would have generated greater interest among potential buyers in 1954 than a portrait of an unknown lady, of Jane Grey, or of Katherine Grey Seymour. And it is perhaps significant that on 2 June 1953, just eight months before Leger acquired this portrait, the United Kingdom had celebrated the coronation of Queen Elizabeth II. International publicity and media attention on a scale never before associated with a coronation accompanied that event, including the first television broadcast of a coronation ceremony. Additionally, not only did the new young queen share a name with the supposed sitter in this portrait, but 1953 had also marked the 350th anniversary of the death of the first Elizabeth. It is not inconceivable that Leger Galleries sought to capitalize in 1954 on the historical events of the preceding year and therefore accepted as essentially factual what was in reality a mere possibility. Piper's very tentative opinion of 1954, in which he expressed only a "reasonable likelihood," would ultimately dictate how every other portrait of the Berry Hill Type was labeled and re-labeled from that point forward.

Roy Strong later relied heavily on Piper's prior judgment, for example, when writing his own studies of the iconography of Elizabeth. Strong re-identified the sitters in the Berry Hill and Syon Portraits, both of which had long been thought to depict Jane Grey, bringing them into conformity with Piper's opinion on the Soule Portrait. But as has been noted, Strong labeled the entire group somewhat ambivalently as "Princess Elizabeth: Perhaps Lady Jane Grey."[6] Strong seemingly did not first carefully consider any alternative sitters before accepting and repeating Piper's opinion. Strong did, however, follow Piper's lead by comparing the facial image depicted across the entire group to several miniature portraits of Elizabeth that appeared as illuminations at the heads of official documents during the first years of her reign.[7] In most of those images, Elizabeth was positioned squared front, much like the sitters of the Berry Hill Type. But unlike portraits of that type, the Elizabethan illuminations depicted the queen crowned and enthroned, and the faces within the many miniature images were little more than two-dimensional cartoons or caricatures (Fig.65).[8]

The illuminations are examples of an iconographic topos of 'monarch enthroned' rather than faithful portraits, as previously noted. Strong seemed to imply, however, that the squared-front positioning was a marker of Elizabeth's portraiture exclusively, without apparent consideration of the many other portraits of decidedly non-royal English women of the Tudor period in which the sitter was similarly positioned squared front.[9] But as has been noted, Strong did express increasing uncertainty in his several successive works on Elizabethan and Tudor portraiture regarding identifying the sitter in the Berry Hill Type as Princess Elizabeth.[10] Yet despite the

Fig. 65: *Document illumination depicting Elizabeth I enthroned*

less-than-definitive nature of Strong's assessment, it has until now seldom been challenged.

Dendrochronological analysis of the wood panel support of the Soule Portrait revealed a terminal intact heartwood growth ring corresponding to the year 1522.[11] No sapwood was present, consistent with the common practice of trimming away that fragile wood during processing. Standard dendrochronology data analysis allows for the removal during panel preparation of between 8 and 24 years worth of sapwood growth rings for the species and geographic origin of this panel, Eastern Baltic oak. Assuming no heartwood was removed, the earliest possible year in which the tree might have been felled would be 1531. If, however, more than 8 years of sapwood growth were removed, or if any heartwood rings were inadvertently removed, the year of felling might extend to as late as 1547 or beyond. Further, the interval between felling and usage was, on average, between 2 and 8 years.[12] Thus, based on the dendrochronological data alone, we can conclude that the Soule Portrait was most probably executed no earlier than 1533 but may date to as late as 1555 or thereafter. But as noted in relation to the Berry Hill Portrait, the costume dates to no earlier than about 1558. We can therefore reliably conclude that the Soule Portrait dates to a period after about 1558 but perhaps before the end of the 1560s, when ruffs became markedly more elaborate. And since that timeframe once again includes precisely the period during which Katherine Grey Seymour was being put forward as Elizabeth's successor, there remains a significant possibility that the Soule Portrait, like the Berry Hill, is a depiction of Katherine Grey Seymour as heir-presumptive to her cousin Queen Elizabeth during the first decade of that queen's reign.

N.B. When the Soule Portrait was photographed by Christie's in 1937 and again by Leger Galleries in 1954, it bore an inscription in the upper right corner: ÆTATIS/ SUÆ 20/ 1602.[13] Piper apparently disregarded the inscription when identifying the sitter, since the dates did not correlate with either Jane Grey or Elizabeth Tudor (neither do they correlate with Katherine Grey Seymour). And he was certainly right to do so. The inscription was painted atop one or more layers of old varnish, indicating that it was not original to the work but was instead applied well after the painting was created. The painting was cleaned and conserved in about 2015, and all remnants of the inscription were removed at that time.

[1] The white fur seen in each of the portraits of the Berry Hill Type should not be mistaken for ermine, sometimes also called miniver. White ermine or miniver fur is not naturally spotted. It is pure, unblemished white. The black spots on ermine garments are achieved by severing the black tip of the stoat's tail and attaching them to the final garment. This creates a relatively small, very sharply demarcated spot of deep, solid black, and those spots are of uniform size across the garment. And the pattern of application is almost always very regularly spaced in a geometric pattern, as seen in Figs. 41 and 42. In contrast, the spots in the fur in the portraits of the Berry Hill Type are relatively large in size, variegated in color from light grey to black, have indistinct margins, occur in a variety of sizes and shapes, and are irregularly spaced. Additionally, the white fur in the Berry Hill Type is depicted as being relatively long, with individual hairs visible at perhaps 2-3 inches in length. Ermine fur is somewhat shorter at 1 to 1.5 inches. The fur seen here is from some animal larger than a stoat, perhaps a lynx or an arctic fox.

[2] Marika Spring, Catherine Higgitt, and David Saunders, "Investigation of Pigment-Medium Interaction Process in Oil Paint Containing Smalt," *National Gallery Technical Bulletin* 26 (2005), 56-70.

[3] *Queen Elizabeth I in coronation robes*, Nicholas Hilliard, ca.1600, unknown materials, 3 ½ in. x 2 ⅕ in., Harley Foundation, Portland Collection, Welbeck Abbey.

[4] David T. Piper to Leger Galleries, 6 May 1954, Object archive of the current owner.

[5] A second letter to Leger Galleries, from James Laver, Keeper of Prints, Drawings and Pictures at the Victoria and Albert Museum from 1938 to 1959 and a noted costume historian, supported Piper's dating of the picture based on the ruff but did not directly address the identification of the sitter. James Laver to Leger Galleries, 1 September 1954, Object archive of the current owner.

[6] Strong, *Portraits of Queen Elizabeth I*, 54. Strong's grouping included the Berry Hill, Soule, and Syon Portraits, plus NPG764.

[7] Strong, *Portraits of Queen Elizabeth I*, 31.

[8] See, for example, the initial illumination of the "Indenture between the Queen and the dean and canons of St George's, Windsor, for performance of statutes concerning the thirteen poor knights," 30 August 1559, National Archives E 36/277.

[9] See, for example, the Rotherwas Portrait on page 80 in this volume, or the many preparatory drawings by Hans Holbein now in the Royal Collection at Windsor in which 8 of 33 non-royal women, or 25%, are positioned squared front.

[10] Strong, *Gloriana*, 52; *Tudor and Jacobean Portraits*, I:109 and II:186.

[11] *Tree Ring Analysis of a Panel Painting: Elizabeth I*, 8 November 2014, Dr Tomasz Wazny, The Laboratory of Tree Ring Research, University of Arizona.

[12] J. Bauch and D. Eckstein, "Woodbiological investigations on panels of Rembrandt paintings," *Wood Science and Technology* 15:4 (1981), 251-263.

[13] National Portrait Gallery, Sitter File for Elizabeth I, photographs marked "Neg #1989" and "sent by Leger Galleries May 1954."

30   The Chawton Portrait

Called Queen Elizabeth I, possibly Katherine Grey Seymour

Unknown artist

Oil on wood panel; 21 in. x 15 in.

1558-1563

Provenance:

> Reputedly Jane Austen (*d.*1817), sister of Edward Austen Knight, Chawton House, Hampshire;
>
> thence by descent with the Knights of Chawton House;
>
> Lionel and/or Edward Knight, by whom sold between 1919 and 1960;
>
> Richard Philp Gallery, London, after 1966;
>
> Weiss Gallery, London, 1995;
>
> Hever Castle and Gardens, Kent.

This portrait differs markedly from others of the Berry Hill Type in that the costume is heavily embellished with gold embroidery, and the sitter wears a gold chain necklace and pendant rather than a knotted strand of beads. The gold pigment used to depict those elements was laid on very thickly, causing it to stand well above the otherwise smooth planar surface of the remainder of the painting. Additionally, the gold embroidery around the ruff and cuffs, the gold necklace and pendant, and the gold aiglettes are all heavily and crudely outlined in black. There is a total absence of highlight and shadow in those elements, causing them to appear entirely two-dimensional. This is in striking contrast to the rendering of the face and of the white fur, both of which exhibit a more sophisticated technique and greater relative degree of realism. And while it is entirely possible that more than one hand worked on the painting simultaneously and within a single studio, the obvious presence of at least two hands requires questioning whether the goldwork was a later addition and not part of the original image.[1] This is especially true when considering the Chawton Portrait in the larger context of the entire Berry Hill Type group. The Chawton Portrait gives the impression of having been deliberately 'improved' and made more suitably 'regal.' But even if the goldwork was indeed a later addition, it was added in the distant past.

The identity of the sitter in the Chawton Portrait was entirely unknown to the painting's nineteenth-century owners. When Richard Davey included it among the twenty listed in the appendix to his *Nine Days' Queen*, he described it as "a curious portrait, probably of Lady Jane Grey, in the possession of J. Knight, Esq., of Chawton House, Alton."[2] The owner of the painting in 1909 was in fact Montagu George Knight, who had inherited the painting as a family heirloom.[3]

Fig. 66: *Elizabeth I, ca.1560-1565*
(shown actual size)

Fig. 67: *Elizabeth I, ca.1565*
(shown actual size)

Several months prior to the publication of Davey's book, Knight sent a photograph of the painting to the Rev. W. J. Loftie of the Burlington Fine Arts Club soliciting Loftie's opinion on the identity of the sitter. Knight's original letter of inquiry is not extant, but Loftie's response survives among the Knight family papers on deposit in the Hampshire Record Office. Writing on 15 June 1909, Loftie informed Knight,

> I have … gone about every day with [the photograph of] the portrait in my pocket. Today Lionel Cust turned up. He said at once 'Queen Elizabeth!' He added, 'There is a miniature of her as Princess by Hilliard which is very like it'___ he could not say where but he had seen it.[4]

The letter implies that Cust reacted almost instinctively on seeing the photograph of the painting, without first conducting focused research or considering other possible sitters. And it is uncertain to which miniature of Elizabeth as Princess he was referring. The two earliest miniatures of Elizabeth known today, both now in the Royal Collection, were in 1909 attributed variously to "British School," to Levina Teerlinc, or to Hans Holbein, but not Nicholas Hilliard (Figs. 66 and 67).[5] Elizabeth's hair is depicted in those miniatures as significantly lighter in color and what might today be called "frizzy," rather than as the darker and soft curls seen in the Chawton Portrait. As of 1909, the earliest known miniature of Elizabeth by Hilliard was dated to 1572, long after she became Queen.[6] Clearly unable to remember where he had seen the miniature said to depict Elizabeth as Princess, Cust may also have incorrectly remembered the reference miniature itself, or that miniature may have been misidentified. In any event, Cust's identification of the sitter in the Chawton Portrait, even if based on only 'gut-instinct,' ultimately outweighed any suggestion by Davey, and the Chawton Portrait became known after 1909 as a depiction of Elizabeth I.

The identification was repeated when the Chawton Portrait was purchased by Richard Philp in the 1960s and was upheld by Strong when Weiss Gallery consulted him in 1995.[7] Strong's opinion was obviously based upon his own previous published research on the iconography of Elizabeth Tudor and thus upon the Soule Portrait and its prior identification by Piper and Leger in 1954. Yet at the time of the exhibition and sale of 1995, the Weiss catalogue included an acknowledgement of the difficulties associated with documenting the early portraiture of Elizabeth Tudor. The catalogue took pains to compare the painting explicitly to both the coronation miniature by Hilliard of circa 1600 (Fig.45, p.160) and an initial illumination attributed to Levina Teerlinc included in an indenture of 1559 issued to the Poor Knights of Windsor in an effort to support the identification as Elizabeth Tudor.[8] No comparisons to portraits of other contemporary historical figures were mentioned in the catalogue.

Scientific dating of the panel on which the portrait was painted has revealed that the work dates to the first years of the reign of Elizabeth I. Dr Ian Tyers of Dendrochronological Consultancy Ltd analyzed the single board of the Chawton Portrait in May 2014. He found that the last heartwood ring corresponded to the year 1534. But unusually, a significant amount of sapwood was retained when the panel was prepared. As has been noted, the methodological standard in dendrochronology requires allowing for the loss during processing of between 8 and 24 years worth of sapwood growth rings for the species and geographic origin of this panel, Eastern Baltic oak. Because this panel actually included 11 sapwood rings, more than the minimum allowance, only 1 to 13 years of additional growth needed to be allowed for in this instance. The last complete sapwood growth ring present corresponded to the year 1545, so that the tree from which the panel came was felled no earlier than 1546, but may have been harvested as late as 1558 or beyond.[9] Given the average interval between felling and usage of between 2 and 8 years, we can conclude that this painting was most probably executed after 1548 and perhaps as late as 1566, based solely on the dendrochronological data.[10] But the evidence derived from the dating of the costume, as discussed previously, requires amending the earliest date to 1558.[11] And because the period between 1558 and 1566 was precisely the one in which Katherine Grey was being put forward as a potential successor to Elizabeth, the results of the dendrochronological study actually serve to include Katherine as a possible sitter rather than to exclude her.

Even the gold embellishment of the costume, whether added by the original artist when copying from the reference image or later and at the behest of a subsequent owner, also allows for consideration of Katherine as the sitter. If the first two portraits of the Berry Hill Type already discussed do indeed depict Katherine, it is entirely conceivable that the original artist of the Chawton Portrait felt compelled to alter her costume so as to bring her appearance into conformity with what was socially and culturally expected of an heir to the crown, as was seen in relation to the early engravings of the Wrest Park Portrait (see p.60). The same rationale might still apply in the event the goldwork was added at the request of some later owner. Or, more simply, either the original artist or a later owner may have wished to differentiate this painting in some way from others of the Berry Hill Type and therefore 're-dressed' the sitter in order to make the portrait unique, similar to the re-dressing seen in the Hastings and Jersey Portraits. But regardless of the motivation for the alteration in the costume, the available evidence and the clear relationship between the Chawton Portrait and the Berry Hill Portrait strongly suggest that the former is a copy of the latter and that the two sitters are the same woman.

[1] A simple radiological examination of the portrait should reveal any underlying image that might include a necklace of white beads, since radiologically opaque lead white was commonly used in the sixteenth century to depict such elements. Administrators at Hever Castle have opted to defer a radiological study until the painting is next scheduled to come up in the long-term conservation rotation.

[2] Davey, *The Nine Days' Queen*, 361.

[3] Montagu George Knight (1844-1914) was the eldest son of Edward Knight (1794-1879) and grandson of Edward Austen Knight (1768-1852). The latter was an elder brother of the author Jane Austen, thus imparting to the portrait its connection to her. Actual personal possession by Jane Austen is unlikely, however, since she resided as a guest at Chawton Cottage in the village of Chawton, rather than at Chawton House. Austen was financially dependent upon her brother and was herself never sufficiently solvent to have been able to spend funds on such luxury pursuits as portrait collecting. She is equally unlikely to have inherited the painting, having come from a very modest background. See Dierdre Le Faye, *Jane Austen: A Family Record*, 2nd ed. (Cambridge: Cambridge University Press, 2004). The few surviving inventories and sale catalogues for the Austen-Knight properties at Chawton in Hampshire and at Godmersham Park in Kent, though incomplete and lacking in detail, do not include any item that can be identified as this portrait. Hampshire Record Office (HRO), Winchester, 39M89/H28, *Catalogue for the sale of furnishings from Godmersham Park, Kent*, 28 April 1875; 39M89/H27, List of furniture brought from Godmersham Park to Chawton House in 1875, including at least four dozen paintings, none identified or described; 39M89/H33/1 and 2, *Catalogue for the sale of furnishings of Chawton Rectory*, 8 August 1912.

[4] HRO, 39M89/F133/2, W. J. Loftie to Montagu Knight, 15 June 1909. Loftie was an antiquarian known primarily as a collector of manuscripts and wrote extensively on a very wide variety of topics. Lionel Cust was Director of the National Portrait Gallery from 1895 to 1909 and co-edited *The Burlington Magazine* from 1909 to 1919. Davey's preface to *Nine Days Queen* was dated September 1909, so that the book must have been published later in that year and thus well after Knight questioned the identity of the sitter in the portrait.

[5] See *Elizabeth I*, British School (formerly Nicholas Hilliard, Levina Teerlinc, or Hans Holbein), ca.1560- 65, watercolor on vellum laid on card, 2 in. diameter round, Royal Collection, RCIN 420944; *Elizabeth I*, British School (formerly Nicholas Hilliard or Levina Teerlinc), ca.1565, watercolor on vellum laid on card, 1 ¾ in. diameter round, Royal Collection, RCIN 420987. Both miniatures were re-attributed to Hilliard in 1999. See Graham Reynolds, *Sixteenth and Seventeenth Century Miniatures in the Collection of Her Majesty the Queen* (London: Thames and Hudson, 1999), 20 and 21. The current identification of the sitter in RCIN420944 is based (very tenuously, in this author's opinion) on the presence of red and white roses adorning the sitter's hairnet. RCIN420987 has been identified based on a cataloguing note written in 1639 by Abraham van der Doort, Surveyor of the King's Pictures from 1625 until 1640, and on comparison to the appearance of the sitter in RCIN420944. Whether either miniature depicts Elizabeth Tudor cannot today be proved.

[6] See *Queen Elizabeth I*, Nicholas Hilliard, 1572, watercolor on vellum, 2 in. x 1 ⁷/₈ in. oval, National Portrait Gallery, NPG 108.

[7] Electronic communication, Mark Weiss, Weiss Gallery, 2 September 2013.

[8] Mark A.F. Weiss, *Tudor and Stuart Portraits 1530-1660* (London: Weiss Gallery, 1995), Item 8: "Elizabeth I, as Princess Royal (?)."

[9] *Tree Ring Analysis of a Panel Painting: Elizabeth I, Hever Castle*, 29 May 2014, Ian Tyers, Dendrochronological Consultancy Ltd, Sheffield.

[10] J. Bauch and D. Eckstein, "Woodbiological investigations on panels of Rembrandt paintings," *Wood Science and Technology* 15:4 (1981), 251-263.

[11] Alternatively, if the panel was stored for more than the usual 2-8 years, or was re-used from some other application such as a previous panel painting or a piece of furniture, the visible portrait may have been produced as a copy at any time after 1558. X-radiography and/or infrared reflectography could potentially resolve this issue by revealing a different underlying image or preparatory drawing.

Queen Jane Grey

31   The Syon Portrait

Posthumous Portrait of Queen Jane Grey Dudley

Unknown artist

Oil on wood panel; 22 in. x 17 ½ in.

circa 1610

Provenance:

William Seymour, 2ⁿᵈ Duke of Somerset (*d*.1660);

Frances Devereux Seymour, Duchess of Somerset (*d*.1674);

Frances Finch Thynne, Viscountess Weymouth (*d*.1712);

Thomas Thynne, 1ˢᵗ Viscount Weymouth (*d*.1714);

Thomas Thynne, 2ⁿᵈ Viscount Weymouth (*d*.1751), by whom gifted to;

Francis Thynne Seymour, Duchess of Somerset (*d*.1754);

Elizabeth Seymour Smithson Percy, Duchess of Northumberland (*d*.1776);

Thence by descent.

The Syon Portrait was the last among the paintings of the Berry Hill Type to have been produced.[1] Dendrochronological analysis by Dr Ian Tyers revealed that the painting dates to no earlier than 1602, almost half a century after the Soule and Chawton Portraits were created.[2] It is therefore clear that the Syon Portrait is a copy derived from its predecessors of the Berry Hill Type. In fact, the Syon Portrait most closely resembles the prototype of the group, the Berry Hill Portrait itself, at least in terms of composition. Both are waist-length portraits, unlike the bust-length Soule Portrait. The Syon Portrait includes the crown of the sitter's headgear and the gold embellishment on the brim, just as is seen in the Berry Hill Portrait, whereas those elements are absent from both the Soule and the Chawton Portraits. The arrangement of the hair in this portrait likewise resembles that depicted in the Berry Hill Portrait rather than the regularly-shaped curls of the Soule and Chawton Portraits. The neck ruff is proportionally equal to the ruff worn by the Berry Hill sitter, but smaller than those of the Soule and Chawton sitters. The knot in the bead necklace conforms to the configuration seen in the Berry Hill Portrait rather than to the awkward-appearing knot of the Soule lady's necklace. The fur of the boa or coat collar is more nearly entirely white like the boa in the Berry Hill Portrait and unlike the more prominently spotted boas worn by the Soule and Chawton sitters. Lastly, the fur accents on the shoulders of the black gown exactly repeat the same elements from the Berry Hill Portrait, while those accents are not fully visible in either the Soule or Chawton Portraits. Considering these close similarities between the Syon Portrait and the Berry Hill Portrait, it seems entirely probable that the Syon was copied directly from the Berry Hill alone, without reference to either the Soule or Chawton Portraits.

One physical feature of the sitter in the Syon Portrait appears quite different from the same element in the Berry Hill Portrait, however. The Syon lady's chin exhibits a pronounced cleft. No such cleft appears in any others of the Berry Hill Type nor, for that matter, in any known portraits of Queen Elizabeth I.[3] Cleft chins are statistically uncommon and more so among women. Of twenty-nine principal portraits considered in this study, for example, only the Syon Portrait depicts a woman with a cleft chin. Further, the development of a cleft chin is known to have a genetic or familial component, causing them to appear across multiple generations of a single family.[4] Significantly, the best known painted portrait of Jane Grey's paternal grandmother, Margaret Wotton Grey, reveals that she may have had a cleft chin.[5] Equally significantly, none of the fully authenticated portraits of Katherine Grey Seymour depict her with a cleft chin.

That the Syon Portrait was originally produced as a depiction of Lady Jane Grey Dudley specifically, rather than of Elizabeth I or Katherine Grey Seymour, is all but certain. The painting's first owner was William Seymour, grandson of Jane's sister Katherine Grey Seymour. William's second wife, Frances Devereux, whom he married in 1617, referred to the painting in her last will and testament of 1674 as "the picture of Queen Jane Grey now hanging in my chamber."[6] Frances survived her husband by fourteen years and inherited from him not only this portrait but also a vaguely-identified portrait of William's grandmother Katherine Grey – probably the double portrait still at Syon House that also includes William's father, Edward Seymour, Viscount Beauchamp of Hache as an infant (Fig.16, page 90). Frances was careful in her will to bequeath the two portraits together in a group that also included a third painting depicting William's first wife, Arbella Stuart. The three portraits constituted a dynastic set that traced a claim to the throne of England held by the Seymours as the senior English line descended from Henry VII via Mary Tudor Brandon, Frances Brandon Grey, Jane Grey Dudley, Katherine Grey Seymour, and Katherine's eldest son (William's father), Edward Seymour. In light of the dendrochronological data situating production of the Syon Portrait in the second or third decade of the seventeenth century, it seems likely that the Syon Portrait was commissioned by Frances's husband William near to the time of their marriage in 1617, leaving little opportunity between then and Frances's will of 1674 for the painting to have become misidentified.

Dendrochonological examination reveals that the portrait was created no earlier than about 1602, as noted above, but the same methodology also reveals a date before which the painting was created, thanks to an unusual circumstance. A smaller copy of the portrait is also held at Syon House and is also on wood panel. Examination of the growth rings in the wood of that smaller panel revealed that the last complete heartwood growth ring corresponds to the year 1618. When the standard minimum of 8 years is added to account for lost sapwood, plus the minimum 2 years for processing and storage, the earliest point at which the smaller copy may have been produced is 1629, the tree having been felled in the year after any last complete growth ring.[7] Thus the larger version, from which the smaller was clearly copied, dates to no earlier than 1602 and probably to no later than about 1626.

That narrower period between 1610 and about 1626 witnessed several critical shifts in the English royal succession that brought the Seymours, especially William, unexpectedly close to the throne. In the first of those events, William Seymour married Arbella Stuart in 1610. Arbella was first cousin to Elizabeth's successor King James VI of Scotland. Many in England thought Arbella's claim to be Elizabeth's heir was superior to James's by virtue of her having been born in England, while James was a foreigner to England.[8] A series of failed plots between 1590 and 1605 actually sought to bring Arbella to the throne in place of James VI, some with and some without her knowledge. Significantly, chief among those plots was that of 1602 involving a plan to marry Arbella to Katherine Grey's son Edward Seymour, Viscount Beauchamp. The marriage was intended to bring together into a single union the two remaining lines of descent from Henry VII, one stemming from Mary Tudor Brandon and the other from Margaret Tudor Stuart. The union would have resolved any concerns about the Stuart line having been passed over by both the Third Act for the Succession of 1543 and Henry VIII's last will and testament. It would also have circumvented any potential for the Seymours to challenge the succession in future by making a Seymour male the progenitor of a new Seymour dynasty through Arbella. A Seymour might even be immediately elevated to the status of co-monarch, similar to the position that had been enjoyed by Phillip of Spain as husband of Mary Tudor.

Arbella was an ambitious woman and an active participant in the plot of 1602, the failure of which earned her a brief period in custody. But Arbella did not give up on a Seymour match and continued to pursue matches with either Edward, his younger brother Thomas, or one of Edward's two sons, Edward and William (the younger Edward eventually married Anne Sackville in July of 1609). Though explicitly forbidden to marry William Seymour, the two were nonetheless finally wed secretly in June of 1610. Both were placed in custody as soon as King James became aware of the forbidden marriage.[9]

The second and third critical events of the 1610s both occurred almost simultaneous with the marriage of Arbella and William. In May, James I's only daughter, Elizabeth, was contracted to marry Frederick V, Elector Palatine of the Rhine. That effectively removed Elizabeth from the English succession since she was expected to relocate to the Rhenish Palatinate. Then in July, Katherine Grey's son Edward died at almost 52 years of age. Any claim he held to the English throne as a descendant of Henry VII in the Grey line thus devolved onto his children, including his second son William, who was by then already engaged to Arbella.

Finally, in November of 1612, Henry Frederick, Prince of Wales died suddenly of typhoid fever. This left only James's second Scottish-born son, 12-year-old Charles, between the sons of the late Edward Seymour and the English throne. Charles had been a sickly child, so much so that he had been considered too unwell to travel from Scotland to London following his father's accession in 1603.[10] He was slow to learn to speak, he stammered, and he had weak legs and ankles.[11] He was thus perceived by many as physically inferior to his deceased elder brother, and there was concern that he too might predecease his father the king. And were Charles indeed to die, and to do so without issue, Arbella was the next heir-in-blood to the Crown, while her new husband was second heir-at-law after his elder brother Edward. Given the animosity held by many Protestants towards James's wife and Charles's mother, the Roman Catholic Anne of Denmark, and the concurrent animosity held by English Catholics towards James himself for his continuation of the anti-Catholic policies of the previous reign, Arbella's and William's ambitions regarding the throne were no mere pretense.

As the second decade of the 1600s rolled on, William Seymour found himself still closer to the throne. Though both he and Arbella had been placed in custody immediately following their marriage, William escaped from the Tower of London in 1611 and fled into exile on the continent. Arbella was immediately transferred from house arrest and to stricter custody in the Tower. She died there in 1615. The English branch of the Stuart family tree ended with her death, leaving the Seymour family with an unobstructed claim to the English throne of James VI & I. Then in 1618,

William's older brother Edward died without issue, leaving William as the senior heir to the crown after Prince Charles. For the next seven years William stood second in line to the throne. He even became heir apparent when Charles, still unmarried and childless, succeeded his father in 1625 as Charles I of England, Scotland, and Ireland. Only the birth of the future Charles II in 1630 finally displaced William as the immediate successor to the English crown.

Following Arbella's death in 1615, William had returned to England and been gradually restored to favor. He married Frances Devereux in 1617, and the couple immediately began producing children. But the period between the death of his own elder brother in 1618 and the birth to King Charles I of Prince Charles in 1630 must have been a particularly heady one for William as next in line to the throne. It was also the most logical period during which he might have commissioned a pair of Seymour dynastic portraits. Though the fragile state of the double portrait on panel of Katherine and her infant son (Fig.16, page 90) has thus far rendered dendrochronological dating unfeasible, it likely dates to this period. Certainly no documentation (inventories, etc.) is currently known that might date the painting to any earlier period.

The current date ascribed to it of about 1562/3 is based entirely on the apparent age of the infant Edward and assumes the painting to have been from the life rather than a later copy. More probably, given Katherine Seymour's committal to the Tower between 1561 and 1563, the double portrait was instead copied at some later date from the Belvoir miniature (Fig.60, page 164). That miniature was in the possession of the Seymour family from its creation until 1750.[12] It is therefore entirely conceivable that the larger version intended for prominent display may post-date the miniature by some considerable time, just as the Syon Portrait of Jane Grey post-dates the Berry Hill, Soule, and Chawton Portraits by over four decades. If so, the double portrait of Katherine and her son plus the Syon Portrait of Jane Grey were likely produced simultaneously and specifically as a part of a dynastic display set that traced William's claim to the throne from Queen Jane, through Katherine as Jane's younger sister and heir, then through Katherine's son Edward Seymour to William himself as Edward's eldest surviving son.

No source image for the Syon Portrait other than the Berry Hill Portrait can today be identified. No pre-existing miniature resembling the pictures of the Berry Hill Type is known, whether in the current collections of the Manners Dukes of Rutland, the Seymour Dukes of Somerset, or the Percy Dukes of Northumberland, or in the historical records and inventories of those families, or elsewhere.[13] Intriguingly, however, Arbella Stuart Seymour is known to have had a personal fondness for Jane Grey as a historical figure. She is said to have requested during her secret pre-nuptial negotiations with the Seymours in the 1590s that the Seymour agent bring with him as a password-like device a small picture of Jane or a sample of her writing, both of which she claimed to be able to recognize.[14] And Arbella was famously compelled by her grandmother, Bess of Hardwick, to share the elder lady's bedchamber, where Bess is known to have kept her own cherished portrait of Jane, the lost Chatsworth Portrait (see Appendix Two).[15] Arbella was therefore likely fully aware of Jane's authentic physical appearance. But tempting as it may be to suggest that the entire Berry Hill Type was based upon the Chatsworth Portrait or some other authentic portrait of Jane Grey, the possibility seems exceedingly unlikely owing to the presence across the group of a ruff that was not yet in fashion at the time of Jane's death early in 1554.

More probably, the Seymours knew the Berry Hill Portrait to be an authentic likeness of Katherine Grey Seymour and therefore adapted that image for use in depicting her sister Jane. Significantly, they did not use the portrait from which the van de Passe engraving had been taken, though that portrait was apparently already relatively well known as a depiction of Jane. Neither did they refer to any portraits of the Streatham, Houghton, or Norris type, though they too were apparently all thought at the time to depict Jane. Perhaps as sisters, Jane and Katherine were known by the Seymours to have had very similar physical appearances. Since the elder Edward Seymour, Earl of Hertford (Katherine's husband and William's grandfather) remained alive until 1621, he could easily have been called upon to attest to Jane's physical appearance and thus to contribute to the distinctive chin shape seen in the Syon Portrait. Edward had known Jane well when both were youths, and their fathers were active together at the court of Edward VI. He was even considered a potential marriage partner for Jane prior to the fall from power in 1551 of his father, the Lord Protector.[16] Whether the elderly Earl could accurately recall Jane's physical appearance is an open question, but perhaps he and his grandson William were aided by whatever transportable portrait Arbella had assumed them to possess. Alternatively, William may have seen the Chatsworth Portrait in his role as Arbella's husband and widower. Of course, this is all simple conjecture, but there was clearly some compelling reason for the artist who created the Syon Portrait to insert an uncommon cleft into the chin. The most logical explanation is that some person associated with the commissioning or production of the Syon Portrait had reliable knowledge of Jane's true appearance, whether through the old Earl of Hertford's memory, existence of some other image now lost, or William's having seen the Chatsworth Portrait. And though the evidence is not conclusive, it seems reasonable to suggest that the Syon Portrait, owing to its unique association with numerous persons in positions to recognize a genuine image of Jane, may well be the closest we shall ever come to an authentic likeness of the Nine Days Queen.

One important copy of the Syon Portrait, in addition to the small copy at Syon mentioned above, survives today at Audley End House, Essex (Fig.68). It is displayed together with another copy of the double portrait of Katherine Grey and her son. Both are on canvas and thought to date to the eighteenth century. The portrait of Jane includes a cleft chin and semi-transparent beads, indicating that it was copied directly from the Syon image rather than from some other of the Berry Hill Type.[17] It is also inscribed in an eighteenth-century hand to identify the lady as "Q^n: Jane Gray [sic] Daugh^{tr} to y$^{[e]}$ Du^{ke} of Suffolk Neice [sic] to King Hen: VIII. & Wife to L^d: Guildfort [sic] Dudley." But the composition was expanded to three-quarter length and to include the lady's right hand. She holds in that hand a book bound in gold-stamped brown leather, and the title of the book is plainly visible on the binding. The lettering, though Greek, identifies the book as Plato's *Phaedo*.

Though the subject *Phaedo* addresses is decidedly metaphysical, it is neither a specifically Christian nor a specifically theological work. It is instead a work of learned philosophy. The inclusion of the book is thus emblematic of Jane's scholarly reputation through specific visual reference to Roger Ascham's account of having found Jane indoors reading that particular book

Fig. 68: *The Audley End copy of the Syon Portrait*

while the rest of her household was out hunting. The book mirrors the focus prior to the beginning of the eighteenth century on Jane's learning rather than on her perceived piety.

The Audley End copy was owned at the beginning of the eighteenth century by Charles Howard, 9th Earl of Suffolk. As a strong supporter of the Act of Settlement, he may even have been the original patron who commissioned the work. Charles and his wife had gone so far as to travel to Hanover prior to the death of Queen Anne in order to court the favor of the future King George I. The Audley End copy was thus likely a visual symbol of the Suffolk allegiance to a succession determined by law rather than blood lineage, similar to others already discussed in this study.

1 An early copy of the Syon Portrait, in somewhat smaller scale, is also held at Syon House. It has been dendrochronologically dated to the second quarter of the seventeenth century. Because it is a direct copy, only the earlier and larger version is considered here.

2 Electronic communication, Dr Ian Tyers, Dendrochronology Consultancy Ltd, 5 December 2012.

3 See, for example, *Elizabeth I as Princess* attributed to William Scrots (fig.8, p.62), the coronation miniature by Nicholas Hilliard (fig.41, p.170), and the two miniatures from the mid 1560s also by Hilliard (figs.42 and 43, p.174). See also the many well-known official portraits of Elizabeth produced during her reign, including the so-called Clopton, Darnley, Ditchley, Sieve, Ermine, Rainbow, and Armada Portraits, as well as the tomb effigy at Westminster Abbey.

4 M.R. Lebow and P.B. Sawin, "Inheritance of human facial features: a pedigree study involving length of face, prominent ears and chin cleft," *Journal of Heredity* 32 (1941), 127-132; B. Vijaya Bhanu and K. C. Malhotra, "A population genetic study of cleft chin in India," *American Journal of Physical Anthropology* 37:3 (November 1972), 367-372.

5 *Lady Margaret Wotton, Marchioness of Dorset*, by follower of Hans Holbein, second half of sixteenth century, oil on panel, 31 in. x 25 ⅝ in., collection of Dr and Mrs Bonheim, Cologne, Germany. The portrait has been dated to no earlier than 1560 and is presumed to have been copied from an original by Holbein, who is known to have created a portrait of Lady Margaret. Significantly, the portrait bears a Lumley cartellino, indicating that it was once owned by John Lumley, who also owned portraits of Jane and Katherine Grey. See Appendix Two: The Lost Portraits, p.183.

6 Longleat House, Seymour Papers, Vol. 6, f. 241, Will of Frances Seymour, 1674 (without day or month).

7 *Tree Ring Analysis of a Panel Painting: Lady Jane Grey, Syon House*, 25 July 2013, Ian Tyers, Dendrochronological Consultancy Ltd, Sheffield. The abrupt halt in 1649-1650 of the importation to England of oak wood from the Eastern Baltic region indicates that the smaller portrait copy was painted no later than about 1650, ten years before William Seymour's death in 1660.

8 See, for example, Robert Parsons, *A Conference About the Next Succession to the Crown of England* (R. Doleman, 1681; reprint of Antwerp, 1595). Others cited a statute from the fourteenth century, *De natis ultra mare* (25 Edw. III 2), that barred persons born under a foreign allegiance from inheriting lands and estates in England. Arbella Stuart was the daughter of Charles Stuart, who was himself the son of Margaret Douglas, granddaughter of Henry VIII's elder sister Margaret Tudor Stuart. Charles Stuart's elder brother (Arbella's uncle) was Henry Stuart, Lord Darnley, first consort of Queen Mary of Scotland and father of James VI of Scotland and I of England. Arbella and James Stuart were thus paternal first cousins.

9 Sarah Gristwood, *Arbella: England's Lost Queen* (Boston: Houghton Mifflin Harcourt, 2003), 141 and 269-292.

10 Richard Cust, *Charles I: A Political Life* (Harlow, Pearson Education, 2005), 2.

11 Pauline Gregg, *King Charles I* (London: Dent, 1981), 11-13.

12 The Rutland miniature descended to Frances Seymour, daughter of Charles Seymour, 6th Duke of Somerset by his second wife. Frances married John Manners, Marquess of Granby in 1750. Their son Charles Manners became 4th Duke of Rutland in 1779. Manners family tradition holds that, upon her father's death in 1748, Frances Seymour had received as a legacy the contents of one room of the Duke of Somerset's London residence and took those possessions into the Manners marriage. The miniature is presumed to have been among the contents of that room, together with a large number of other items still in the Manners's possession and known to have originated there. Electronic communication, Harvey Proctor, Private Secretary to the Duke and Duchess of Rutland, 17 December 2013.

13 Electronic communication, Harvey Proctor, Private Secretary to the Duke and Duchess of Rutland, 17 December 2013; Electronic communication, His Grace the Duke of Somerset, 29 January 2010. A fire in 1816 at the Rutland seat of Belvoir Castle destroyed a large number of pictures, but no portrait of Jane Grey was included in the list of lost items. See Irvin Eller, *The History of Belvoir Castle: From the Norman Conquest to the Nineteenth Century* (London: R. Tyas, 1841), 127-132.

14 Gristwood, *Arbella*, 145.

15 Gristwood, *Arbella*, 132-133.

[16] One myth states that Jane Grey and Edward Seymour were actually contracted to marry, the contract being voided by the Lord Protector's attainder in 1551. No documentation survives to confirm that myth, however. See Ives, *Lady Jane Grey*, 184; de Lisle, *Sisters*, 29 and 66.

[17] Similarly, the portrait on canvas of Katherine and her son now at Audley End House is a precise copy of the version on panel at Syon House, indicating that it too was copied directly from the Syon version rather than from either the miniature or the version now at Petworth House.

APPENDIX ONE: THE SPINOLA LETTER

Throughout the past century every historian discussing Jane Grey, whether in writings for the general public or for a rigorously scholarly audience, has based any physical description of Jane on the content of a work published in 1909 by the novelist-turned-historian Richard Davey. Each of those modern writers has assumed Davey's evidence for Jane's appearance to be authentic and valid. I followed their lead and cited Davey in my own PhD dissertation and in my earliest published work on portraiture of Jane Grey, though I did note that the letter had yet to be confirmed.[1]

Leanda de Lisle was the first to offer any critical commentary on Davey's evidence, in an article that appeared in the magazine *The New Criterion* in September 2009.[2] De Lisle had come to question the authenticity of the document while writing her collective biography of the Grey sisters, *The Sisters Who Would Be Queen: Mary, Katherine, and Lady Jane Grey: A Tudor Tragedy*. She was "niggled" that no historian writing after 1909 had ever bothered to confirm Davey's source, leading her to investigate more carefully where others had not. She eventually contacted me, and I related to her that my own search for the original document had proven fruitless, despite combing through dozens of archival catalogues and corresponding with all of the principal archives in Genoa. De Lisle conducted her own investigation and ultimately concluded that the document was, in her judgment, a "forgery." She was able to detail in her resulting essay the likely inspirations for the details contained in the imaginary document, ranging from the famous highly-fictionalized painted depiction of Jane's execution by Paul Delaroche to nineteenth-century books on costume history and even to authentic ambassadorial descriptions of Jane's cousin Queen Mary. The issue of Jane Grey's physical appearance has, of course, been central to my extensive research on her early portraiture. Having erred by citing Davey in my analysis of the Fitzwilliam Portrait, I thereafter resolved to set Davey firmly aside. I returned to his account early in 2014, hoping to sort out in my own mind, once and for all, whether or not Davey was at all reliable in his description of Jane's physical appearance.

Davey made his description of Jane's physical appearance part of a narration of her ritual entry into the Tower of London upon becoming queen on 10 July 1553. Davey placed the description within the supposed eye-witness account of an Italian visitor to London who was able to view the ceremonial procession. According to Davey, that witness's account was included in a letter sent home to Genoa, where the letter eventually became part of an unnamed Genoese archive. Davey significantly altered the fictional letter over the course of two separate publications, however, and the changes between those two versions allow for easily confirming that the letter is nothing more than the former-novelist's creation to fill a conspicuous void in the authentic documentary record.

Davey published his first version of the letter in 1906 in *The Pageant of London*, a romantic account of the history of the City from Roman times to 1900. He sought to enliven his recitation of the historical facts with a series of colorful vignettes, one of which was the description of Jane's entry into the Tower. The fourth chapter of the second volume of *Pageant* covered the reign of Mary I, beginning with the abortive reign of Queen Jane. There Davey claimed to quote from "an Italian MS [i.e., manuscript] of the period, the original of which is in Genoa" which he stated was written by "the Genoese merchant *Bartolomeo* Spinola" [emphasis added].[3]

A little before three, in the afternoon of the tenth of this month, I hurried, with some of our clerks, to see the new Queen land, and enter the Tower. There was with her a great crowd of magnificently dressed gentlemen and women, who proceeded and followed her, all very stately. The Duke of Northumberland, her father-in-law, who is a very fine big man, was dressed in crimson velvet, and gave her his hand to alight from the barge. This lady Jane, who is the daughter of the Duke of Suffolk, is very small, so small indeed, that she had to be raised on chopine made after the Venetian fashion, and nearly a foot in height, which were, however, concealed by her robes, and made her walk totteringly, so that, in order not to tumble, she had to lean on her husband's arm. She is pretty, with very small features, red hair, and much freckled. Her dress was of green velvet, bordered in gold. Her train of purple velvet was of great length, lined with ermine, and was upheld by her mother the Lady Frances, niece to Henry VIII. This was much commented upon, for many thought the crown should have come first to her, she being the late King's niece, and not to her daughter. But there is a good deal of religion about this matter, this lady having been brought up a staunch Protestant, and the Protestants wish her to be the head of the nation and of the Church. Her husband is a very fine tall young man. He has a bright complexion, like a woman, and very fair curly hair. His garments were of white velvet and white satin, and he was constantly bowing and smiling most pleasantly. But the crowd was very silent. None the less, the people knelt when the Queen passed, according to the custom of this country. Northumberland's wife was in this procession, but I do not know the names of the other lords and ladies, who were numerous, most gaily dressed, and all of them chatting and laughing cheerfully as they passed along. When they entered the Tower the gates were closed.[4]

Certain details within the letter do not sustain careful scrutiny, however. Most obviously, the author used the very particular term "Protestant" to describe Jane. Yet that word was not in common usage in 1553, when the letter was supposedly written.[5] Roman Catholic writers of the mid-sixteenth century tended instead to describe non-Catholics as "heretics," a generic term in that early period for anyone with non-orthodox beliefs.[6] Further, the writer stated that English Protestants as a group "wish [Jane] to be the head ... of the Church", a statement so patently historically inaccurate that it is impossible for a contemporary foreign observer, even if relying on mere street-gossip, to have made such an error. Women were utterly barred from positions of theological authority among both Roman Catholics and the non-Catholic reformers, in England as well as on the continent. Edward's own Devise for the Succession had inherently assumed that Mary would renounce any claim to be Supreme Head of the Church in England and restore the Church to (male) papal authority. There were even concerns expressed elsewhere about how the issue of the supremacy should be handled were Elizabeth ever to ascend the throne unmarried.[7] These two details alone expose the Spinola letter as an anachronistic figment of Davey's imagination.

Davey seems to have become aware of these issues, since he corrected them in the next outing of the letter three years later. He also made other alterations that served to increase the verisimilitude of the letter. Writing in *Nine Days' Queen: Lady Jane Grey and Her Times*, Davey quoted again from the letter, though in this later instance the author's name was changed from *Bartolomeo* to *Baptist* Spinola. And for second outing, Davey added a footnote containing significant detail about Spinola, including that he was knighted, that he remained in London throughout the reigns of Edward VI and Mary and into that of Elizabeth, that Elizabeth once paid him "an enormous sum—

probably for supplies of Genoa velvet and brocade", and that he was frequently mentioned in the State Papers of the period.[8] Such peripheral detail in regard to the supposed writer of the letter lent to the letter itself an impression of seeming authenticity. Further, Davey altered the manner in which he presented the letter, adding parenthetical and bracketed inclusions of discursive clarifications and phrases in Italian, both of which implied that he had translated the letter from an authentic Italian original.

> To-day [the date is not given, but possibly it figured on the cover, now lost : it was, of course, 10th July 1553] I saw Donna Jana Groia [an Italianisation of Grey] walking in a grand procession to the Tower. She is now called Queen, but is not popular, for the hearts of the people are with Mary, the Spanish Queen's daughter. This Jane is very short and thin, but prettily shaped and graceful. She has small features and a well-made nose (*ben fatta ha il naso*), the mouth flexible and the lips red. Her eyes are sparkling and red (*rossi* – a sort of light hazel often noticed with red hair). I stood so long near Her Grace, that I noticed her colour was good, but freckled. When she smiled she showed her teeth, which are white and sharp. In all, a *graziosa persona* and *animata* [animated]. She wore a dress of green velvet stamped with gold, with large sleeves. Her headdress was a white coif with many jewels. She walked under a canopy, her mother carrying her long train, and her husband Guilfo [Guildford] walking by her, dressed all in white and gold, a very tall strong boy with light hair, who paid her much attention. The new Queen was mounted on very high *chopines* [clogs] to make her look much taller, which were concealed by her robes, as she is very small and short. Many ladies followed, with noblemen, but this lady is very *heretica* and has never heard Mass, and some great people did not come into the procession for that reason.[9]

As mentioned above, the inclusion of Italian phrases, even the "Italianization" of Jane's noble style and name, lent the letter an air of seeming authenticity. Likewise, the phonetic spelling of Guildford's name suggested that the writer found the name foreign to his Italian ear, in the same way that Spanish writers of the period so often referred to English noblemen as "Milord" (i.e., My Lord), almost as though that was their given name. Even Davey's inclusion of the reference to chopines would have rung true for any reader already familiar with the exceedingly popular (and equally flawed) earlier work of Agnes Strickland, in which she too described Jane wearing that same style of platform shoe, though not in any specific situational context.[10] Note, however, that any references to "Protestants" and to a contemporary desire that Jane become Supreme Head of the Church have been omitted and reduced to a statement in historically correct terminology that she was "heretica" and had never heard Mass.

Other aspects of the letter, beyond its textual content, also lend it a semblance of authenticity. The supposed-author's surname Spinola, for example, was and still is very common among Genoese families. Further, several men by that surname were indeed documented in the State Papers as living in England at various points throughout the sixteenth century, just as Davey claimed, including several with the forename Baptist (or Baptista). Some also happened to be merchants. Yet a significant number of those called Baptist(a) Spinola were Florentine or Venetian rather than Genoese, an important distinction if the supposed letter was written to a recipient in Genoa and stored in a Genoese archive. These non-Genoese included the Florentine Luke Baptista Spinola, who is recorded residing in England in as early as 1519.[11] Others, though Genoese, were soldiers rather than merchants, such as Captain Giovanes Baptista Spinola, who in 1545 offered his services to Henry VIII and promised to bring with him one thousand soldiers and a number of shipbuilders.[12] Yet another Baptista Spinola, together with his Genoese compatriot Horatio Pallavicino, served as the Elizabethan government's financial agent for moving funds between London and the Low Countries during the two decades preceding the Spanish Armada of 1588.[13] Given this abundance of men named Baptista Spinola mentioned in the State Papers and other sources, many of whom were indeed merchants originating in Genoa, such a name and occupation were logical choices for Davey's supposed witness to Queen Jane's entry into the Tower on 10 July 1553.

Davey's *Nine Days' Queen* contained numerous other obvious fabrications developed to fill documentary voids, indicating alacrity on his part to fictionalize wherever he thought it might be useful. In regard to Jane's christening, for example, he stated that her maternal grandmother sent her a "rich bowl with a chiseled cover," and that various material favors were afterward dispensed to the local citizenry from the church steps, yet Jane's birth and christening are entirely undocumented.[14] Her mother Lady Frances is described as dining daily in a solitary state, a claim that notably aided in portraying Frances as a cold and heartless mother, yet there is absolutely no documentation surviving to detail the daily routines of the Grey household.[15]

Such repeated and unsupported fabrications reduce *Nine Days' Queen* from the realm of biography to that of historical fiction. We must, therefore, dismiss the Spinola letter as mere fiction, just as de Lisle has earlier argued. Unless some reliably authentic contemporary document, not yet known, is discovered in an obscure archive, or until some equally reliable life portrait can be fully authenticated, we cannot and will not know anything whatsoever about the physical appearance of Jane Grey beyond the very vague and subjective statements from observers in the period that she was "pretty" or "beautiful."

[1] J. Stephan Edwards, *'Jane the Quene': A New Consideration of Lady Jane Grey, England's Nine Days Queen* (PhD dissertation, University of Colorado – Boulder, 2007), 264, note 82.

[2] Leanda de Lisle, "Faking Jane: On Lady Jane Grey & a historical forgery uncovered," *The New Criterion*, September 2009.

[3] Richard Davey, *The Pageant of London* (London: Methuen, 1906), 82.

[4] Davey, *Pageant*, 82–83.

[5] The modern word "Protestant" is derived from the Latin "protestantem," meaning "those who protest." It was first used at the Diet of Speyer in 1529 to describe very narrowly those followers of Martin Luther who protested the ruling of the Diet of 1526 that had severely curtailed church reform within the territories of the Holy Roman Empire. As a descriptor of a wider doctrinal system of belief, the term "Protestant" did not enter common usage in any language until the end of the sixteenth century.

[6] See, for example, Giordano Ziletti, *Lettere di Principi, le qvali si scrivono o da principi, o a principi, o ragionano di principi, Libro Primo* (Venice: Appresso Giordano Ziletti, 1569), ff.5r–v.

[7] Soon after Elizabeth actually did become queen, a compromise was reached under the Act of Supremacy of 1559 by which Elizabeth was named Supreme Governor (rather than Head) of the Church, implying temporal administrative guardianship rather than personal theological control.

[8] Davey, *Nine Days' Queen*, 252–253 and note 2.

[9] Davey, *The Nine Days' Queen*, 253.

[10] Strickland, *Lives of the Tudor Princesses*, 138. Strickland's own reference to Jane wearing chopines is bolstered by a citation to the very popular essayist Isaac Disraeli (father of the Prime Minister Benjamin Disraeli) and his *Curiosities of Literature*, a widely-read three-volume collection of essays on a variety of subjects, including historical fashions. Yet Disraeli never mentioned chopines by name, and mentioned Jane Grey only once, in a footnote and as a friend of Roger Ascham ("Autographs" in *Curiosities of Literature*, New Edition [London: Frederick Warne and Co., 1858], Vol. 3, 165, n.107). Strickland's description of Jane wearing chopines would appear to be as imaginative as Davey's.

[11] Julius de Medici to Thomas, Cardinal Wolsey, 16 March 1519, *Letters and Papers, Foreign and Domestic, Henry VIII*, Volume 3: 1519-1523 (1867), 39.

[12] Giovanes Baptista Spinola to Nicholas Wotton, 18 February 1545, *Letters and Papers, Foreign and Domestic, Henry VIII*, Volume 20 Part 1: January–July 1545 (1905), Item 217/2, 90–101.

[13] Lawrence Stone, *An Elizabethan: Sir Horatio Palavicino* (Oxford: Clarendon Press, 1956), 59 and 73.

[14] Davey, *Nine Days' Queen*, 15–16.

[15] Davey, *Nine Days' Queen*, 21.

APPENDIX TWO: THE LOST PORTRAITS

This study has striven to be as comprehensive as possible in surveying early portraits said to depict Lady Jane Grey Dudley. Nonetheless, there are undoubtedly some surviving portraits that were inadvertently overlooked owing to their being closely held in private collections and not yet known either to scholars or to the general public. Additionally, a small number of others that *are* known could not be included on account of having been "lost" since their last documented notice and there being no known photographs of them. This appendix details efforts to locate those lost portraits in the hope that by raising awareness they may someday be recovered and studied.

The Chatsworth Portrait

As noted in the Introduction to this study, an inventory compiled in about 1560 of the personal possessions of Bess of Hardwick held at Chatsworth House included a portrait of Lady Jane Grey.[1] Given the close nature of the relationship between Bess and Jane, it is all but certain that the portrait was a fully authentic likeness, perhaps even *ad vivum*, from the life. The painting cannot today be identified as having survived, though at least one portrait incorrectly said to depict Jane Grey is known to have survived in the collection of Bess's descendants: the Portland Portrait. Various inventories and travel diaries offer occasional hints after 1560 regarding the history of the painting owned by Bess, however, allowing tentative tracing of the Chatsworth Portrait from the sixteenth century through to its likely destruction early in the nineteenth century.

Chatsworth House was still a relatively modest house at the end of the sixteenth century, and though only recently built, it was but one of Bess's many residences. Her ancestral home, nearby Hardwick Hall, was older and becoming old-fashioned. Bess therefore set about building New Hardwick Hall in the 1590s, doing so on a palatial scale and using an innovative new architectural style. New Hardwick Hall quickly became a marvel of its day and was furnished accordingly. Bess is known to have moved some of her furnishings from Chatsworth House to Hardwick Hall, but it is not clear whether the portrait of Jane Grey was among the items moved before Bess's death in 1608. An earlier separate inventory of Chatsworth House taken in 1559 did not include any pictures or paintings whatsoever, making it impossible to locate the painting there prior to the subsequent inventory of about 1560.[2] Likewise, an inventory of Chatsworth prepared in 1601 to accompany Bess's will also did not list any paintings, though it seems improbable that the house was entirely devoid of pictures. In contrast, an inventory from the same year for Bess's two houses at Hardwick —the Old Hall and the New Hall—enumerates a total of more than 140 pictures, including 67 portraits, and details the subject content of all but 20.[3] No portrait of Jane Grey was listed at either Old or New Hardwick Hall, however. In all likelihood, the painting was still at Chatsworth in 1601, but the Chatsworth inventorist chose for unknown reasons not to include any paintings in his list.

Any inventories that may have been taken of Chatsworth House and Hardwick Hall over the following 150 years have failed to survive. The next extant accounting dates to 1764 and covers both residences, but it is frustratingly vague. A large number of pictures were counted in batches at Chatsworth House in that year, but only a handful were individually identified by subject matter. Most of those depicted either religious scenes or family members then still living. Similarly, the inventory for New Hardwick Hall simply stated the total number of pictures in a given room, only very rarely identifying their subject matter. Of note, however, is a statement that 32 pictures from the Long Gallery had recently been cleaned, while another 36 old pictures were considered unworthy of preservation.[4] This latter observation set a pattern followed by most Chatsworth and Hardwick inventorists over the following half-century. In 1792, for example, a "Catalogue of the Moveable Pictures" included notice of "Twenty eight very old pictures much defaced and the greater part of them cannot be made out."[5] No portrait of Jane Grey was listed in either house in 1792, probably because it had by that time fallen into such disrepair that it was no longer identifiable.

Despite the failure of inventories from the seventeenth and eighteenth centuries to identify any portrait of Jane Grey at either Chatsworth House or Hardwick Hall, a succession of visitors to one or both of the houses in the eighteenth century left accounts of their visits that are of some limited use. The well-known engraver George Vertue visited both Chatsworth and Hardwick in 1727, for example, though he made no mention of a portrait of Jane at either house.[6] Yet Vertue noted only the few pictures that piqued his personal interest, so that his failure to mention a portrait of Jane Grey cannot be interpreted to mean that none was there. The travel diarist John Byng, Viscount Torrington did report a portrait of Jane "much neglected" and hanging in the Great Drawing Room when he visited Hardwick Hall in 1789.[7] And when a Mrs Radcliffe visited five years later, in 1794, she observed paintings carelessly stacked on chairs or on the floor, though she did not describe any of them.[8] At the time of Mrs Radcliffe's visit, New Hardwick Hall was undergoing significant renovation at the direction of the 5th Duke of Devonshire, during which process paintings were of necessity moved about both within Hardwick and between the Devonshire residences. A significant number of paintings were even removed from Chatsworth to Hardwick in order to redecorate what had become the Duke's preferred residence.[9] The old portrait of Jane seen at Hardwick by Byng may well have been among those removed to there from Chatsworth at some point prior to 1789 and was quite possibly the same as the picture owned by Bess in 1560. The renovations of the 1790s would have been a logical occasion on which to reassess the value of the twenty-eight defaced and neglected paintings inventoried in 1792 at both Chatsworth and Hardwick Hall and to discard those no longer thought to be of value. No written account survives in the Devonshire archive to confirm any deliberate destruction of old and defaced pictures, however.

Following the death of the 5th Duke of Devonshire in 1811, a number of additional inventories were again compiled. The Cavendish's London residence of Devonshire House was inventoried for the first time, though the several hundred paintings there were once again simply counted collectively by room rather than being individually described. Nonetheless, the Devonshire House inventorist did feel compelled to make explicit mention of a portrait in the Middle Drawing Room that was attributed to the seventeenth-century artist Anthony Van Dyck and curiously said to depict "the Dutchess[sic] of Suffolk and Lady Jane Grey."[10] A contemporary inventory of Chatsworth House also counted paintings collectively rather than itemizing them individually, making it impossible to determine whether Bess's portrait of Jane Grey had survived at either Devonshire House or Chatsworth House.[11] The inventory of 1811 for Hardwick Hall differed, however, in that extensive descriptive detail was included for the many individual paintings held there. None were thought to depict Jane. But perhaps reflecting the earlier reports of defaced portraits, at least nine portraits of women that could no longer be identified were recorded in 1811. One full-length was suspected to depict Arbella Stuart, while a half-length was said to of "a Lady supposed to be Queen."[12] The other seven were entirely beyond recognition. And a further "Twenty other Old Portraits and Paintings various, [were] very much defaced and Bad."[13]

A second and more visual window onto the collection at Hardwick Hall also appeared at around the time of the death of the fifth duke. The prolific artist David Cox the Elder began a series of visits to Hardwick Hall in 1811 and that would span the artist's entire working life, until his death in 1859. Cox created numerous images of the interior of the house, especially the newly refurbished Long Gallery and the multitude of pictures it contained. Working variously in pencil, watercolors, and oils, Cox left a valuable visual record of the appearance of the interior of Hardwick Hall during the first half of the nineteenth century. But while his works make it clear that the Long Gallery held a large number of portraits that likely dated to the sixteenth century, Cox was an early precursor of Impressionism. Cox's depiction of the artwork held in the Long Gallery thus lacks the depictional realism necessary to identify the sitters in any of the portraits included in his own paintings of the Gallery.

A portrait of Jane Grey was documented as hanging in the Long Gallery in the nineteenth century, but the source document is undated, making it impossible to know whether Cox may have seen it during one of his visits to Hardwick Hall.[14] Neither can we know whether it was the same poartrait as that seen by Byng in the Great Drawing Room in 1789, since the document does not describe the portrait in any detail. But it had disappeared again by 1860, when Lady Louisa Cavendish Egerton compiled a catalogue of the pictures at Hardwick Hall.[15] She listed just over 300 pictures, none of which were said to depict Jane Grey. Four were of unidentified women, two of which were dated to the late-seventeenth century, and a third had been newly acquired in the nineteenth century.[16] The fourth was not described.

Five years later, Sir George Scharf, Director of the National Portrait Gallery, surveyed over 300 pictures at Hardwick Hall, though he offered descriptions of the content of only 261, including over a dozen identified using the single word "Unknown."[17] Then in 1903, Cecil Foljambe, Lord Hawkesbury created a printed catalogue of the collection at Hardwick Hall. Foljambe counted "four curious paintings on panels, supposed to have come from the old Hall," though he did not record their content.[18] Neither did he find any picture that could today be identified as a potential depiction of Jane Grey. Foljambe did, however, observe that a large number of portraits of royal sitters known to have hung at Hardwick Hall in 1601 were no longer present in 1903, including portraits of several kings ante-dating the Tudor period. Those portraits probably comprised a portrait set and, unlike the portrait of Jane Grey, none were created during the sitters' lifetimes. Thus Bess's portrait of Jane is unlikely to have been part of that group. Finally, the Courtauld Institute's Photographic Survey found no portrait of Jane Grey at Hardwick Hall in 1972, and no such portrait is recorded there in the current collection database of the National Trust, which acquired Hardwick Hall in 1959. Neither is there any portrait there with any potential for being a "lost" portrait of Jane mistakenly identified as some other person.[19] Likewise, no portrait known or said to depict Jane Grey is currently held at Chatsworth.[20] Neither are there at Chatsworth any sixteenth-century portraits of unidentified women or of wrongly-identified women who might actually be Jane Grey.[21] In all likelihood, Bess of Hardwick's authentic portrait of Jane Grey was one of the many found to be "much defaced" or "bad" late in the eighteenth century and thus not worth preserving. The picture was almost certainly discarded or deliberately destroyed before the middle of the nineteenth century.

The Lumley Portrait

A second potentially authentic portrait of Jane was recorded in the sixteenth century in the collection of John Lumley, 1st Baron Lumley. An accounting of the furnishings in Lumley's various residences was compiled in 1590. The resulting inventory included almost 300 paintings, three of which are relevant to this study. All three were described by the compiler of the inventory as "Pictures of a Smaller Scantlinge," or portraits of less than full length, to be distinguished from those "caryinge the fowrme of the whole Statuary," or full lengths. The first such scantling related to this study was itemized as "Of Quene Katherin Parre, last wife to K:H:8."[22] As discussed elsewhere in this volume, the scantling of Parr can today be identified as the Northwick Portrait. The second scantling was listed as "Of the Lady Katheryn Graye, married to the Earle of Hertfourde," which was perhaps related to the portraits of the Berry Hill Type. The last was "Of the Lady Jane Graye, executed."[23] The current whereabouts of Lord Lumley's portrait of Jane Grey are not known, but it is entirely likely that the painting was an authentic likeness of Jane Grey.

John Lumley married his first wife, Jane (or Joan) Fitzalan, in 1552, barely a year before the succession dispute that briefly brought Jane Grey Dudley to the throne. Jane Fitzalan was the daughter of Henry Fitzalan, Earl of Arundel, by Fitzalan's first wife Catherine Grey. Catherine Grey Fitzalan was Jane Grey's paternal aunt, thus making Jane Fitzalan a first cousin to Jane Grey. Further, Jane Fitzalan was born in about 1537 and within a year of her cousin Jane Grey, and their two families certainly knew each other. It is altogether likely that the two Janes were themselves well acquainted through both family interaction and their common circulation in the social circles surrounding the Henrician and Edwardian royal courts. It therefore follows that Jane Fitzalan Lumley—and quite probably John Lumley as well—would have been able to distinguish with certainty a portrait of her cousin Jane Grey and, conversely, to discredit any portrait that did not depict Jane Grey within a reasonable degree of accuracy.

The details of Lumley's acquisition of the portrait of Jane Grey are not known, so that today we can only speculate on its origins. Lumley did inherit Nonsuch Palace in 1580 from his father-in-law, Henry Fitzalan, and the collection there is usually said to have constituted the core of Lumley's own larger collection. But the picture of Jane Grey is unlikely to have originated at Nonsuch. Henry VIII began construction of the palace in 1538, though it was not entirely finished when the King died in 1547 (and when Jane Grey was not more than 11 years old). His successor Edward VI let out the palace on a long-term lease and thus did not use the residence himself. Queen Mary initially continued the lease following her own accession in 1553, but ultimately sold Nonsuch to Fitzalan in 1556. He completed construction of the palace in 1559 and soon after entertained Queen Elizabeth there. Given Fitzalan's history of initially supporting the efforts to elevate Jane Grey to the Crown at the expense of Mary and Elizabeth, however, together with Elizabeth's own famous distaste for all three Grey sisters, it would have been exceedingly impolitic for him to have displayed within the palace any portrait of his niece-by-marriage. And while it is true that Fitzalan briefly supported Katherine Grey as Elizabeth's successor when the latter suffered a near-fatal illness in 1562, he very soon shifted his support to Mary Stuart, in largest part because Mary shared Fitzalan's own Roman Catholic faith and Katherine did not. Since it is therefore unlikely that Fitzalan already held a portrait of Jane Grey at Nonsuch when John Lumley inherited the palace from him, Lumley must have acquired the painting through deliberate purchase and as a likeness that he, his wife, or both recognized as their executed cousin. And because both Lumleys were undoubtedly aware of Jane Grey's true appearance, it is improbable that the portrait was misidentified when the distinctive Lumley cartellinos were applied toward the end of the sixteenth century.[24]

Tracing the subsequent disposition of the Lumley Portrait of Jane Grey has proven all but impossible. At John Lumley's death in 1609, a portion of the collection passed to Thomas Howard, 21st Earl of Arundel. The portrait of Jane Grey was not listed among the almost 600 paintings owned by the Howards in 1655, however.[25] But the bulk of Lumley's collection passed to his cousin, Richard Lumley, who was later created Viscount Lumley in 1628. Richard's descendant in the sixth generation, George Lumley-Saunderson, 5th Earl of Scarborough, finally sold off much of the Lumley collection in 1785 and 1807. By the time of those sales, a significant percentage of the Lumley portraits had already lost there cartellini inscriptions, as evidenced by the large number of portraits described in the sale catalogues as simply "A Lady" or "A Gentleman." At least five half-length portraits of women were not able to be identified and none of either Katherine Parr or Jane Grey were included in either sale.[26]

Richard Lumley, 13th Earl of Scarbrough, has confirmed that the current Lumley collection at Sandbeck Park contains only one portrait on wood panel that is both a half length and depicts a woman. But that portrait reliably dates to the first decade of the sixteenth century, long before Jane Grey was born.[27] And while many of the portraits formerly in the sixteenth-century Lumley collection have been located elsewhere over the past few decades, the portrait said to depict Jane Grey has not.[28] It must for now be numbered among the "lost" portraits of Jane Grey.

The Harrington Portrait

Included among the many portraits said to depict Jane Grey itemized by Richard Davey in *Nine Days' Queen* was,

> a splendid portrait ... exhibited at the Derby Art Exhibition in 1841. It belonged to a Mr Harrington, who inherited it from two ancient ladies, the Misses Grey of Derby, in the possession of whose family this picture had been for many generations.[29]

Davey appears to have embellished from an earlier submission to the antiquarian journal *Notes and Queries* made in 1854 by Thomas Russell Potter, in which Potter sought further information on the painting.[30] No answer to Potter's query ever appeared in *Notes and Queries*, perhaps because Potter was himself mistaken in regard to one crucial detail: there was no Derby Art Exhibition in 1841.[31] Potter undoubtedly meant instead the Derby Mechanics' Institute Exhibition of 1839, which did indeed include a portrait of Jane Grey.[32]

Potter understood the picture to have been "once in the possession of the late Mr Harrington, of Breaston, Derbyshire, [and] ... *supposed* [sic] to have been identical with that in the Derby Exposition of 1841 ... an undoubted original." Potter elsewhere stated that Harrington had "procured it from Risley Hall, a seat of a branch of the Greys."[33] "The late Mr Harrington" can be only Benjamin Harrington, who owned the manor of Breaston, just one mile from Risley Hall, until his death in December 1817.[34] Harrington's last will and testament dated 13 November 1817 was witnessed by, among others, the Reverend John Hancock Hall, the owner of Risley Hall.[35] This indicates a close relationship between Harrington and Hall and supports the claim that Harrington "procured" the portrait from Risley Hall, whether by gift or purchase.

John Hancock Hall had inherited Risley from his maternal uncle, John Hancock, who in turn had purchased the whole of Risley manor in 1772 from Sir Willoughby Aston, 6th Baronet.[36] The Astons had never lived in Risley Hall, however, preferring nearby Risley Lodge instead. The Hall had therefore been let to a series of tenants after 1743, until it was finally demolished in 1757. John Hancock undertook the building of a new Risley Hall in the 1790s.[37] There is no surviving documentation to indicate whether Hancock simply moved the portrait said to depict Jane Grey from the old Lodge to the new Hall, or whether he purchased it in the 1790s to decorate his new house. But if Hancock acquired the portrait as an included furnishing of Risley Lodge in the sale of 1772, we may be able to deduce the possible appearance of the portrait.

The Astons of Risley Hall and Lodge were distant heirs-male of Anchitell Grey, second son of Henry Grey, 1st Earl of Stamford. Anchitell was himself a distant cousin of Henry Grey, 1st Duke of Kent and the purchaser in 1701 of the Wrest Park Portrait. And while it is unlikely that Anchitell had time before his death in 1702 to commission a copy of his cousin's newly-acquired portrait called "Lady Jane Grey," it is entirely possible that his spinster daughter Elizabeth may have done so. As Anchitell's sole surviving but female child, Elizabeth retained a life interest in (but not ownership of) Risley Hall and Lodge until her death in 1721. Elizabeth Grey never married, yet throughout her life she affected the title "Mrs." She may therefore be the homophonic "Misses Grey of Derby" alluded to in later centuries by Potter and Davey. If so, it is entirely likely that the Harrington Portrait was itself an early copy of the Wrest Park Portrait.[38]

There is only scant evidence for tracing the disposition of the Harrington Portrait in the years following the death of Benjamin Harrington in 1817. By his last will and testament, Harrington established a trust to benefit his eldest daughter's two surviving sons, Alexander Harrington Foxcroft and John Foxcroft. Three trustees were named: Harrington's son-in-law Alexander Foxcroft of Nottingham, Thomas Slater of Nottingham, and Francis Jessop of Derby. In order to facilitate the trustees' ability to generate revenue from the estate during his grandsons' minorities, Harrington further did "give and bequeath ... all ... household Goods and Furniture, Plate, Books, and Pictures" into the legal possession of the three trustees for the term of their trusteeship, with all to be restored to the Foxcroft boys upon either reaching the age of 21 years.[39] The Foxcrofts resided primarily in Nottingham, thus the trustees let out Breaston to tenants between 1817 and 1829.[40] Two years after reaching his legal majority in 1827, Alexander Harrington Foxcroft sold Breaston, in April of 1829.[41] Ownership of the portrait called "Lady Jane Grey" appears to have been entirely transferred to one of the Harrington trustees sometime between 1817 and 1829, however. The catalogue for the exhibition at the Derby Mechanics' Institute in 1839 identifies the owner of the portrait of Jane Grey included in that showing as "F. Jessop." This was surely the "Francis Jessop of Derby" named as a trustee in Harrington's will.[42] Jessop was Mayor of Derby in 1840–41 and a frequent contributor to local charities and cultural events. In January of 1851, at the advanced age of 68 years, Jessop sold his country villa in the village of Quarndon where he had been living with his wife Anne, their second son William, and five servants.[43] The catalogue for the sale listed as item number 141 a portrait of Lady Jane Grey in a carved gilt frame.[44] No further description of the painting was offered, and no buyer's name or sale price were recorded in the surviving copy of the catalogue. The Harrington Portrait thus disappeared from the historical record when it was sold by Jessop in 1851.

Other Lost Portraits

A number of additional portraits said to depict Jane Grey are mentioned in various books, inventories, and archives, though none can today be readily located. Davey cited, for example, a "sweetly pretty contemporary Tudor portrait, reputed to be that of Lady Jane Grey," in the possession of Colonel Horace Walpole at Heckfield Place, Hampshire.[45] Heckfield had originally been built in the eighteenth century by John Lefevre, but was completely rebuilt in the mid nineteenth century by his son-in-law Charles Shaw-Lefevre, 1st Viscount Eversley. At his death in 1888, Lord Eversley was survived by two daughters, Helena and Elizabeth. The two women married cousins from the St John-Mildmay family, leaving Heckfield Place to be sold in 1895 to Lt. Colonel Horace Walpole, himself a distant cousin of the Walpole Earls of Orford. Following Walpole's death in 1919, the property passed eventually to Mrs Colin Davey (no apparent relation to the author Richard Davey), who periodically sold portions of the contents of the house during the 1940s and 1950s. No inventory, auction catalogue, or sale record for Heckfield Place that might mention a portrait of Jane Grey has yet been identified, however. Heckfield Place itself has been resold at least twice since the 1980s and is at this writing reportedly being converted into a luxury hotel. The current owners have confirmed that no sixteenth-century portraits remain at the house.[46] The portrait thought to depict Jane Grey was most probably sold by Mrs Colin Davey prior to 1960, but no record of that sale has yet been discovered, and the whereabouts of the portrait remain unknown.

A further half-dozen portraits said to depict Jane Grey were recorded in 1804 by the engraver George Perfect Harding in his three-volume manuscript *List of Portraits, Pictures, In Various Mansions, of the United Kingdom*. Harding surveyed a vast number of houses, both large and small, throughout the United Kingdom, but we can only wonder at why he listed so few portraits of Jane and failed to mention many that were in houses he did visit and that were already well-known. Because he was an engraver seeking subject matter, perhaps he deliberately overlooked images that had already been popularized by others of his craft. Only one of those mentioned by Harding had previously been engraved: the Wrest Park Portrait.[47] Two others, the Jersey and Bodleian Portraits, had not yet been published as engravings.[48] A fourth was owned in 1804 by Christopher Roberts Wren, fourth-generation descendant of the seventeenth-century architect Sir Christopher Wren, of Wroxhall Abbey, Warwickshire. Wroxhall was sold in 1861 and soon demolished, to be replaced by a new mansion in 1866. The estate was eventually liquidated in 1995 and the last contents of the house were removed, their disposition unknown today.

Harding also noted a portrait at Dalkeith Palace in 1804 in the collection of the Duke of Buccleuch that was said to depict Jane. The sitter in that portrait had "long hair, black and very thick; [and was] not handsome."[49] It was not included in an inventory of Dalkeith taken in 1911, however.[50] Finally, Harding listed a portrait of Jane Grey at Warwick Castle, home at that time to George Greville, 2nd Earl of Warwick and a great collector of portraits in particular.[51] According to mid-nineteenth-century inventories, the portrait hung in the Blue Boudoir, where the Warwick collection of paintings attributed to Holbein were gathered.[52] Yet the portrait was not mentioned in a mid-nineteenth-century detailed guidebook to the house, though that guidebook listed and described many dozens of portraits in virtually every part of the house.[53] Significant sales of portraits from Warwick Castle were held in 1903, 1936, and 1968. The portrait is reportedly not at Warwick Castle today.[54]

Perhaps in imitation of both Byng and Harding, Prince Frederick Duleep Singh visited a large number of houses in Norfolk and subsequently published an account of the portraits he saw in those houses. Singh noted a portrait said to depict Jane at Ketteringham Hall, home of the antiquarian Sir John Peter Boileau. Singh provided a detailed description of the painting:

> H[ead] and S[houlders]. Body, face and blue eyes all turned towards the sinister [i.e., the viewer's left], fair hair parted and flat, roll over each ear, and small row of rolls over the head, black cap on the head falling at the side and behind. Dress: Black with white fur round the neck and down the front, also on each side of the arms. Blue Background, Min[iature]. Square. Age 18.[55]

Though the description is in many ways remarkably consistent with the appearance of the Bodleian Portrait, that painting was already at the Bodleian Library by the time Singh visited Ketteringham Hall. The house was sold to the Duke of Westminster in 1948 and used as a preparatory school and college until 1968. Ketteringham Hall is now owned by the Chapman family, which has redeveloped it as rental spaces for small businesses. It is not currently known whether the portrait seen at Ketteringham by Singh in the nineteenth century is still in the house today, but the non-residential uses to which the house has been put over the past half century suggest not.

One other type of source also refers to portraits of Jane Grey. Among the manuscripts held by the British Library is an inventory of paintings at Penshurst Place, home of the Sidney family since 1552. Compiled in the 1740s for Mrs Elizabeth Sidney Perry, item 43 in the inventory was identified as a portrait of Jane Grey. The painting was not described in any detail, but no portrait said to depict Jane Grey is at Penshurst today, and no record of the sale of such a painting at public auction after 1740 is known.[56]

Finally, the Heinz Archive and Library at the National Portrait Gallery maintains manuscript index card files on a large number of sitters. One of those files lists portraits of Jane Grey that various researchers have reported to the NPG over the past 150 years. Some of those portraits are covered by this study, including the Jersey Portrait formerly at Stowe House, the Chatsworth Portrait removed to Hardwick Hall, and the copy of the Syon Portrait now at Audley End. Others are eighteenth- and nineteenth-century copies of misidentified originals, such as a copy owned by the Scottish antiquary David Laing of the Althorp Portrait, exhibited at the Manchester Art Exhibition of 1857, and later noted by Scharf in the 1860s.[57] Yet another was a fanciful eighteenth-century portrait most recently sold through Bonham's in 2005.[58] And a miniature by Henry Bone is noted in the NPG card file, but it was produced around 1825 and was based on the Hastings Portrait.[59]

Several portraits noted in the NPG card file have disappeared from the collections that held them at the time they were first reported. A portrait recorded in the 1860s at Longleat, seat of the Marquis of Bath, was not included in a catalogue of portraits at that residence published less than twenty years later, for example.[60] Neither was it discovered during the Courtauld Institute's survey of the pictures at Longleat in the middle of the twentieth century.[61] Another was reportedly seen in 1797 at Duff House, home of the Earl of Fife, but was no longer present there in 1999.[62] The painter Robert Crozier of Manchester owned a bust-length portrait of Jane on wood panel that was recorded in the card file by Scharf in 1857, but it too has vanished. And the collection of Mrs Elizabeth Lawrence of Studley Royal Park, North Yorkshire, likewise included a portrait said to depict Jane Grey, though none is held there today.[63]

One final apparently "lost" portrait remains to be considered. It was included in successive exhibitions of paintings by Old Masters held at Burlington House in 1872 and 1880.[64] The work was loaned on both occasions by George C Handford, a London architect and surveyor known for having amassed a large collection of historical portraits.[65] Handford disposed of a portion of his collection in 1887, and his portrait of Jane was sold through Christie, Manson, and Woods on 15 January of that year.[66] The inclusion of the portrait of Jane Grey in the sale was made the focus of pre-sale advertising, indicating that the painting was perceived to be of considerable significance.[67] Both the catalogue and the pre-sale advertising noted that the portrait had previously been in the collection of "Sir J. South" as well as at Gilston Park House, Hertfordshire. Since Gilston was demolished and its contents sold in 1851, we can deduce that the painting originated there, was purchased by the astronomer Sir James South at the sale of 1851, and was sold upon South's death in 1867 to George Handford. No buyer was recorded at the time of the Christie sale in 1887, however, making it almost impossible to determine the painting's current whereabouts. The Burlington House exhibition catalogues offered a detailed description of the painting.

> Portrait of Lady Jane Grey (?). François Clouet, called Janet. Bust, nearly full face; headdress hanging down behind; black dress, trimmed with gold; gold chain around neck and waist; hands clasped in front; greyish background with coat of arms on l[eft]. Dated, on r[ight].; "1566." (Compare date of Lady Jane Grey's death.) Panel, 12 by 9 ½ in.[68]

Several aspects of the description are worthy of special notice. Firstly, the work was attributed to the French artist Clouet, much like the Tayler, Berry Hill, and Soule Portraits. And as with those three portraits, the attribution is quite probably incorrect. Clouet never worked in England, very rarely depicted women full face, and equally rarely included the hands of adult sitters within the composition.[69] Further, the size of the panel—12 x 9 ½ inches—was remarkably similar to that of the Berry Hill Portrait—12 ½ x 9 inches. The written description of the composition of the portrait was also strikingly similar to what is actually seen in the Berry Hill Portrait: full face, hands clasped in front, and a black dress. Though the description indicated bust length, it nonetheless described a gold chain around the sitter's waist, implying that the composition was actually half-length, again much like the Berry Hill Portrait. But the remainder of the description was reminiscent of the Chawton Portrait: dress trimmed with gold and a gold chain around the neck. And like the Soule Portrait, the Handford painting bore an inscribed date. Whether that date was original to the work or, as was the case with the Soule, a later addition cannot now be determined, however.

The seemingly unanswerable question arises: Was the Handford Portrait another variant of the Berry Hill Type? The many described similarities certainly seems to leave the possibility open. Further, the inscribed date of 1566 allows equally for the painting to be either an early portrait of Elizabeth I or a portrait of Katherine Grey Seymour. But if the coat of arms included in the image were original rather than a later addition, the failure of subsequent owners and dealers to readily identify those arms as royal effectively eliminates Elizabeth Tudor as the sitter. Records of both the Grey and the Seymour arms should have been readily available for comparison to what was depicted in the painting, however, so that failure to identify the arms suggests more probably that the painting depicted some woman unrelated to the Tudor-Stuart line of succession. But as long as the painting remains among the "lost" portraits of Lady Jane Grey Dudley, we cannot reach a definitive conclusion.

[1] White, *'that whyche ys nedefoulle and nesesary,'* II:389-415. Appendix Three is a transcription in full of the inventory. See also Chatsworth House, Devonshire Manuscripts (MSS) H/143/6.

[2] Devonshire MSS H/143/2. Though the inventory is catalogued as dating to 1553, White notes that the manuscript is undated but is almost certainly related to an attached deed dated August 1559. See White, *'That whyche ys nedefoulle'*, 373-374. Construction of Chatsworth began in 1552.

[3] National Archives (NA), PROB 11/111, ff. 196v–208r, will and inventories of Elizabeth, Dowager Countess of Shrewsbury; White, 'That whyche ys nedefoulle,'464-472. It is not clear why the Hardwick Hall inventories should be so thorough in listing and identifying so many pictures while the Chatsworth inventory fails to list any at all. The Hardwick inventories are, in general, more detailed in other respects as well, so that the difference may lie in a lack of diligence on the part of the Chatsworth inventorist. See also Devonshire MSS H/279/9-10.

[4] Devonshire MSS, CH36/7/0, f.26v.

[5] Devonshire MSS CH36/7/1A; CH36/7/2, 90-91 and 137-140.

[6] "The Vertue Notebooks – Vol. VI," *Journal of the Walpole Society*, Volume XXX (London, 1955 and 1968), 72-73.

[7] John Byng, *The Torrington Diaries: Containing the Tours through England and Wales of the Hon John Byng (later 5th Viscount Torrington) Between the Years 1781 and 1794*, edited by C. Bruyn Andrews, introduction by John Beresford (London : Eyre & Spottiswoode, 1934-38), II:32.

[8] Lindsay Boynton, ed., *Hardwick Hall Inventories of 1601* (London: The Furniture History Society, 1971), 11.

[9] Mark Girouard, Alistair Laing, et al., *Hardwick Hall* (National Trust Ltd., 1989 and 2006), 18.

[10] Devonshire MSS, CH36/5/5, f.26v. Since van Dyck was not active in London until almost a century after Jane's death and is not known to have painted sixteenth-century subjects, the portrait, the artist, or both must have been misidentified. No mention of any double portrait of Frances and Jane Grey has yet been uncovered in any other source material.

[11] Devonshire MSS, CH36/5/3.

[12] Devonshire MSS, CH36/5/, ff. 25v and 26v.

[13] Devonshire MSS, CH36/5/, f.27r.

[14] Devonshire MSS, *Diagram of the Long Gallery at Hardwick with an inventory of the pictures there*, undated, nineteenth century. "Item 22: Lady Jane Grey."

[15] Cecil George Saville Foljambe, Baron Hawkesbury (later 1st Earl of Liverpool), "Catalogue of the Pictures at Hardwick Hall," *Journal of the Derbyshire Archaeological and Natural History Society* XXV (June 1903), 103-158.

[16] Foljambe, "Catalogue of the Pictures at Hardwick Hall," 132 and 133.

[17] National Portrait Gallery, Heinz Archive and Library, Papers of Sir George Scharf, NPG 7/1/3/3/1/2, ff.167r passim.

[18] Foljambe, "Hardwick Hall," 37.

[19] Electronic communication, Carol Wilson, Hardwick Hall, 15 August 2007.

[20] *Catalogue of Paintings in the Collection of the Duke of Devonshire* (bound typescript, 1933). This is the current Devonshire Collection curator's working copy.

[21] The sole sixteenth-century panel portrait of an unidentified woman, Item Number 450 in the 1933 *Catalogue*, is in storage and was not accessible at the time of my site visit. It has never been photographed. The *Catalogue* states, however, that the work was originally attributed to Antonis Mor but later re-attributed by Lionel Cust to Frans Pourbus the Younger. Mor did not visit England until late in 1553, after Jane had been imprisoned. He is thus very unlikely to have painted a portrait of Jane Grey, and it would have been exceedingly impolitic of Bess of Hardwick to commission him for such a portrait at that juncture. Both Frans Pourbus the Elder (1545-1581) and his son Frans Pourbus the Younger (1569-1622) were active in the Low Countries rather than in England and both well after Jane's death in 1554.

[22] Lionel Cust, "The Lumley Inventories," *The Sixth Volume of the Walpole Society* (Oxford: Oxford

University Press, 1918), 25.

23 Cust, "Lumley Inventories," 26.

24 Jane Lumley died in 1576, probably before the cartellinos were painted, but John Lumley would nonetheless have ensured the proper identification of the sitter, even as late as 1590.

25 Mary F.S. Hervey, *The Life Correspondence and Collections of Thomas Howard, Earl of Arundel* (Cambridge: Cambridge University Press, 1921), 473-495.

26 Search of the Getty Research Institute's *Provenance Index Database*, Christie's sale of 18 June 1785, Sale Catalog Br-A4197; Christie's sale of 8-11 August 1785, Sale Catalog Br-A4205; Thomas Dawson auction house, sale of 2-7 November 1807, Sale Catalog Br-532 and sale of 16-19 December 1807, Sale Catalog Br-538; Cust, "Lumley Inventories," 31-35 .

27 Richard Lumley, Earl of Scarbrough, 13 March 2014, Electronic communication. The sole half-length on panel depicting a female is inscribed "Lady Margaret" and dated to 1509.

28 Catharine MacLeod, Tarnya Cooper, and Margaret Zoller, "A List of Portraits in the Lumley Inventory," in *The Lumley Inventory: Art Collecting and Lineage in the Elizabethan Age*, edited by Mark Evans (London: The Roxburghe Club, 2010), Appendix Three.

29 Davey, *Nine Day' Queen*, 362.

30 Thomas Russell Potter, "Lady Jane Grey," *Notes and Queries* Series 1, Vol. IX, Issue 234 (April 22, 1854), 373.

31 A second exhibition was held in Derby in 1843, but no portrait of Jane Grey was displayed at that later event. See W. Bemrose, *Catalogue of the articles comprised in the exhibition, held for the benefit of the Town and County Museum, 1843* (Derby Town and County Museum, 1843).

32 Derby Local Studies Library, Ref. 4181, *Catalogue of articles contained in The Exhibition of the Derby Mechanics' Institute, 1839*, Item no. 137, "Portrait of Lady Jane Grey, unknown artist."

33 Thomas R. Potter, *The History and Antiquities of Charnwood Forest* (London: Hamilton, Adams and Co., 1842), note, bottom of page 126.

34 John Timbs, *Ancestral Stories and Traditions of Great Families Illustrative of English History* (London: Griffith and Farran, 1869), 404.

35 NA, PROB 11/1604, ff. 188-190; Daniel and Samuel Lysons, *Magna Britannia: Vol. 5: Derbyshire* (London: T. Cadell and W. Davies, 1817), clxviii and 251. The Rev. John Hancock Hall (d.1859) should not be confused with his son, also named John Hancock Hall, barrister, who pre-deceased his father in 1845.

36 Lysons, *Magna Britannia*, 251.

37 Alistair Plant, "Lost Houses – Risley Hall," Images Online, <http://www.countryimagesmagazine.co.uk/lost_houses/risley-hall/>. Accessed 20 June 2014.

38 At least three early copies of the Wrest Park Portrait are documented, though the locations of only two are known today. Of the two known, the first and presumed earliest was produced in the middle of the eighteenth century for Harry Grey (1715-1768), 4th Earl of Stamford. It was held at Enville Hall until the beginning of the twentieth century, when it was removed to Dunham Massey at the behest of Roger Grey, 10th Earl of Stamford. See Christie, Manson & Woods, Ltd., *The Estate of the Late Lord Stamford, Dunham Massey, Altrincham, Cheshire. Valuation at Current Market Prices. Pictures, Drawings, Prints, Porcelain, Silver, Miniatures, Objects of Vertu and Books.* 1977, p.10: "[In] The Great Hall. Holbein. [£]350. Portrait of a Lady half length, wearing brown dress, white collar and headdress, holding a half opened book - 29 ½ x 23 in."; National Trust Collection, Dunham Massey, DUN.P.31, *A lady called Lady Jane Grey*, English School, oil on canvas, 29 ½ in. x 23 in. The second surviving copy, also now at Dunham Massey, is believed to date to late in the eighteenth century. See Christie, *Estate of the Late Lord Stamford*, p.37: "[In] The Staircase Hall Outside the Stone Parlour. Eworth. [£]200. Portrait of a Lady, half length, wearing a brown dress and white cap, holding a half open book - 29in by 24in.", National Trust, Dunham Massey, DUN.P.12, *? Lady Jane Grey*, English School, oil on canvas, 29 in. x 24 in. A third apparent copy was sold through Christie's in 1931 by Sir John Foley Grey, 8th Baronet and owner of Enville Hall from 1914 until his death in 1938. See Christie, Manson & Woods, Ltd., *Catalogue of pictures by old masters: the property of Sir John Foley Grey, Bart*, 27 February 1931, Lot 114.

39 NA, PROB 11/1604, ff. 188r–190r.

40 Alexander Foxcroft resided in the parish of St Nicholas in Nottingham in 1804. *See The Lady's magazine: or, Entertaining companion for the fair sex*, November 1804 (London: G and J Robinson, 1804), 615. Alexander and Sarah Foxcroft's son Herbert died in October 1817 and was buried at the Priory Church of St Anthony, Lenton, Nottinghamshire. See John Thomas Godfrey, *The History of the Parish and Priory of Lenton in the County of Nottingham* (London and Derby: Bemrose and Sons, 1884), 257. Alexander Foxcroft was an overseer of the poor for Lenton in 1820 and 1821. Godfrey, *History ... of Lenton*, 338.

41 "Breaston, Derbyshire to be sold by auction," *Derby Mercury*, 22 April 1829. The notice of sale makes no mention of the contents of the house, which had probably been removed in 1817 prior to the house being let to tenants. Alexander Harrington Foxcroft died exactly one year after the sale of Breaston, on 17 April 1830, at the age of 24, perhaps as the ultimate result of a compound fracture of the leg sustained in a carriage crash in Nottingham on 17 April 1827. See "A distressing accident," *Derby Mercury*, 25 April 1827.

42 Derby Local Studies Library, Ref. BA 352/16464, *Modern Mayors of Derby – sketches, biographical, historical and reminiscent of the Mayors of Derby* (Derby: Hobson,1909).

43 NA, HO107/2144/51, Census Returns of England and Wales, 1851, 22. Son William died two years later, in June of 1867. Francis and Anne Jessop's eldest son, Francis Johnson Jessup, died shortly after his brother, on 28 July 1867 and was survived by one son, Francis Robert Jessop, and six daughters. See Llewellyn Jewitt, "Memorial Note to the Rhyming Tour," *The Reliquary and Illustrated Archaeologist: A Quarterly Journal*, Vol. VIII, 1867-8 (London: Bemrose, 1868), 106-107.

44 Derby Local Studies Library, Ref. BQ 333.33/44634, *Catalogue... [of contents] at the villa of Francis Jessopp, Esq., (Quarndon, near Derby - who is changing abode)* 1856 January 21st -24th, 14.

45 Davey, *Nine Days Queen*, 362. It is likely that Davey was once again simply mistaken in his understanding, since he notes that the portrait exhibited at Derby in either 1839 or 1841 was "mentioned by Howard." That would seem to refer to George Howard, the nom-de-plume of Francis Charles Laird, author of *Lady Jane Grey and her Times*. That book was published in 1822 however, almost two decades before any Derby Exhibition and was largely a work of fiction. Further, Howard/Laird made no mention within his volume of any portraits of Jane Grey.

46 Louise Remington, Heckfield Place, electronic communication, 13 April 2010.

47 NPG, Heinz Archive and Library, George Perfect Harding, *List of Portraits, Pictures, In Various Mansions, of the United Kingdom* (manuscript bound in three volumes, 1804), II:246.

48 Harding, *List of Portraits*, I:44 and III:186 and 191.

49 Harding, *List of Portraits*, II:55.

50 Henry Scott, *Catalogue of the Pictures at Dalkeith House* (Privately printed, 1911).

51 Harding, *List of Portraits*, II:301.

52 Aaron Manning, Warwick Castle, electronic communication, 16 October 2014.

53 Henry T. Cooke, *An Historical and Descriptive Guide to Warwick Castle ... and other places of interest in the neighborhood*, 6th edition (Warwick: Henry T Cooke, 1849).

54 Aaron Manning, Warwick Castle, electronic communication, 16 October 2014.

55 Frederick Duleep Singh, *Portraits in Norfolk Houses* (Norwich: Jarrold and Sons Ltd., 1927), 361.

56 Maryann Webster, Secretary to Viscount De L'Isle, electronic communication, 9 October 2014.

57 *Catalogue of the Art Treasures of the United Kingdom Collected at Manchester in 1857* (London: Bradbury and Evans, 1857), 132; Heinz Archive and Library, Papers of George Scharf, 16/C/1/146. The painting, item number 382, was noted in the catalogue to have been "engraved by Dibdin." See Thomas Dibdin, *The Bibliographical Decameron* (London: Shakespeare Press, 1817), III: unnumbered leaf following page 248.

58 *British and Continental Pictures*, Bonhams, Knightsbridge, Sale Number 11632, 10 May 2005, Lot Number 76, "Portrait of a young woman, said to be Lady Jane Grey." Buyer unknown.

59 The miniature is reportedly now in a US collection. Bone's dated preparatory drawing is held by the NPG as accession number D17222.

[60] *Biographical Catalogue of the Portraits at Longleat* (London: Elliot Stock, 1881).

[61] *Courtauld Institute Photographic Survey of Longleat*, typescript, 1954.

[62] *Duff House Catalogue of Paintings and Sculpture*, introduction by Timothy Clifford and Stephen Lloyd (National Gallery Scotland, 1999).

[63] Studley Royal is today part of the Fountains Abbey estate owned by the National Trust. No portrait potentially identifiable as Jane Grey and held there is mentioned in the NT's online collection database.

[64] *Exhibition of the Works of the Old Masters*, 1872 (London: William Clowes and Sons for the Royal Academy, 1872), 22. "Item 208: Portrait of Lady Jane Grey by François Clouet, called Janet; panel; 12 x 9 in.; Lent by George C. Handford, Esq."; *Exhibition of the Works of the Old Masters ... including a special collection of works by Holbein and his school* (London: William Clowes and Sons for the Royal Academy, 1880), 32, Item 154.

[65] Walter H. Godfrey, *Survey of London, Volume 2: Chelsea, Part 1* (1909), 54-60.

[66] Christie's Manson & Woods, sale of 15 January 1887, Lot 282, "Lady Jane Grey by François Clouet, called Janet." The catalogue explicitly notes that the painting was exhibited at Burlington House in 1872 and 1880. Handford gifted a second portrait, depicting the travel-writer Jean Chardin, to the Royal Society in June 1887. See Royal Society accession number 9680.

[67] *The Athenaeum*, no.3089 (8 January 1887), 51.

[68] *Exhibition of the Works of the Old Masters ...* (1880), 32.

[69] See, for example, the 128 portrait drawings by Clouet now in the Musée Condé at Chantilly.

BIBLIOGRAPHY

MANUSCRIPTS

British Library
>Additional 33230
>Arundel 97
>Egerton 1636
>Harley 2342
>Royal 18C XXIV
>Chatsworth House

Catalogue of Paintings in the Collection of the Duke of Devonshire, bound
>typescript, 1933.

Devonshire Manuscripts

Essex Record Office
>Barrett Lennard Family Records

Fitzwilliam Museum, Cambridge
>Object File PD.1-1963

Hampshire Record Office, Winchester
>Knight Family Papers

Leeds Probate Registry
>Will of Sophia Matilda Heathcote, Widow

Longleat House
>Seymour Papers

Minneapolis Institute of Art
>Object File for Accession Number 87.6

National Archives (UK)
>E 36/277
>E 101/631/44
>LR 2/118
>LR 2/120
>PROB 11/37
>PROB 11/111
>SP 12/31/25

National Portrait Gallery, Heinz Library and Archive
>George Perfect Harding, List of Portraits, Pictures, In Various Mansions, of the
>>United Kingdom
>George Scharf Papers
>Object File for NPG764

Object File for NPG4451
>Sitter File for Elizabeth I
>Sitter File for Katherine Parr
>Sitter File for Lady Jane Grey

Oxford University
New College 328/1
Society of Antiquaries (London)
706A

PRINTED

Acts of the Privy Council. Vol. 4. Edited by John Roche Dasent. London: HMSO, 1892.

Alford, Stephen. T*he Early Elizabethan Polity: William Cecil and the British Succession*. Cambridge: Cambridge University Press, 2002.

"Art Treasures in Fire." *The Times of London*, 1 October 1949.

Ascham, Roger. *The Scholemaster*. London: John Daye, 1570.

"An Authentic Portrait of Lady Jane Grey?" *The Times of London*, 5 July 1965.

Baetjer, Katherine. "Buying Pictures for New York: The Founding Purchase of 1871." *Metropolitan Museum Journal* 38 (2004).

Banks, John. *The Innocent Usurper*. London: Printed for R. Bentley, 1694.

Barrett-Lennard, Thomas. *An Account of the families of Barrett and Lennard*. 1908.

Bauch,J. and D. Eckstein. "Woodbiological investigations on panels of Rembrandt paintings." *Wood Science and Technology* 15:4 (1981), 251-263.

Bemrose, W. *Catalogue of the articles comprised in the exhibition, held for the benefit of the Town and County Museum, 1843*. Derby Town and County Museum, 1843.

Bent, J. Theodore Bent. "The English in the Levant." *The English Historical Review* 5:20 (October 1890), 654-664.

Bethan, William. *The Baronetage of England*. London: E. Lloyd, 1805.

Bhanu, Vijaya and K. C. Malhotra. "A population genetic study of cleft chin in India." *American Journal of Physical Anthropology* 37:3 (November 1972), 367-372.

Biographical Catalogue of the Portraits at Longleat. London: Elliot Stock, 1881.

Bolland, Charlotte and Tarnya Cooper. *The Real Tudors: Kings and Queens Rediscovered*. London: National Portrait Gallery Publications, 2014.

Boynton, Lindsay, ed. *Hardwick Hall Inventories of 1601*. London: The Furniture History Society, 1971.

Briefel, Aviva. *The Deceivers: Art Forgery and Identity in the Nineteenth Century*. Ithaca: Cornell University Press, 2006.

Brotton, Jerry. *The Sale of the Late King's Goods: Charles & and his Art Collection*. London: Pan Books, 2007.

Burnet, Gilbert. *The History of the Reformation of the Church of England: The second part, of the progress made in it till the settlement of it in the beginning of Q. Elizabeth's reign*. London: Printed by T[homas] H[odgkin]for Richard Chiswell, 1681.

Byng, John. *The Torrington Diaries: Containing the Tours through England and   Wales of the Hon John Byng (later 5th Viscount Torrington) Between the Years 1781 and 1794*. 4 volumes. Edited by C. Bruyn Andrews, introduction by John Beresford. London : Eyre & Spottiswoode, 1934-38.

The Catalogue and Description of King Charles I's Capital Collection. London: W. Bathoe, 1752.

Catalogue of articles contained in The Exhibition of the Derby Mechanics' Institute, 1839.

Catalogue of Important English Pictures circa 1550 – circa 1880 from the Northwick Collection. Christie's, London, 25 June 1965.

Catalogue of the Art Treasures of the United Kingdom Collected at Manchester in 1857. London: Bradbury and Evans, 1857.

Catalogue of the late Lord Northwick's Extensive and Magnificent Collection of Ancient and Modern Pictures ... at Thirlestane House, Cheltenham. London: J. Davy and Son, 1859.

Catalogue of the more important part of the collection of Italian and English pictures, the property of Thomas Wright, Esq., of Upton Hall, Newark. Christie and Manson, 7 June 1845.

Catalogue of pictures by old masters: the property of Sir John Foley Grey, Bart. Christie, Manson & Woods, Ltd., 27 February 1931.

Chaloner, Thomas. *Elegy on the untimely death of the most Protestant divine Lady Jane Grey.* London: Thomas Vautrollerius, 1579.

Chapman, Hester. *Lady Jane Grey.* London: Jonathan Cape, 1962.

"Circle of the Master of the Female Half Lengths." *The Collectors: Old Master Paintings.* Edited by Roy Bolton. Exh. cat., 2009.

A collection of proceedings and trials against state prisoners; ... from the Norman conquest to this present time. London: Printed for J. Wilcox, 1741.

Collins, Arthur. *Historical Collections of the Noble Families of Cavendishe, Holles, Vere, Harley, and Ogle.* London, 1752.

A conference between the Lady Jane Grey and F. Fecknam a Romish priest, concerning the blessed sacrament; whilest she was prisoner in the Tower of London, and was beheaded on the Green there, Feb. 12. 1554. Together with her behaviour and last speech and prayers at her suffering. London, 1688.

The Contents of Fulbeck Hall, Lincolnshire. Sotheby's, London, 8 October 2002.

Cooke, Henry T. *An Historical and Descriptive Guide to Warwick Castle ... and other places of interest in the neighborhood.* 6th edition. Warwick: Henry T. Cooke, 1849.

Cumming, Valerie, C. W. Cunnington, P. E. Cunnington. *Dictionary of Fashion History.* Oxford: Berg, 2010.

Cust, Lionel. "The Lumley Inventories." *The Sixth Volume of the Walpole Society.* Oxford: Oxford University Press, 1918.

Cust, Richard. *Charles I: A Political Life.* Harlow, Pearson Education, 2005.

Davey, Richard. *The Nine Days Queen: Lady Jane Grey and her Times.* London: Methuen, 1909.

de Lisle, Leanda. "Faking Jane: On Lady Jane Grey & a historical forgery uncovered." *The New Criterion.* September 2009.

--------------------. *The Sisters Who Would Be Queen: The Tragedy of Mary, Katherine and Lady Jane Grey.* Hammersmith: Harper Press, 2008.

De Marchi, Neil. "The Antwerp-Mechelen Production and Export Complex." *In His Milieu: Essays on Netherlandish Art in Memory of John Michael Montias.* Edited by Amy Golhany, Mia Mochizuki, and Kisa Vergara. Amsterdam: Amsterdam University Press, 2007.

de Mirimonde, Albert P. *Sainte-Cécilie: Métamorphoses d'un thème musical*. Geneva: Minkoff, 1974.

Dibdin, Thomas Frognall. *The Bibliographical Decameron; Or, Tens Days Pleasant Discourse Upon Illuminated Manuscripts, and Subjects Connected With Early Engraving, Typography, and Bibliography*. London: W. Bulmer and Company, 1817.

Digby, Anne. "Victorian values and women in public and private." *Victorian Values*. Edited by Thomas C. Smout. Oxford: Oxford University Press for the British Academy, 1992.

Disraeli, Isaac. *Curiosities of Literature, New Edition*. London: Frederick Warne and Co., 1858.

Dobson, Michael and Nicola J. Watson. *England's Elizabeth: An Afterlife in Fame and Fantasy*. Oxford: Oxford University Press, 2002.

Dodd, M.H. "Cecilia Bodenham: A Portrait by Holbein." *Notes and Queries*, 2nd series, XI (March 20, 1915), 231.

Drabble, John. "Thomas Fuller, Peter Heylyn and the English Reformation." *Renaissance and Reformation*, new series, 3 (Spring 1979), 168-188.

Duff House Catalogue of Paintings and Sculpture. Introduction by Timothy Clifford and Stephen Lloyd. National Gallery Scotland, 1999.

Du Mortier, Bianca M. "Features of Fashion in the Netherlands of the Seventeenth Century." *Netherlandish Fashion in the Seventeenth Century*. Introduction by Johannes Pietsch. Riggisberg: Abegg-Stiftung, 2012.

Edwards, J. Stephan. "Framing a Life in Portraits: A 'New' Portrait of Mary Nevill Fiennes, Lady Dacre," *British Art Journal* XIV:2, 14-20.

----------------------------------. *'Jane the Quene': A New Consideration of Lady Jane Grey, England's Nine Days Queen*. PhD diss., University of Colorado at Boulder, 2007.

----------------------------------. "A New Face for the Lady." *History Today* 55:12 (December 2005): 44-45.

----------------------------------. "On the Date of Birth of Lady Jane Grey." *Notes and Queries* 54:3 (September 2007), 240-242.

----------------------------------. "A Further Note on the Date of Birth of Lady Jane Grey." *Notes and Queries* 55:2 (June 2008), 146-148.

Eller, Irvin. *The History of Belvoir Castle: From the Norman Conquest to the Nineteenth Century*. London: R. Tyas, 1841.

The Estate of the Late Lord Stamford, Dunham Massey, Altrincham, Cheshire. Valuation at Current Market Prices. Christie, Manson & Woods, Ltd., 1977.

Evans, Joan. *English Jewelry from the fifth century A.D. to 1800*. London: Methuen and Company, 1921.

Evans, Mark, ed. *The Lumley Inventory and Pedigree: Facsimile and Commentary on the Manuscript in the Possession of the Earls of Scarborough*. Roxburghe Club, 2010.

Exhibition of Portrait Miniatures. London: Burlington Fine Arts Club, 1889.

Exhibition of the Works of the Old Masters, 1872. London: William Clowes and Sons for the Royal Academy, 1872.

Exhibition of the Works of the Old Masters ... including a special collection of works by

Holbein and his school. London: William Clowes and Sons for the Royal Academy, 1880.

Fellman, Bruce. "Looking for Lady Jane." *Yale Alumni Magazine*. May/June 2007.

Ferguson, George. *Signs and Symbols in Christian Art*. Oxford: Oxford University Press, 1954.

Fischel, Anna, et al., ed. *Fashion: The Definitive History of Costume and Style*. New York: Dorling Kindersley for the Smithsonian Institute, 2012.

Foljambe, Cecil George Saville. "Catalogue of the Pictures at Hardwick Hall." *Journal of the Derbyshire Archaeological and Natural History Society* XXV (June 1903), 103-158.

Foster, John. *Alumni Oxonienses 1500-1714: Abannan – Kyte*. London: Parker and Company, 1891.

Fuller, Thomas. *The Church History of Britain: From the Birth of Jesus Christ Until the Year MDCXLVII*. Edited by J.S. Brewer. 6 volumes. Oxford: Oxford University Press, 1845.

Ganz, Paul. *Hans Holbein D.J.: Der Meisters Gemälde in 252 Abbildungen*. Stuttgart: Deutsche Verlags-Anstalt, 1912.

Gilchrist, Alexander. *Life of William Blake*. 2 volumes. London: MacMillan, 1880.

Gildon, Charles. *Remarks on Mr Rowe's Tragedy of the Lady Jane Grey, and all his other plays*. The English Stage Series, vol. 48. New York: Garland Publishing, 1974.

Giorgi, Rosa. *Saints in Art*. Translated by Thomas Michael Hartmann. Los Angeles: Getty Publications, 2003.

Girouard, Mark, and Alistair Laing, et al. *Hardwick Hall*. National Trust Ltd., 1989 and 2006.

Godfrey, John Thomas. *The History of the Parish and Priory of Lenton in the County of Nottingham*. London and Derby: Bemrose and Sons, 1884.

Godfrey, Walter H., ed. *Survey of London, Volume 2: Chelsea, Part 1*. 1909.

Gordon, Delahay. *General History of the Lives, Trials, and Executions of All the Royal and Noble Personages, that have Suffered in Great-Britain and Ireland for High Treason, and other crimes*. 3 volumes. London: J. Burd,   1760.

Goulding, Richard. *The Welbeck Abbey Miniatures belonging to His Grace the Duke of Portland*. Oxford, 1916.

Graz, Marie-Christine. *Jewels in Painting*. Milan: Skira, 1999.

Gregg, Pauline. *King Charles I*. London: Dent, 1981.

Grey, Jane, Lady. *An epistle of the Ladye Iane, a righte vertuous woman, to a learned man of late falne from the truth of Gods most holy word, for fear of the worlde read it, to thy consolacion: whereunto is added the communication that she had with Master Feckenham vpon her faith, and belefe of the sacraments: also another epistle whiche she wrote to her sister, with the words she spake vpon the scaffold befor she suffered, anno. M.D.Liiii*. London: John Day, 1554.

Gristwood, Sarah. *Arbella: England's Lost Queen*. Boston: Houghton Mifflin Harcourt, 2003.

Grosvenor, Bendor, ed. *Lost Faces: Identity and Discovery in Tudor Royal Portraiture*. London: Philip Mould Ltd, 2007.

Gurnis-Farrell, Musa. "Martyr Acts: Playing With Foxe's Martyrs on the Public Stage." In *Religion and Drama in Early Modern England: The Performance of Religion on the Renaissance Stage*, edited by Jane Hwang Degenhardt and Elizabeth Williamson. Farnham: Ashgate Publishing, 2011.

Hackenbroch, Yvonne. *Renaissance Jewelry*. London: Sotheby Park Bernet, 1979.

Hales, John. *A Declaration of the Succession of the Crowne Imperiall of Inglande*. London: 1563.

Hamilton, Edward. *The Sanctus: A Collection of Sacred Music, Full and Complete in Every Department; Adapted to the Worship of All Protestant Denominations*. Boston: Phillips, Sampson & Company, 1857.

Harrison and Willis, Messers. *The Great Jennens Case*. Sheffield: Pawson and Brailsford, 1879.

Hayward, Maria. *Rich Apparel: Clothing and the Law in Henry VIII's England*. Farnham: Ashgate, 2009.

Hervey, Mary F.S. *The Life Correspondence and Collections of Thomas Howard, Earl of Arundel*. Cambridge: Cambridge University Press, 1921.

Heylyn, Peter. *Ecclesia Restaurata, or, the Reformation of the Church of England*. London: H. Twyford, T. Dring, J. Place, and W. Palmer, 1661.

Hind, Arthur M. *Engraving in England in the Sixteenth and Seventeenth Centuries*. Cambridge: Cambridge University Press, 1955.

The History and Fall of the Lady Jane Grey. London: Printed by J. Watts for J. Roberts, 1725.

A History of the County of Warwick. Vol. 6. Edited by Louis F. Salzman. Oxford: Oxford University Press, 1951.

Hoekstra, Rosemarijn. "Images of Dress in the Golden Age of Dutch Painting." *Costume* 33 (1999), 36-45.

Holland, Henry Holland. *Heroωlogia Anglica hoc est, clarissimorvm et doctissimorvm aliqovt [sic] Anglorvm qvi florvervnt ab anno Cristi M.D. vsq' ad presentem annvm M.D.C.XX viuae effigies vitae et elogia*. Arnhem: Jan Janson Arnemuiden, 1620.

Hussey, Christopher. "Melton Constable, Norfolk, the Seat of Lord Hastings." *Country Life* 64:1652 and 1653 (15 and 22 September 1928), 364-370 and 402-409.

Ives, Eric. *Lady Jane Grey: A Tudor Mystery*. Oxford: Wiley-Blackwell, 2009.

-----------. "Tudor Dynastic Problems Revisited." *Historical Research* 81:212 (2008), 255-279.

Jacks, Leonard. *The Great Houses of Nottinghamshire and the county families*. Nottingham: W. and A.S. Bradshaw, 1881.

James, Susan E. *The Feminine Dynamic in English Art, 1485-1602: Women as Consumers, Painters and Partrons*. Stroud: Ashgate, 2009.

------------------. *Kateryn Parr: The Making of a Queen*. Stroud: Ashgate, 1999.

------------------. "Lady Jane Grey or Queen Kateryn Parr?" *The Burlington Magazine* 138:1114 (Jan., 1996), 20-24.

Jensen, Robin. *Living Waters: Images, Settings and Symbols of Early Christian Baptism*. Leiden: Brill, 2011.

Jones, Ann Rosalind and Peter Stallybrass. *Renaissance Clothing and the Materials of Memory*. Cambridge: Cambridge University Press, 2000.

Jones' Views of the Seats, Mansions, Castles, Etc. of Noblemen and Gentlemen in England, Wales, Scotland, and Ireland. London: Jones and Company, 1829.

Keate, George. *An Epistle from Lady Jane Grey to Lord Guildford Dudley*. London: Printed for R. and J. Dodsley, 1757.

Kim, Keechang. *Aliens in Medieval Law: The Origins of Modern Citizenship*. Cambridge: Cambridge University Press, 2000.

Kingsley-Smith, Jane. "Mythology." *A New Companion to English Renaissance Literature and Culture*. 2 volumes. Edited by Michael Hattaway. Chichester: Wiley-Blackwell, 2010.

Klarwill, Victor von, ed. *Queen Elizabeth and Some Foreigners: Being a series of hitherto unpublished letters from the archives of the Hapsburg family*. Translated by T.H. Nash. New York: Brentanos, 1928.

Knecht, R.J. *Francis I*. Cambridge: Cambridge University Press, 1982.

Korda, Natasha. *Labors Lost: Women's Work and the Early Modern English Stage*. Philadelphia: University of Pennsylvania Press, 2011.

Lady Jane Grey: An Historical Tale in Two Volumes. London: Minerva Press, 1791.

The Lady's magazine: or, Entertaining companion for the fair sex. November 1804. London: G and J Robinson, 1804.

"Landscape paintings returned to hall." *The Newark Advertiser*, 1 November 2013.

Lebow, M.R. and P.B. Sawin. "Inheritance of human facial features: a pedigree study involving length of face, prominent ears and chin cleft." *Journal of Heredity* 32 (1941), 127-132.

Lees-Milne, James. *Tudor Renaissance*. London: T. Batsford Ltd, 1951.

Le Faye, Diedre. *Jane Austen: A Family Record*. 2nd edition. Cambridge: Cambridge University Press, 2004.

Letters and Papers, Foreign and Domestic, of Henry VIII. Edited by J.S. Brewer. London: Longmans and HMSO, 1875.

The Letters of Horace Walpole, Earl of Orford. 9 volumes. Edited by Peter Cunningham. London: Henry G. Bohn, 1861.

Levine, Mortimer. *The Early Elizabethan Succession Question, 1558-1568*. Stanford: Stanford University Press, 1966.

The life, death and actions of the most chast, learned, and religious lady, the Lady Iane Gray, daughter to the Duke of Suffolke. Containing foure principall discourses written with her owne hands. The first an admonition to such as are weake in faith: the second a catechisme: the third an exhortation to her sister: and the last her words at her death. London: G. Eld, for John Wright, 1615; London: Printed by I. H[aviland] for John Wright, 1629 and 1636.

Luke, Mary. *The Nine Days Queen: A Portrait of Lady Jane Grey*. New York: William Morrow, 1986.

Lygon, William. *Catalogue of the Pictures, chiefly historical portraits, at Madresfield Court*. London: William Clowes and Sons, 1927.

Lysons, Samuel. *Magna Britannia: Vol. 5: Derbyshire*. London: T. Cadell and W. Davies, 1817.

Marsden, Jean I. *Fatal Desire: Women, Sexuality, and the English Stage, 1660-1720.* Ithaca: Cornell University Press, 2006.

Marshall, Alan. "The Westminster Magistrate and the Irish Stroker: Sir Edmund Godfrey and Valentine Greatrakes, Some Unpublished Correspondence." *The Historical Journal* 40:2 (1997), 499-505.

Meroff, Deborah. *Coronation of Glory: The Story of Lady Jane Grey.* Grand Rapids: Zondervan Publishing, 1979.

Mikhaila, Ninya and Jane Malcolm-Davies. *The Tudor Tailor: Reconstructing Sixteenth-Century Dress.* Hollywood: Costume and Fashion Press, 2006.

Modern Mayors of Derby – sketches, biographical, historical and reminiscent of the Mayors of Derby. Derby: Hobson,1909.

Mueller, Janel. *Katherine Parr: Complete Works and Correspondence.* Chicago: University of Chicago Press, 2011.

Murphy, Beverley A. *Bastard Prince: Henry VIII's Lost Son.* Stroud: Sutton, 2001.

Needham, Paul. *Twelve Centuries of Book- bindings, 400-1600.* New York: Pierpont Morgan Library, 1979.

"New Holbein Is Found." *New York Times*, 28 June 1913.

"Nostell Priory 'mystery' painting on display." *Yorkshire Evening Post*, 1 April 2010.

Parsons, Robert. A *Conference About the Next Succession to the Crown of England.* R. Doleman, 1681; reprint of Antwerp, 1595.

Peterson, M. Jeanne. *Family, Love, and Work in the Lives of Victorian Gentlewomen.* Bloomington: Indiana University Press, 1989.

Pictures in the Collection of J. Pierpont Morgan at Princes Gate and Dover House, London. Introduction by T. Humphry Ward. London: Privately Printed, 1907.

"A Picture's Romantic History." *The Morning Post* (London), 28 June 1913.

Plowden, Alison. *Lady Jane Grey and the House of Suffolk.* New York: Franklin Watts, 1986.

--------------------. *Lady Jane Grey: Nine Days Queen.* Stroud: Sutton Publishing, 2003.

Podaras, Evangelia. "Identity Questioned in Painting of 'Lady Jane'." *Yale Daily News*, 2 November 2007.

Polden, Patrick. "Stranger Than Fiction: The Jennens Inheritance in Fact and Fiction." *Common Law World Review* 32 (2003), 3:211-247 and 4:338-367.

Poole, Reginald Lane and Kenneth Garlick. *Catalogue of Portraits in the Bodleian Library.* Oxford: Oxford University Press, 2004.

Potter, Thomas R. *The History and Antiquities of Charnwood Forest.* London: Hamilton, Adams and Co., 1842.

Potter, Thomas Russell. "Lady Jane Grey." *Notes and Queries* Series 1, Vol. IX, Issue 234 (April 22, 1854), 373.

Powers, Elizabeth. "Choice/Choosing." *Encyclopedia of Comparative Iconography: Themes Depicted in Works of Art.* Edited by Helene E. Roberts. Chicago: Fitzroy Dearborn Publishers, 1998.

Preston, Joseph H. "English ecclesiastical historians and the problem of bias, 1559-1742." *Journal of the History of Ideas* 32:2 (April-June 1971), 203-220.

Propert, John Lumsden. *The History of Miniature Art: With Notes on Collectors and*

Collections. London: MacMillan and Company, 1887.

----------------------------. *Catalogues of Miniatures, Enamels, Pastels, and Waxes, at 112, Gloucester Place, Portman Square*. London: William Clowes and Sons, 1890.

Reynolds, Nigel. "The true beauty of Lady Jane Grey." *The Telegraph (*London), 5 March 2007.

Robinson, George T. "Decorative Plaster Work." *Journal of the Society of Arts* 2005:39 (24 April 1891), 439-453.

"The Rotherwas Holbein." *The Times of London.* 28 June 1913.

Rowe, Nicholas. *Lady Jane Grey: A Tragedy, in five acts.* Edinburgh: Apollo Press, 1782.

Rowlands, John. *Holbein: The Paintings of Hans Holbein the Younger.* Boston: David R. Godine, 1985.

Russell, Douglas A. *Period Style for the Theater.* Boston: Allyn and Bacon, 1987.

"Saying it with flowers: Starkey unveils the face of Lady Jane Grey." *Antiques Trade Gazette*, 5 March 2007.

Scarisbrick, Diana. *Jewellery in Britain 1066-1837: A Documentary, Social, Literary and Artistic Survey.* Wilby: Michael Russell, 2000.

----------------------. *Tudor and Jacobean Jewellery.* London: Tate Publishing, 2000.

Schuessler, Melanie. "French Hoods: Development of a Sixteenth-Century Court Fashion," *Medieval Clothing and Textiles.* Vol. 5, edited by Robin Netherton and Gale R. Owen-Crocker. Woodbridge: Boydell and Brewer, 2009, 129-160.

Schwarz, Angela. "They cannot choose but to be women: Stereotypes of femininity and ideals of womanliness in late Victorian and Edwardian Britain." In *Political Reform in Britain, 1886–1996: Themes, Ideas, Policies.* Edited by Ulrike Jordan and Wolfram Kaiser. Bochum: Brockmeyer, 1997.

Scott, Henry. *Catalogue of the Pictures at Dalkeith House.* Privately printed, 1911.

Sherman, John. "Three Portraits by Andrea del Sarto and his circle." *The Burlington Magazine* 102:683 (February 1960), 58-63.

Sherrow, Victoria, ed. *Encyclopedia of Hair: A Cultural History.* Greenwood Publishing Group, 2006.

Sim, H. Colin. "Mary Magdalene, Musician and Dancer." *Early Music* 8:4 (October 1980), 460-473.

Singh, Frederick Duleep. *Portraits in Norfolk Houses.* Norwich: Jarrold and Sons Ltd., 1927.

Snook, Edith. "Jane Grey, 'Manful' Combat, and the Female Reader in Early Modern England." *Renaissance and Reformation* 32:1 (Winter 2009), 47-81.

Spencer-Churchill, E. George. *Northwick Rescues, 1912-1961.* Evesham: Sharp Bros., 1961.

Spies, Martin. "The Portrait of Lady Katherine Grey and Her Son: Iconographic Medievalism as a Legitimation Strategy." *Early Modern Medievalisms: The Interplay Between Scholarly Reflection and Artistic Production.* Leiden: Brill, 2010.

Spring, Marika, Catherine Higgitt, and David Saunders. "Investigation of Pigment-Medium Interaction Process in Oil Paint Containing Smalt." *National Gallery Technical Bulletin* 26 (2005), 56-70.

Stone, Lawrence. *An Elizabethan: Sir Horatio Palavicino*. Oxford: Clarendon Press, 1956.

Strickland, Agnes. *Lives of the Queens of England: From the Norman Conquest*. 12 volumes. London: H. Colburn, 1841-48.

----------------------. *Lives of the Tudor Princesses, including Lady Jane Gray* [sic] *and her sisters*. London: Longmans, Green, and Company, 1868.

Strong, Roy. *English Icon: Elizabethan and Jacobean Portraiture*. New Haven: Yale University Press, 1987.

--------------. *Gloriana: The Portraits of Queen Elizabeth I*. London: Thames and Hudson, 1987.

--------------. *Portraits of Queen Elizabeth I*. Oxford: Clarendon Press, 1963.

--------------. *Tudor and Jacobean Portraits*. 2 volumes. London. HMSO. 1969.

--------------. *The Tudor and Stuart Monarchy: Pageantry, Painting, and Iconography*. Woodbridge: Boydell Press, 1998.

Strype, John. *Historical Collections of the Life and Acts of the Right Reverend Father in God John Aylmer*. London: Printed by W. Bowyer for Brabazon Aylmer, 1701.

Tait, Hugh. "The girdle-prayerbook or 'tablett': an important class of Renaissance Jewellery at the court of Henry VIII." *Jewellery Studies* 2 (1985), 29-57.

Taylor, Ida A. *Lady Jane Grey and Her Times*. New York. D. Appleton and Company. 1908.

Taylor, James D. *The Letters of Lady Jane Grey, the Nine Days Queen, 1553: Containing letters from, to, and about Lady Jane Grey*. Jefferson, N.C.: MacFarland Press, 2003.

Taylor, Lou. *Mourning Dress: A Costume and Social History*. Routledge, 2009.

Timbs, John. *Ancestral Stories and Traditions of Great Families Illustrative of English History*. London: Griffith and Farran, 1869.

Vermeylen, Filip. "Exporting Art Across the Globe: The Antwerp Art Market in the Sixteenth Century." *Nederlands kunsthistorisch jaarboek* 50 (1999), 12-29.

von Boehn, Max. *Modes & Manners: Ornaments; Lace, Fans, Gloves, Walkingsticks, Parasols, Jewelry and Trinkets*. J. M. Dent and Sons, 1929.

Waagen, Gustav Friedrich. *Galleries and Cabinets of Art in Great Britain*. London: John Murray, 1857.

Waterhouse, Ellis. *Catalogue of the exhibition of works by Holbein and other masters*. London: Royal Academy of Arts, 1950–51.

Weiss, Mark A.F. *Tudor and Stuart Portraits 1530-1660*. London: Weiss Gallery, 1995.

White, Gillian. *'That whyche ys nedefoulle and nesesary': The Nature and Purpose of the Original Furnishings and Decoration of Hardwick Hall, Derbyshire*. Ph.D. diss., University of Warwick, 2005.

Whitelock, Anna. *The Queen's Bed: An Intimate History of Elizabeth's Court*. London: Bloomsbury Publishing, 2013.

Wilcox, R. Turner. *The Mode in Hats and Headdress: A Historical Survey with 190 Plates*. New York: Dover Publications, 2008.

Wilkinson, Joseph. *Worthies, Families, and Celebrities of Barnsley and the District*. London: Bemrose and Son, 1883.

Wilson-Chevalier, Kathleen. "Sebastian Brant: The Key to Understanding Luca Penni's
    Justice and the Seven Deadly Sins." *The Art Bulletin* 78:2 (June 1996), 236-263.

Wyatt, M. Digby. "On the Foreign Artists Employed in England in the Sixteenth Century,
    and Their Influence on British Art." In *Papers Read at the Royal Institute of
    British Architects*. London, 1867.

Yarwood, Doreen. *Illustrated History of World Costume*. London: Dover Publications,
    2011.

Young, Edward. *The Force of Religion; or, Vanquish'd Love*. London: Printed by E. Curll
    and J. Pemberton, 1714.

Zarin, Cynthia. "Teen Queen: Looking for Lady Jane Grey." *The New Yorker*, 15 October
    2007, 46-55.

Ziletti, Giordano. *Lettere di Principi, le qvali si scrivono o da principi, o a principi, o
    ragionano di principi, Libro Primo*. Venice: Appresso Giordano Ziletti, 1569.

WEBSITES

Bendor Grosvenor, "A Rare Tudor Survival," *Art History News*, 15 March 2012.
    <http://arthistorynews.com/articles/1149_A_rare_Tudor_survival>.

Foxe, John. *The Unabridged Acts and Monuments Online* or *TAMO*, 1563 edition.
    Sheffield: HRI Online Publications, 2011.
    <http//www.johnfoxe.org>

Getty Research Institute's *Provenance Research Database*.
    <http://www.getty.edu/research/tools/provenance/search.html>

Historical Portraits, Philip Mould Ltd.
    <http://www.historicalportraits.com>

Lady Jane Grey Internet Museum.
    <http://www.bitterwisdom.com/ladyjanegrey/>

National Portrait Gallery, Online Collection Database.
    <http://www.npg.org.uk/collections.php>

Printed in the USA
CPSIA information can be obtained
at www.ICGtesting.com
LVHW072345091024
792475LV00028B/21